Spotlight
on FCE

Alastair Lane

Exam Booster with key

HEINLE
CENGAGE Learning™

Australia • Brazil • Japan • Korea • Mexico • Singapore • Spain • United Kingdom • United States

Spotlight on FCE Exam Booster with key
Alastair Lane

Publisher: Bryan Fletcher

Development Editor: Liz Driscoll

Assistant Editor: Amanda Cole

Project Manager: Howard Middle

Content Project Editor: Natalie Griffith

Art Editor: Natalie Griffith

Manufacturing Buyer: Maeve Healy

Marketing Manager: Marcin Wojtynski

Text Designer: Oxford Designers & Illustrators

Cover Designer: Co Studio

Photo Researcher: Erika W. Hokanson

Illustrator: Paul Cemmik, Mark Draisey, Kathrin Jacobsen, Piet Luthi

Practice Test: Process ELT

Audio: Martin Williamson, Prolingua Productions

Printer: Canale

Cover image: Erol Taskoparan | egotrips.de

ISBN 978-1-4240-1678-5

Heinle
High Holborn House, 50-51 Bedford Row
London WC1R 4LR

Cengage Learning is a leading provider of customized learning solutions with office locations around the globe, including Singapore, the United Kingdom, Australia, Mexico, Brazil and Japan. Locate our local office at: **international. cengage.com/region**

Cengage Learning products are represented in Canada by Nelson Education, Ltd.

Visit Heinle online at **http://elt.heinle.com**
Visit our corporate website at www.**cengage.com**

Author's acknowledgement
The author would like to thank Yvonne Lane for her invaluable help on this project.

Printed in Italy
1 2 3 4 5 6 7 8 9 10 11 10 09

Contents

Overview of the exam

The First Certificate in English examination consists of five papers, each worth an equal 40 marks of the maximum 200 marks. Grades A, B and C represent a pass grade. Grades D and E are a fail. It is not necessary to achieve a satisfactory grade in all five papers in order to receive a final passing grade.

PAPER 1 (1 HOUR)

Reading

- Three parts (a variety of texts and comprehension tasks).
- You must answer all three parts.
- 30 questions in total (You have 1 hour).
- You receive two marks for each correct answer in Parts 1 and 2, and one mark for each correct answer in Part 3.

Part 1: Multiple choice
You read a text and answer eight multiple choice questions. Each question has four possible answers (A, B, C or D).

Part 2: Gapped text
You complete a text with seven missing sentences. There is one extra sentence which you should not use.

Part 3: Multiple matching
You read one or more texts (often four shorter texts) and match prompts to parts of the whole text. There are 15 prompts.

PAPER 1

See the following pages for Paper 1 exam tasks:
Part 1 38, 78, 102, 110, 126
Part 2 22, 54, 70, 94, 118
Part 3 6, 14, 30, 46, 62, 86

PAPER 2 (1 HOUR 20 MINUTES)

Writing

- Two parts.
- You must answer both parts.
- Two questions to answer in total (You have 1 hour 20 minutes).
- You receive equal marks for each question.

Part 1: A letter or email
This part has one question and you must answer it. You read some text and respond with a letter or email. Your answer must be 120–150 words.

Part 2: An article, an essay, a letter, a report, a review or a story
This part has four possible questions and you answer one only with 120–180 words:

Questions 2–4 can ask you to write an article, an essay, a letter, a report, a review or a story. You read about a situation and then write a response using the correct type of text.
Question 5 also asks you to write similar types of texts but based upon the set reading text that you can study for the exam (optional).

PAPER 2

See the following pages for Paper 2 exam tasks:
Part 1 12, 20, 28, 34, 82, 108, 132
Part 2 44, 52, 60, 68, 74, 92, 100, 116, 124

PAPER 3 (45 MINUTES)

Use of English

- Four parts.
- You must answer all four parts.
- 42 questions in total (You have 45 minutes).
- You receive one mark for each correct answer in Parts 1, 2 and 3, and two marks for each correct answer in Part 4.

Part 1: Multiple-choice cloze
This is a cloze test with twelve gaps and four possible options for each one.

Part 2: Open cloze
This is a cloze test with twelve gaps. You complete each gap with one word.

Part 3: Word formation
You read a text with ten gaps. There is a word-stem after each gap. You must change the form of the word and complete the gap.

Part 4: Key-word transformations
There are eight questions. Each question has a lead-in sentence. Then a key word is given. You must use this word in a second gapped sentence so that it has the same meaning as the first.

PAPER 3

See the following pages for Paper 3 exam tasks:
Part 1 19, 33, 43, 67, 84, 91, 99, 107, 131
Part 2 11, 43, 51, 67, 76, 107
Part 3 11, 19, 27, 36, 59, 99, 115, 123, 131
Part 4 27, 51, 61, 76, 84, 91, 115, 123

PAPER 4 (APPROXIMATELY 40 MINUTES)

Listening

- Four parts.
- You must answer all four parts.
- 30 questions in total (approximately 40 minutes).
- You receive one mark for each correct answer in all four parts.
- Text types: you hear four different sets of recordings (*monologues* or *interacting speakers*). *Monologues* could include answerphone messages, radio documentaries and features, announcements, instructions, news, lectures, reports, speeches, advertisements and stories. *Interacting speakers* could include conversations, radio plays, interviews, discussions, quizzes and transactions. After you listen, you have five minutes to write your answers onto the answer sheet.

Part 1: Multiple choice
You listen to eight short unconnected recordings. Each one is about 30 seconds long. For each recording you answer a question with three answers to choose from.

Part 2: Sentence completion
You listen to someone talking or a conversation. It lasts about three minutes. You have to complete ten sentences with words you hear on the recording.

Part 3: Multiple matching
There are five short recordings and you match five questions to the correct option. There are six possible options.

Part 4: Multiple choice
You listen to a longer text with more than one speaker. You have seven questions and each one has three options to choose from.

PAPER 4

See the following pages for Paper 4 exam tasks:

Part 1 10, 18, 50, 90, 113

Part 2 26, 58, 83, 106

Part 3 35, 66, 75, 122

Part 4 42, 98, 130

PAPER 5 (APPROXIMATELY 14 MINUTES)

Speaking

- Four parts.
- You must answer all four parts.
- You take the Speaking test with another candidate.
- The interlocutor (examiner talking to you) asks you questions and gives you prompts (pictures and words) which you may have to talk about or discuss with the other person.
- You are assessed on your performance throughout.

Part 1: Conversation between interlocutor and each candidate (asking and answering)
This is general interactional and social language – a conversation between the interlocutor and each candidate. You will answer questions on topics such as home, family and personal interests. This part will last approximately three minutes.

Part 2: An individual 'long turn' for each candidate with a short response from the second candidate
You look at two photographs and the interlocutor asks you to talk about them (describing, comparing and giving an opinion). The other candidate listens, then has to respond at the end of your talk. Each candidate's turn should last approximately one minute, with a further 20 seconds given for the other candidate to respond and comment on what you have said.

Part 3: A two-way conversation between the candidates, with a decision-making task
Both candidates are given spoken instructions with written or visual stimuli. You work together in a collaborative task (exchanging ideas, expressing opinions, agreeing and/or disagreeing, speculating, suggesting, evaluating, reaching a decision through negotiation). Your discussion should last three minutes.

Part 4: A discussion on topics related to the collaborative (Part 3) task
The interlocutor now joins in the discussion (from Part 3) and asks further questions to each candidate so that it is a three-way conversation lasting four minutes. The focus here is expressing and justifying opinions, and agreeing and/or disagreeing,

PAPER 5

See the following pages for Paper 5 exam tasks:

Part 1 13, 133

Part 2 29, 36, 85, 93, 125, 133

Part 3 21, 45, 53, 61, 69, 77, 101, 133

Part 4 109, 114, 133

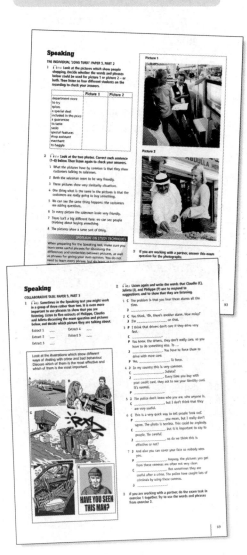

1 Friends and family

☐ I know words to describe family connections, page 8.

☐ I know some phrasal verbs with *out*, page 8.

☐ I know how to use the present simple and present continuous, page 9.

☐ I know how to use the present perfect simple and present perfect continuous, page 9.

☐ I know how to change *-ic* adjectives to adverbs, page 10.

☐ I know how to use intonation in questions, page 13.

EXAM CHECKLIST

☐ I have practised the multiple matching question from the Reading paper, page 6.

☐ I have practised the multiple matching question from the Listening paper, page 10.

☐ I have practised the word formation question from the Use of English paper, page 11.

☐ I have practised the open cloze question from the Use of English paper, page 11.

☐ I have practised how to organise my ideas in the Writing paper, page 12.

☐ I have practised the opening conversation from the Speaking paper, page 13.

Reading

MULTIPLE MATCHING: PAPER 1, PART 3

1 **You are going to read an article about a family choosing a name for a baby. For questions 1–10 choose from the people (A–D). The people may be chosen more than once.**

Which person

1 does not like their name? ___

2 is not concerned about other people's opinion of the name? ___

3 wants to make a change from tradition? ___

4 had trouble because of their name? ___

5 is happy to give the baby a name which doesn't come from their own country? ___

6 doesn't suggest a name for the baby? ___

7 says their name is not very modern? ___

8 wants the baby to have the first name of another family member? ___

9 has changed their opinion of the name because of recent events? ___

10 has a name which is not understood in other countries? ___

2 **Now read the text again and find words that mean the following:**

1 pregnant (introductory paragraph) _____

2 a difficult decision (introductory paragraph) _____

3 the history and culture of a nation or people (paragraph A) _____

4 very pleased or excited (paragraph A) _____

5 to other countries (paragraph B) _____

6 when people attack or laugh at someone in an unkind way (paragraph C) _____

7 almost (paragraph D) _____

8 become an adult (paragraph D) _____

The Name Game

Steven and Maria have been married for two years and now Maria is expecting their first child. They know the baby will be a boy, but now they have a dilemma which is very familiar to couples who come from different countries. Steven is from Scotland and Maria from Greece, and they have to decide whether to give their baby a British or a Greek name. We spoke to Steven's family in Inverness and Maria's family in Thessaloniki.

A Dimitra, Maria's mother

Of course I'm just happy that I'll be a grandmother! Maria is my only child. My husband was from a different generation and his parents were very proud of our Greek heritage, so they gave him the name Aristotélos. He was a wonderful man and I've been a widow for ten years now, so I'd be thrilled if they named the baby after his grandfather. It would be a bit unusual though because, here in Greece, we normally give the first-born baby a name from the father's side of the family.

B Hamish, Steven's brother

Steven and Maria said that they think the baby needs to have a name that works in both countries, something very international. I personally don't think that should be a big issue. Take my name: it's very common here in Scotland, but when I go overseas, people don't understand it because they've never heard it before. But that's only a problem when you meet people. I'm Scottish and I'm proud I have a Scottish name. I think they should just choose a name that's interesting.

C Hilary, Steven's uncle

It's always a problem naming a baby and everyone has an opinion. But I can only give my personal experience. My parents gave me a name that's quite old-fashioned and could be a man or a woman's name, and I've never been fond of it. I had a lot of bullying when I was at school because of it. So that's what they have to be most careful about. What's wrong with James or John? They're common names.

D Maria

Everybody keeps asking me what name I'm going to give my baby and I just don't know what to do. Practically everyone I know has suggested a name to me, except Steven! He's as worried as I am. Originally, I was worried because our plan was to live in Britain and I was worried that the baby wouldn't know about his own culture. Luckily, Steven has just found a job in Athens and I now know our child will grow up here in Greece. So, I think it would be fine for him to have a British name, if we can think of a nice one. I have told Steven though that we must give the baby Aristotélos as a middle name. That's very important for my family.

Vocabulary

FAMILY CONNECTIONS

1 **Complete the crossword.**

Across

1 This is someone you are going to marry.

4 This is a formal word for the person you are married to: it could be a man or a woman.

6 Two children born on the same day to the same mother.

7 Your son is married to your daughter-_ _ - _ _ _ _ .

Down

2 The son or daughter of your uncle and aunt.

3 The members of your family.

4 Your brothers and sisters.

5 When you talk about your family, including all the grandparents, uncles, aunts etc. that do not live with you, you talk about your _____ family.

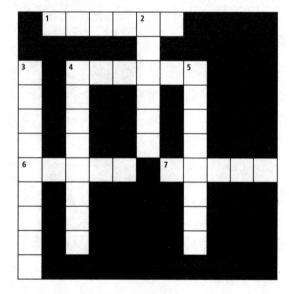

2 *Out* has many different meanings in phrasal verbs. Look at the phrasal verbs in **bold** in the sentences (1–4) below. Then match the pictures (a–d) to the sentences.

1 Two of them really **stand out** from the others. ___

2 I think we should **keep out** of that field. ___

3 I'm **locked out**! ___

4 Everyone else is enjoying themselves and I'm **missing out**. ___

3 **Look at the sentences (1–6). Match the phrasal verbs in the sentences with the definitions (a–f).**

1 I've just **found out** that the exam is on Tuesday not Wednesday. ___

2 Three prisoners **broke out** of jail last night and are still on the run. ___

3 Can I **hand** some invitations **out**? I'm having a party next week. ___

4 Do we need these old books or shall we **throw** them **out**? ___

5 I couldn't **get out** of work until nine o'clock because I was so busy. ___

6 Sarah's been **going out** with Ian for six months now. ___

a put something in the rubbish

b discover

c be in a relationship

d leave

e distribute

f escape

Grammar

PRESENT SIMPLE AND PRESENT CONTINUOUS

1 Underline the correct form of the verb.

1 Our children *grow up / are growing up* really fast.

2 On Sundays the whole family *eats / is eating* lunch together.

3 The situation *changes / is changing* dramatically at the moment.

4 My son-in-law *speaks / is speaking* English, French and German.

5 *Do you usually send / Are you usually sending* your grandmother a present on Mother's Day?

6 Andrea isn't here because *she plays / she is playing* with her nieces in the garden.

7 Statistically, families *get / are getting* smaller.

2 Complete the sentences with the verb in brackets. Decide if the verb is being used as a state or an active verb.

1 My aunt _____ a house in London and another in the South of France. (own)

2 We _____ of sending the children to a language school this summer. (think)

3 She _____ that you know the answer. (not / believe)

4 You can't use the bathroom because Denise _____ a shower. (have)

5 I _____ Francesco's new girlfriend. (like)

6 I love your lemon cheesecake. It _____ great! (taste)

SPOTLIGHT ON STUDY TECHNIQUES

A learner's dictionary such as the Collins Cobuild will give you a lot of information about verbs. It can tell you if the verb is transitive or intransitive, and it can also tell you if the verb is a state verb. State verbs are usually identified with an instruction such as 'not used in the progressive tenses'.

State verbs tend to be verbs of the mind or thinking: *think, know, remember, forget.*

They also cover possession: *have, own, possess.*

Verbs of the senses are also typically state verbs: *taste, smell, sound,* etc.

PRESENT PERFECT SIMPLE AND PRESENT PERFECT CONTINUOUS

3 Look at the pictures of Rachel. They show recent activities. Write sentences using the words in brackets and the present perfect or present perfect continuous.

1 _____ (write / five letters)

2 _____ (jog)

3 _____ (clean / house)

4 _____ (break / a plate)

5 _____ (make / cake)

6 _____ (work /computer)

Spelling

Changing -ic adjectives to adverbs
When an adjective ends in -ic, make the adverb by
adding -ally to the ending. Note that the adverb is
spelt -ll-.
Example: dramatic ➡ dramatically

1 **Complete the sentences by changing the adjectives in
the box into adverbs.**

economic   genetic   logic   periodic
sympathetic   tragic

1 My uncle doesn't visit all the time, but he comes here

_____.

2 _____, my grandfather died of malaria
when he was just 38.

3 If x+7=20, _____ x must be 13.

4 _____, the country looks good:
unemployment is low and there are lots of jobs.

5 Many people buy organic vegetables because they are

worried about _____ modified food.

6 If you are a doctor, you need to listen

_____ to your patients' problems.

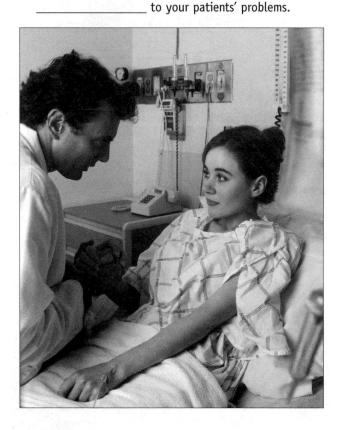

Listening: friends and family

MULTIPLE CHOICE: PAPER 4, PART 1

1   🎧1.1 **You will hear eight people talking about their
family and friends. For questions 1–8, choose the
best answer (A, B, or C). Remember to listen to the
recording twice.**

1 You hear two friends meeting. Where are they?
   A in a restaurant
   B in a shop
   C at the cinema

2 You hear a girl talking about her evening. Who is
   she looking after?
   A her brothers and sisters
   B her cousins
   C the children of her friends

3 You hear a man talking about a friend. Why did he
   argue with his friend?
   A His friend was laughing at him.
   B His friend broke his sunglasses.
   C His friend never phones him.

4 You hear a woman talking about her marriage
   plans. Who is she marrying?
   A a soldier
   B an accountant
   C a doctor

5 You hear a woman talking to her neighbour. What
   is the problem?
   A He has lost some money.
   B He is worried about work.
   C He can't get into his house.

6 You hear a woman talking about her family. What
   does she say about her brother?
   A He is very good looking.
   B He looks different to everyone else in the
     family.
   C He is the only person in the family who has
     lived abroad.

7 You hear a boy talking about his brothers. What
   does he say about them?
   A They have a different mother to him.
   B They are twins.
   C They are younger than him.

8 You hear a man talking about his wife. Where did
   he meet her?
   A at school
   B at work
   C at a party

Use of English

WORD FORMATION: PAPER 3, PART 3

1 Read the text below. Use the word given in capitals at the end of some of the lines to form a word that fits in the gap in the same line. There is an example at the beginning (0).

I used to think that jogging was a form of **(0)** ....*madness*........... .	**MAD**
I was never interested in **(1)**	**FIT**
I much preferred to spend my time in **(2)** .... activities.	**CULTURE**
But last year I was working with a **(3)** .... sports	**PROFESSION**
agency in my job. My company provided **(4)** .... for a lot of	**SPONSOR**
their athletes and as a present they gave me and my family free **(5)** .... of my local	**MEMBER**
gym. My life was transformed! I went two or three times a week and **(6)** .... I was going	**EVENTUAL**
every day. My kids like it too. They go swimming there and play tennis. It's helped them get rid of a lot of **(7)** .... in the	**RESTLESS**
evenings, so we don't have that problem any more. I've also hired a **(8)** .... trainer to	**PERSON**
help me. We've agreed that thirty minutes is the perfect **(9)** .... for our	**LONG**
sessions. I don't have the **(10)** .... to exercise for more than half an hour at a time.	**STRONG**

OPEN CLOZE: PAPER 3, PART 2

2 Read the text below and think of the word which best fits each gap. Use only one word in each gap. There is an example at the beginning (0).

In Britain **(0)** ......*everybody*...... knows a mother-in-law joke. It might seem strange, but they are a member of the family **(1)** .... every comedian makes jokes about. Well I'm very happy to say that I am really good friends with my mother-in-law. We got on fantastically well from the first moment we met and we **(2)** .... never fallen out.

(3) .... name is Tracy, and she and my father-in-law, Don, have been like second parents to me. My wife and I go round to their house for lunch every Sunday and they normally visit us **(4)** .... least once a week. I think the reason we get on so well is **(5)** .... we have the same sense of humour. There are always loads **(6)** .... jokes and funny stories whenever we meet.

At the moment, my wife **(7)** .... expecting our first child. Don and Tracy are very excited about **(8)** .... first grandchild. Every time they visit, they bring a new present **(9)** .... the baby and want to hear all the latest news.

As **(10)** .... as my wife, Don and Tracy also have a son: my brother-in-law, Peter. He works overseas, **(11)** .... we don't see him very often. He works as **(12)** .... chef on a cruise ship and his cooking is amazing. **(13)** .... he is in the country, he always stays with us. We often go out **(14)** .... the evenings to watch the football together. So you can see, I'm very happy **(15)** .... my in-laws.

Writing: organising your ideas

COMPULSORY TASK: PAPER 2, PART 1

1 When taking the Writing test, it is essential to answer the question correctly. Look at the exam question below and decide which of the subjects (1–8) you must include in your answer.

1 A description of interesting locations that you went to.

2 What the weather was like.

3 What your accommodation was like.

4 A description of some food.

5 A description of how you travelled around the country.

6 Your general impressions of the trip.

7 Your opinion of the people in Charlotte's country.

8 A description of your trip to the capital city.

You have received an email from your friend Charlotte. Read the email and the notes you have made. Then write an email in 120–150 words using all your notes. You must use grammatically correct sentences with accurate spelling and punctuation in a style appropriate to the situation.

Hi _____

I hope you had a great time visiting my country last week. I'm really sorry that I wasn't able to meet you, but I had to study for my final exams. I'd love to know everything about your trip!

it was great!   museums galleries

What kind of places did you visit? Did you go to the capital city? Where did you stay while you were there?

three days   friendly youth hostel

You know our cooking is world famous, so did you manage to eat any famous local dishes?

yes – absolutely delicious

I want to hear all the news!
Speak soon
Charlotte

2 Before you start writing, it is important to organise your ideas and plan your answer. You have to write between 120 and 150 words in Part 1 of the Writing test. So you need to write about three paragraphs. Make one main idea the subject of each paragraph. Look again at your answers in exercise 1. How can you organise these five ideas into three paragraphs?

paragraph 1

_____

paragraph 2

_____

paragraph 3

_____

3 Adam has written an answer to Charlotte's email. Match the teacher's comments (a–g) with the numbers on the email (1–7). Which of the teacher's comments is a compliment?

a Don't repeat the same word!

b Don't write a list – tell me more information.

c Just one paragraph?

d This answer is too short. You need to tell me more.

e Where is the rest of the greeting?

f This is well written.

g Spelling!

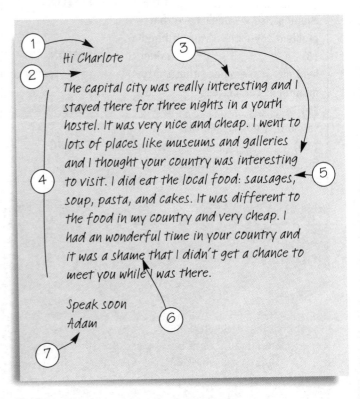

Hi Charlote

The capital city was really interesting and I stayed there for three nights in a youth hostel. It was very nice and cheap. I went to lots of places like museums and galleries and I thought your country was interesting to visit. I did eat the local food: sausages, soup, pasta, and cakes. It was different to the food in my country and very cheap. I had an wonderful time in your country and it was a shame that I didn't get a chance to meet you while I was there.

Speak soon
Adam

4 Now write your own answer to the exam question in exercise 1.

....

....

....

....

....

....

....

....

....

....

....

Speaking: answering questions

OPENING CONVERSATION: PAPER 5, PART 1

1 🎧1.2 **At the start of the Speaking test, the interlocutor asks some general questions. Often these questions will be about your family. Listen to two students, Julieta and Philippe, in the first part of the Speaking test. What answers do they give to the following questions?**

1 Do you live alone or do you live with your family?

2 Do you come from a large family or a small family?

3 What do your parents do?

2 **Julieta and Philippe made the following mistakes in the interview. Correct the mistakes in these sentences.**

1 We are four in my family.

2 I have one older sister, Ana, who has twenty-four years.

3 I don't have some brothers and sisters.

4 My father is teacher and my mother works as doctor.

3 **If you are working with a partner, look at listening script 1.2 on page 156. Role-play the interview, with one person being the interlocutor and the other the student. Ask and answer questions. Then swap roles and repeat the role-play.**

Pronunciation

1 **Work in pairs. Ask and answer the questions.**

1 What do you enjoy doing in the evening?

2 Where are you planning to go this evening?

3 Do you like surfing the Net?

4 Which sites on the World Wide Web do you recommend visiting?

5 What TV programmes do you like watching?

2 🎧1.3 **Listen to the questions in exercise 1. Which question has a different intonation? Why?**

SPOTLIGHT ON PRONUNCIATION

Intonation in questions
Remember that in questions with a question word (*who, what, when, why*, etc.), intonation falls at the end of the question. In questions with no question word (*Do you like ... ? Have you got ... ?*, etc.), intonation rises at the end.

3 **Look at the questions (1–7). Decide if the intonation falls or rises at the end of the question.**

1 Are you good at learning languages?

2 Where do you go when you have to study?

3 Do you think you'll pass the exam?

4 Which do you think is hardest: listening in English, speaking or writing?

5 Have you got a lot of work to do at the moment?

6 Will you be working this weekend?

7 What book are you reading at the moment?

4 🎧1.4 **Listen and check your answers.**

5 **If you are working with a partner, ask and answer the questions in exercise 3.**

2 Jobs and work

LANGUAGE CHECKLIST

- ☐ I know words to describe jobs and applications, page 16.
- ☐ I know some phrasal verbs with *off*, page 16.
- ☐ I know which jobs are spelt *-or*, page 17.
- ☐ I know phrases for making comparisons, page 17.
- ☐ I know how to pronounce words with the schwa /ə/, page 18.

EXAM CHECKLIST

- ☐ I have practised the multiple matching question from the Reading paper, page 14.
- ☐ I have practised the Part 1 extracts + multiple choice question from the Listening paper, page 18.
- ☐ I have practised the multiple-choice cloze question from the Use of English paper, page 19.
- ☐ I have practised the word formation question from the Use of English paper, page 19.
- ☐ I have practised how to expand points in the Writing paper, page 20.
- ☐ I have practised the collaborative task from the Speaking paper, page 21.

Reading

MULTIPLE MATCHING: PAPER 1, PART 3

1 You are going to read an article about four people who have their dream job. For questions 1–15, choose from the people (A–D). The people may be chosen more than once.

Which person

1 is not completely happy? ___

2 gets their motivation from someone else in their family? ___

3 does not own their own house? ___

4 suffered from prejudice? ___

5 thought they wouldn't get their dream job when they were younger? ___

6 got their dream job through introductions to other people? ___

7 earns less money doing their dream job? ___

8 finds it difficult to do any work? ___

9 was criticised by their family? ___

10 does long hours? ___

11 was resented by their colleagues? ___

12 lives abroad? ___

13 did not continue their education after high school? ___

14 is a workaholic? ___

15 doesn't want to buy or own a lot of things? ___

2 Find these words and phrases (1–8) in the text. Then match the definitions (a–h) to the words and phrases.

1 in my teens ___

2 opened the door ___

3 nepotism ___

4 out of the blue ___

5 royalties ___

6 lacking ___

7 running ___

8 bothered ___

a managing or controlling a business

b using family connections to get unfair advantages at work or in society

c money that an author or creative person gets from selling a book, CDs, etc.

d gave someone an opportunity

e aged 13–19

f concerned, worried

g suddenly, from nowhere

h missing, absent

DREAM JOB

Is it really possible to find your dream job? For many people it seems a complete impossibility, but we spoke to four people who say that they have their dream job. The question is: are they happy?

A Zvonimir, Croatia

Ever since I was a very small child, I loved to play basketball and I always hoped to be a professional player. Although I played all the time when I was a kid, I was very small for my age. I always felt I had no chance. Thankfully, in my teens I did finally grow quite fast, but I'm still not as tall as many of the other players out there.

When I was eighteen, I had the choice of going to university or joining a very small local team to play basketball full-time. For me the decision was easy and although my parents thought I was mad, I knew it was the only thing I wanted to do. I have been playing for the team for two years now and although I still live at home, I am sure that one day everything will change. My real dream is to play in the NBA in the USA. I'm only twenty, so I still have time!

B Patricia, UK

I absolutely love my job, but I would never have thought of it as my dream job because it's the only job that I ever wanted to do. I was very fortunate in that my father worked as a TV director and when I was growing up, he used to take me along to the studio to watch the recordings. When I left school, I asked him if he could help me get a career in directing. He told me what were the best places to study and he also introduced me to his contacts. They were the people who opened the door to me.

But even though my father worked in the business, it doesn't mean that I've had an easy ride. Lots of people said that I only got the job because of nepotism. But I had to work twice as hard as everyone else because I was a woman. When I started work in the 1970s, there were very few female directors working in TV.

C Tove, Sweden

It took me a long time, but I finally have my dream job. I am an artist and illustrator for children's books. I am based half the year here in Uppsala and the rest of the year in New Zealand. It's this that makes my dream job. I always loved the thought of living my life this way. I never really wanted very much and I was never interested in possessions. I only managed to buy my house in the end because out of the blue a book I was working on became very popular. With the royalties from that, I was able to buy my house in New Zealand.

The funny thing is that I don't feel absolutely content. Even though I have the lifestyle that I always wanted, I still feel there is something lacking in my life. Sometimes I think I was better off when I was working towards my dream. Now I have it, the motivation's gone. I used to work weekends and evenings all the time, but now I can spend days looking out of the window.

D Jose, Portugal

Who would believe that I have my dream job? I work twelve hours a day running a small export company from a small office outside of Porto. I never go on vacation, I eat lunch in ten minutes at my desk and I often work through the weekend.

It's my dream job because I always wanted to run my own company, to be my own boss. I left my old job as a sales manager for a multinational last year. It wasn't easy making my mind up and I had actually been thinking about it for ages. In fact, I've actually taken a pay cut to do this. That hasn't bothered me too much though because I knew what I wanted and I was prepared to take risks to get it. But it's not just watching the company grow and make profits. I also know that my daughters will benefit from any success that I may have.

Vocabulary

JOBS AND APPLICATIONS

1 **Complete the puzzle. What is the word in grey?**

1 Personal characteristics, such as patience.

2 An employer makes you _____ by giving you some money and asking you to leave the company.

3 A manager has to _____ with problems.

4 You send an application _____ to a company to tell them you want a job.

5 When you work more than your usual hours and you get paid some more money.

6 A system where workers can choose when they start and finish work.

7 When your company gives you more money (two words: 3, 4).

8 A document that gives the history of your education and your working life.

9 When a company asks an employee to leave, perhaps because they have done something wrong.

10 To find and give a job to a new employee.

11 To tell your employer that you will leave your job.

12 When you decide to leave your job, you have to give this to your employer.

13 New employees learn about their job on a _____ programme.

14 Extra benefits you get from your job.

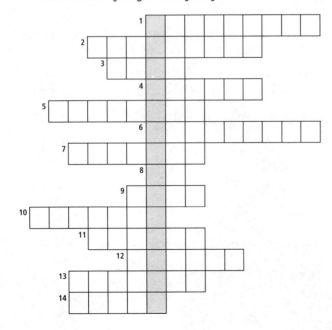

2 *Off* has many different meanings in phrasal verbs. Look at the phrasal verbs in **bold** in the sentences (1–6) below. Then match the pictures (a–f) to the sentences.

1 They worked really hard and eventually the project **came off**! ____

2 There was a problem in Alaska, so we **sent** Julia **off** to fix it. ____

3 I **took** the day **off** because there wasn't much to do in the office. ____

4 The company is **laying off** six hundred staff because there isn't enough work. ____

5 We realised that they were never going to pay the money, so we **wrote** the debt **off**. ____

6 He had a very stressful year, but his hard work **paid off** when they asked him to be the new boss. ____

a   b

c   d

e   f

3 **Look again at the sentences in exercise 1. In which sentence(s) does *off* mean the following?**

a had a successful result ____ ____

b to another place ____

c to cancel/remove ____ ____

d not at work ____

Spelling

Jobs with -or

Several jobs in English end with a schwa sound /ə/.
The most common spelling is -er.
Example: teacher

However, some other jobs are spelt -or.
Example: actor

1 Write the job for each picture.

1 _____

2 _____

3 _____

4 _____

5 _____

6 _____

7 _____

8 _____

Grammar

MAKING COMPARISONS

1 Look at the sentences below. Five of them contain a mistake. Find and correct the mistakes.

1 The harder you work, the quick you get promotion.

2 I don't think my new job is as interesting than my old one.

3 People in London are much more highly paid than people in the rest of Britain.

4 We're more busier this year than last year.

5 London is the expensive city in Europe.

6 I think that writing reports is the least interesting part of my job.

7 Working as a manager is difficulter than working as a secretary.

2 Put the words from the box into the sentences below. Add one word to each sentence.

> a almost any as bit far like

1 You need to go on a training course to learn how to use the new program. It's a more complicated than the software we were using before.

2 The new office is as good the old one.

3 I have to do lot more overtime in my new job than in my old one.

4 My job is too easy. I want a job with more responsibility.

5 The job in Berlin pays €30,000 and the one in Madrid pays €29,000. So the money is the same.

6 My new project is easy. It isn't anything the project that I've just finished. That one was a nightmare!

7 I don't think working as a journalist is more difficult than working as an editor.

Listening: Do you like your job?

1 🎧2.1 **You will hear eight people talking about their job. For questions 1–8, choose the best answer (A, B or C).**

1 You hear a man complaining about his job. Where is he?
   A in the staff canteen
   B at his desk
   C at home

2 You hear a woman talking about her new job. How does she feel?
   A worried
   B delighted
   C disappointed

3 You hear two people complaining about their boss. What do they complain about?
   A his qualifications
   B the amount of work he gives to people
   C the way he speaks to people

4 You hear a man talking on the telephone. Who is he speaking to?
   A his boss
   B his secretary
   C his business partner

5 You hear two people speaking in a café. What do they want to do?
   A take a career break
   B quit their jobs
   C go back to study at university

6 You hear a woman talking about her job. What is she describing?
   A her working conditions
   B who she works with
   C where she works

7 You hear a woman describing her day at work. What did she like about it?
   A It was a lot of fun.
   B She did something very important.
   C Her boss congratulated her.

8 You hear a man talking about something he has been working on. What is it?
   A a job application
   B secretarial work
   C an advertising campaign

Pronunciation

SPOTLIGHT ON PRONUNCIATION

The schwa (1)
The most important sound in English is also the smallest sound: the schwa /ə/. In English words, syllables that are unstressed are often pronounced /ə/.

Sometimes the schwa appears more than once in the same word.
Example: position /pəzɪʃən/

1 🎧2.2 **Listen to the words below. The stress in each word is underlined. The sound in *italics* is the schwa /ə/.**

   doct*or*   b*i*gger   *a*pply

2 🎧2.3 **Look at the words below. Underline the stress. Which syllables are pronounced with the schwa /ə/? Listen to check your answers.**

   organisation   qualification
   possessions   powerful
   international   certificate
   information   computer

SPOTLIGHT ON PRONUNCIATION

The schwa (2)
Small words like articles (*the, a*), prepositions (*of, to, from*), auxiliary verbs (*do, can*), and conjunctions (*and, but*) have two pronunciations. The pronunciation with the schwa /ə/ is called the weak form. We use the weak form in everyday speech and the strong form when we need to stress the word.

3 🎧2.4 **Listen to two versions of each sentence below. In which sentence (a or b) is the word in *italics* pronounced with the schwa /ə/?**

   1 I need to speak to you *and* Gary. ___
   2 Karen is *the* best manager I have worked with. ___
   3 I *can* help you if you like. ___
   4 You *should* get a letter from her boss. ___

4 🎧2.4 **Listen again to the sentences in exercise 3. Which other words are pronounced with the schwa /ə/?**

5 🎧2.4 **Listen again to the first sentence in each pair in exercise 3. Listen to the stronger form of the words in *italics*.**

6 **If you are working with a partner, practise together reading the sentences in exercise 3, using both pronunciations.**

Use of English

1 Use the word given in capitals at the end of each sentence to form a word that fits in the gap. The word in each pair of sentences is formed the same way. There is an example at the beginning (0).

0 a I have been working for this .....organisation... for ten years. **ORGANISE**

   b Companies in this country have an .....obligation..... to give training to their employees. **OBLIGE**

1 a Can you make an .... of the security situation in the company? **ASSESS**

   b The new artwork and furniture has made a big .... to the appearance of the offices. **IMPROVE**

2 a Have you got an .... form for the job? **APPLY**

   b We do most of our .... by email. **COMMUNICATE**

3 a The new advertising campaign has been extremely .... **SUCCESS**

   b It's .... that Richard will be at the meeting tomorrow. He's got so much work to do. **DOUBT**

4 a When you apply for a new job, you should provide a .... from your previous employer. **REFER**

   b I don't believe in the .... of life on other planets. **EXIST**

5 a We need to recruit someone with the .... to speak French and German. **ABLE**

   b There is no .... between our company and your company. **SIMILAR**

2 Read the text below and decide which answer (A, B, C or D) best fits each gap. There is an example at the beginning (0).

They say that if you want to (0) .....earn..... a lot of money, you should (1) .... to be a plumber, (2) .... the reality is that plumbers actually only command an annual (3) .... of £25,000. Nevertheless, more women are currently (4) .... from their office jobs and entering the profession.

Why? Well, plumbing gives women a feeling of (5) .... as there is a real result at the end of the day. This (6) .... to people who have only ever worked in offices organising the work of other people.

There is a skills shortage in the UK at the moment across the construction (7) .... and employers are turning to women to fill the gap. A number of schemes have also started to help women make the career change. For example, a college in Wales is (8) .... a qualification in plumbing which is only for female students.

Women do often still need (9) .... to enter a male-dominated world. Some employers won't accept women at all. In (10) .... to fighting against this prejudice, some women plumbers also complain that people try to take advantage of them by not paying. 28-year-old Pauline Brown, who has starred in a government advertising campaign to encourage women to (11) .... up plumbing, takes a no-nonsense approach. She says, "I have a policy of same-day payment – if (12) .... try to avoid paying, I'll rip the work out and take my materials away."

	A	B	C	D
0	win	collect	<u>earn</u>	pay
1	train	educate	instruct	practise
2	however	despite	furthermore	although
3	payment	wages	cash	salary
4	resigning	sacking	quitting	leaving
5	achievement	completion	relaxation	victory
6	pleases	satisfies	appeals	delights
7	manufacturing	factories	industry	working
8	instructing	preferring	presenting	offering
9	determination	defiance	aggression	obsession
10	combination	excess	development	addition
11	put	take	begin	make
12	buyers	purchasers	shoppers	clients

Writing: expanding points

1 In Part 1 of the Writing test, it is important to give extra information to develop each of your points. Look at the exam question below. Match the three points (A–C) from the exam question to the sentences with extra information (1–6).

You have seen this advertment in a newspaper.

Tour guides wanted

We are looking for people to work as tour guides around the city castle and museum. Applicants should be available to work throughout the summer (July to August) and be aged 21–65.
In addition, the ideal applicant will:
- have an interest in history Ⓐ
- have good communication skills Ⓑ
- be able to speak at least one foreign language Ⓒ

Please write requesting an information pack to Julian Hinchcliffe at the address below.

---

1 I often speak in front of groups as I act in a local theatre club. ___

2 On my course, I have visited very many castles and learned about how they worked. ___

3 In addition to which, I presented a student radio programme when I was at High School. ___

4 I am a native speaker of Japanese and I have been working in English for the last year as an au pair in London. ___

5 As well as studying this subject, I also enjoy reading books about this period. ___

6 I have also completed a German course at B1 level. ___

2 Now look at the student's answer to the exam question in exercise 1. Place the sentences (1–6) from exercise 1 into the gaps (a–f) in the letter.

Dear Mr Hinchcliffe

I am writing to you to request an information pack for a Tour guide position.
I am currently studying Archaeology at the University of London. ª_____ ᵇ_____

You mentioned that you were looking for candidates with good communication skills.
ᶜ_____ ᵈ_____

I am also able to speak three languages.
ᵉ_____ ᶠ_____

I look forward to your reply.

Yours sincerely,
Mineko Kamimura

3 Now write your own answer to the exam question in exercise 1.

....
....
....
....
....
....
....
....
....
....
....
....
....
....
....
....

Speaking

COLLABORATIVE TASK: PAPER 5, PART 3

SPOTLIGHT ON STUDY TECHNIQUES

A large part of the Speaking test is a discussion between you and your partner. It is often possible to choose someone from your class as your partner before the exam itself. If you can arrange this early on in the course, you can practise with your partner a lot before the exam and get used to talking and listening to each other. The Speaking sections in this workbook will give you the opportunity to work with a partner. Use these to study together before the exam.

---

1 **If you are working with a partner, look at the pictures. Imagine that you are going to take a part-time job while you are studying at university. Decide together which job is the best one. When you are speaking, use the phrases below and tick (✔) each one after you have used it.**

___ Working as X is (much) better than working as Y ...
___ This seems like a better / the best (idea)
___ I don't think it's anything like as (good) as ...
___ It looks fairly similar to ...
___ How do you think it compares to ...?
___ Is it much different from ...?

2 🎧 2.5 **Listen to two students in Part 3 of the Speaking test, Claudio and Eleni. Which of the pictures in exercise 1 do they forget to talk about?**

3 🎧 2.5 **Listen again. Complete the phrases that Claudio and Eleni use to ask for each other's opinion.**

1 Which picture should we _____ with?

2 What do you think about _____?

3 Do you think _____?

4 So how does the office job _____ to the job here?

5 Why do you _____ that?

6 Which job would you go _____?

3 Sport and leisure

LANGUAGE CHECKLIST

- ☐ I know words to describe sports and pastimes, page 24.
- ☐ I know how to talk about obligation and necessity, page 25.
- ☐ I know how to spell adjectives ending -ful, page 25.
- ☐ I know how to pronounce /v/, /w/ and /b/, page 26.
- ☐ I know how to pronounce -age, page 29.

EXAM CHECKLIST

- ☐ I have practised the gapped text question from the Reading paper, page 22.
- ☐ I have practised the sentence completion question from the Listening paper, page 26.
- ☐ I have practised the key word transformation question from the Use of English paper, page 27.
- ☐ I have practised the word formation question from the Use of English paper, page 27.
- ☐ I have practised writing a review from the Writing paper, page 28.
- ☐ I have practised the individual 'long turn' from the Speaking paper, page 29.

Reading

GAPPED TEXT: PAPER 1, PART 2

1   You are going to read an article about the Japanese sport of sumo. Seven sentences have been removed from the article. Choose from the sentences (A–H) the one which fits each gap (1–7). There is one extra sentence which you do not need to use.

A   It is a **sacred** area which only wrestlers, referees and judges are allowed to enter.

B   For higher-ranked wrestlers the schedule is a little less **demanding** as they can rise later and get straight down to a five-hour training session.

C   But this short period is full of action, as the two huge fighters attempt to push each other out of the ring.

D   Once this entrance is complete, the wrestlers throw a handful of salt into the air.

E   The head of the stable will help the fighter to select one that is also a **talisman**.

F   The biggest difference between sumo and other major sports is the complete lack of celebration by the winner.

G   Although its main purpose is to protect the fighters, it has also determined the fighting style of the sport.

H   For young trainees in particular it is a hard life.

2   Now match the words in **bold** in the sentences and the text to the definitions (1–10) below.

1   very difficult _____

2   an object that gives you good luck _____

3   a fight between two wrestlers or boxers _____

4   easy to win, without real competition _____

5   make your body larger (fatter or more muscular) _____

6   a kind of thick soup _____

7   the bottom part of your feet _____

8   a very strong hold on something _____

9   of religious importance, holy _____

10 find evidence in history _____

A beginner's guide to Sumo
Japan's national sport

Sumo has its origins in mythology. The Japanese god Take-mikazuchi won control of the islands of
5 Japan after defeating a rival god in a sumo contest. Although this is just a legend, it shows the importance that Japanese
10 people attach to this sport. Historians are able to **trace back** sumo as we know it today over 1,500 years.

Modern sumo wrestlers
15 live and train in a *beya* or 'stable'. There are 49 of these in Japan, each of which is run by a former wrestler. **(1)** _____ These
20 lowest-ranked wrestlers get up at about 4am, clean the building, prepare the food for the main meal and put in some practice. **(2)** _____ The main meal of the day is a rich **stew** that provides the wrestlers with enough calories to **bulk up**. To ensure they gain the maximum weight, they go to sleep straight after the meal.

25 It is in the *beya* that wrestlers choose their fighting names. **(3)** _____ It will pay due respect to the tradition of the *beya* and bring good luck throughout his fighting career – in theory at least.

The *dohyo* is the ring in which the sumo tournaments take place. **(4)** _____ The fighting area itself is a circle 15 feet in diameter covered in a thin layer of sand.

30 The *mawashi* is the belt that the wrestlers wear. It is made of silk and measures ten yards long by two feet wide. It is folded in six, then wrapped round the wrestler's waist. **(5)** _____ There are 70 winning moves, nearly all of which involve getting a **grip** of some kind on the opponent's belt. On many occasions, the **bout** is effectively over when one of the combatants has achieved a grip on his opponent's belt.

35 The average sumo match lasts little more than six seconds. **(6)** _____ A fighter also wins by forcing their opponent to touch the ring around the fighting area with a part of the body other than the **soles** of the feet. Many of these bouts are **one-sided**, as many wrestlers succeed with the first attack, but two well-matched fighters can produce a fabulous contest.

Once the bout is over, the referee points to the victor, and the two wrestlers bow to each other
40 before leaving the ring. **(7)** _____ Only when he is out of sight of the public can the victor show his excitement over his triumph. This ensures that order and respect, or *rei*, is maintained throughout the sport.

Vocabulary

SPORTS AND PASTIMES

1 Write the sport for each picture.

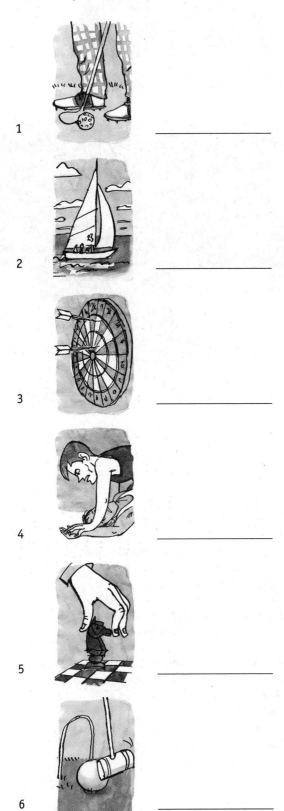

1 _____

2 _____

3 _____

4 _____

5 _____

6 _____

2 Read the descriptions and decide which sports they describe.

1 You fire arrows from your bow and you try to hit the target.

_____

2 You can play this sport on an indoor court or on the beach and you try to hit a ball over a net with your hands.

_____

3 This is a bit like dancing. You do this with other people in a swimming pool and you all try to move at the same time to music.

_____

4 You hit a little white ball over a net using bats.

_____

5 It's a bit like rugby. You play it in the USA, and players wear helmets and protective pads. The biggest game is the Superbowl.

_____

6 You play this on a court where you hit a ball over a net using rackets. You can play it indoors, on a grass court or a clay court.

_____

7 This is a sport where you hit a shuttlecock over a net with a racket.

_____

8 This is where you throw a very hard ball at ten wooden objects, which you try to knock down.

_____

9 You do this in the mountains. It's a bit like skateboarding except that your board doesn't have any wheels.

_____

10 You wear white clothes and you wear a belt which is a different colour, depending on how good you are. You fight your opponents using your hands, arms, feet and legs, and you try to throw them to the ground.

_____

3 Look at the sentences below. Six of them contain a mistake. Find and correct the mistakes.

1 I like table games like chess and backgammon.

2 I've been playing the drums for about five years.

3 We played tennis on a grass park. It was really different to playing on clay.

4 We played golf yesterday and Sarah won me!

5 Zinedine Zidane used to play by Juventus and Real Madrid.

6 We lost the game 5–1.

7 We played a game of football at our local stadium, but the court was terrible.

8 I think darts is my favourite play.

Grammar

OBLIGATION AND NECESSITY

1 Read the sentence beginnings (1–6). Match the endings (a–f) to the beginnings to make complete sentences.

1 Last year you had to book a court ___

2 You're supposed to wear proper tennis shoes, ___

3 You mustn't buy tickets from the ticket touts waiting outside the stadium ___

4 You don't have to buy tickets before the game ___

5 You needn't buy a tennis racket ___

6 I needn't have bought a tennis racket on holiday ___

a because I've got one you can borrow.

b because it's illegal.

c before you went to play tennis.

d because nobody wanted to play with me.

e because you can buy them on the day.

f but most people don't.

2 Put the words from the box into the sentences below. Add one word to each sentence.

are better could don't have to wasn't

1 Laura ride a bike when she was five: she learned really quickly.

2 When we got to the slopes, we discovered that we needn't brought our skis.

3 You need to buy bowling shoes. You can rent them at the bowling alley.

4 You supposed to wear special shoes when you play golf.

5 I wasn't able beat Suzanne at tennis.

6 You had start training if you want to run the marathon in July.

7 Andy able to save the goal.

Spelling

Adjectives with -ful
Adjectives do not end -full except for the word full itself. This is a very common spelling mistake.
Example: careful ~~carefull~~

1 Find twelve adjectives ending -ful in the wordsearch. Words can be found vertically, horizontally and diagonally.

a	d	e	l	i	g	h	t	f	u	l	l	c
g	k	r	o	d	k	t	l	h	p	w	f	o
o	e	t	e	u	p	m	v	o	a	g	o	l
l	x	w	a	a	w	a	e	p	f	y	r	o
b	w	c	m	o	d	i	w	e	i	j	g	u
e	g	o	n	h	z	f	b	f	b	b	e	r
a	r	e	n	c	t	u	u	u	u	e	t	f
u	a	i	f	d	v	b	n	l	h	l	f	u
t	t	y	a	o	e	v	e	n	t	f	u	l
i	e	w	s	s	r	r	p	a	n	r	l	x
f	f	p	o	w	e	r	f	u	l	l	l	a
u	u	o	z	r	e	u	j	u	b	y	d	n
l	l	g	r	a	c	e	f	u	l	l	m	r

25

Listening: footvolley

1 In Part 2 of the Listening test, you will need to complete some sentences or notes. You can anticipate some of the answers. Look at the notepad below. Which answers do you think will be:

a a number?   c an adjective?

b a place?   d something else?

There are [**1**   ] players on a footvolley team.

Each team can only kick the ball [**2**   ] times before it goes over the net.

You lose a point if the ball goes out of the [**3**   ]

Footvolley comes from [**4**   ]

Footvolley was originally a [**5**   ] for football games.

Vera has coached the sport in [**6**   ]

They held the Birmingham tournament indoors because Birmingham doesn't have a [**7**   ]

Vera showed her [**8**   ] in São Paolo.

Vera thinks one day footvolley will be in [**9**   ]

Vera likes footvolley because games are [**10**   ], but they also have a good atmosphere.

---

2 🎧 3.1 **Now you will hear an interview about the sport of footvolley. For questions 1–10, complete the sentences. You will need to write a word or a short phrase in each gap.**

Pronunciation

1 🎧 3.2 **Listen and number the pictures 1–6.**

2 **Work with a partner. Read the sentences to each other.**
   1 Vincent will visit Valerie in Vienna.
   2 We worked very well this week.
   3 We will wait with the van.

SPOTLIGHT ON PRONUNCIATION

/v/, /w/ and /b/
To make a /v/ sound, press your front teeth on your bottom lip. To make a /b/ sound, press your lips together. Your teeth should not touch your lips.

---

3 **Now practise /v/ and /b/.**
   1 Bob's brother Vivian brought a box of vegetables.
   2 Valerie borrowed that valuable bracelet.
   3 Did Vanessa buy vanilla or blackberry ice cream?

4 🎧 3.3 **Listen and circle the words you hear.**

---

vote boat **van** **ban** **vase** **bars**
vending *bending* very berry *vest*
best *via* buyer

Use of English

KEY WORD TRANSFORMATIONS: PAPER 3, PART 4

1 Complete the second sentence so that it has a similar meaning to the first sentence, using the word given. Do not change the word given. You must use between two and five words, including the word given. There is an example at the beginning (0).

0 You won't be able to win the competition.
CHANCE
You have ..*no chance of winning*.. the competition.

1 You're not allowed to go on the court if you're not wearing the right shoes.
MUST

You .... on the court if you're not wearing the right shoes.

2 Diana plays the guitar really well.
AT

Diana .... playing the guitar.

3 We tried really hard, but we couldn't beat the other team.
ABLE

We tried really hard, but we .... beat the other team.

4 We play cricket sometimes.
FROM

We play cricket ....

5 It's very important to tell the coach that you can't play tomorrow.
HAD

You .... the coach that you can't play tomorrow.

6 You shouldn't use the swimming pool if there isn't a life guard on duty.
SUPPOSED

You .... use the swimming pool if there isn't a life guard on duty.

7 It's not necessary to watch the game tomorrow if you don't want to.
HAVE

You .... watch the game tomorrow if you don't want to.

8 Jake always beats me at tennis.
KEEPS

Jake .... me at tennis.

WORD FORMATION: PAPER 3, PART 3

2 Read the text below. Use the words given in capitals at the end of some of the lines to form a word that fits in the gap in the same line. There is an example at the beginning (0).

After a lot of campaigning, last year the city council agreed to hold a local swimming (0) ..*championship*.. . They did however demand that all	**CHAMPION**
(1) .... in the competition should come from the local area. Unfortunately, there were not	**CONTEST**
enough local (2) .... who wanted to take part. It does not	**INHABIT**
take a lot of (3) .... to realise that the more people who compete, the more money the competition will raise. So, as they had	**INTELLIGENT**
received a lot of (4) .... from people in other towns who wanted to take part, the organisers decided that anyone resident in the state could compete. Eventually, they had over a	**CORRESPOND**
thousand (5) .... I was one of the organisers, so I was delighted that the competition was taking place as arranging it had taken a	**ENTER**
lot of (6) .... from all of us. I could never have imagined the	**PATIENT**
(7) .... we had in arranging this event. Although it was	**DIFFICULT**
(8) .... , we decorated the pool for the competition. It was worth doing this as the decorations looked really (9)	**EXPENSE**
	IMPRESS
The swimming races went well and all our swimmers were (10) .... , even if we didn't win any of the gold medals.	**COMPETE**

Writing: a review

COMPULSORY TASK: PAPER 2, PART 1

1 Complete the student's answer to the exam question below with the words from the box.

amazed	bored	disappointed	excited
amazing	boring	disappointing	exciting

> Write a review in response to this advertisement.
>
> **World Sports**
> World Sports magazine is preparing a special edition with your favourite memories of sports events. All readers are invited to send us a review of a sports event that you have attended with the title *A memorable sports event*.
>
> Reports should include the background to the event and what was special about it for you. All submissions should be 100–150 words.

A memorable sports event
Last year our local team was in the cup final. I was especially [1] _____ because I had won tickets to the game! It was the first time I had seen a match in the stadium and it was very [2] _____ being there.

Before the game, the atmosphere was [3] _____: everyone was singing and shouting. When we got to our seats, we were even more [4] _____ because we were on the halfway line – we had the best seats in the stadium!

There were no goals and afterwards the newspapers said it was [5] _____, but I never felt [6] _____ in the stadium: for one thing the game ended with penalties. Unfortunately, we only scored two penalties and we lost. It was so [7] _____! Anyway, I had a great time despite the result, but my father was really [8] _____. For us, it was a very memorable sports event.

2 Now write your own answer to the exam question in exercise 1.

....
....
....
....
....
....
....
....
....
....
....
....
....
....

Speaking

INDIVIDUAL 'LONG TURN': PAPER 5, PART 2

1 🎧 3.4 **In Part 2 of the Speaking test, you have to describe and contrast a pair of photographs for about a minute. Listen to two students doing the individual 'long turn' and talking about the photographs below. Which student does not answer the interlocutor's question? (Note that in the exam you and your partner will always have different pairs of photographs to talk about.)**

2 🎧 3.4 **Listen again and complete the sentences with useful words for comparing photographs.**

1 So the first picture is indoors _____ the second picture is outdoors.

2 _____ I like chess, I prefer the second activity.

3 Both pictures _____ people in competitions.

4 In each picture there's a different _____ of competition.

5 So cycling _____ harder, but I think chess is the most difficult activity.

3 **If you are working with a partner, ask and answer the interlocutor's question for the photographs. The question is in listening script 3.4 on page 158.**

Pronunciation

> ### SPOTLIGHT ON PRONUNCIATION
>
> **Words ending in -age**
> Words ending -age are usually pronounced /ɪdʒ/ not /eɪdʒ/.
> Example: marriage ➡ /mærɪdʒ/
>
> There are some exceptions however. One-syllable words are usually pronounced /eɪdʒ/.
> Example: page ➡ /peɪdʒ/
>
> Some verbs that begin en- are also pronounced /eɪdʒ/.
> Example: engage ➡ /ɪngeɪdʒ/
>
> Some words are pronounced /aːʒ/. These words originally come from French.
> Example: sabotage ➡ /sæbətaːʒ/

1 **Complete the table with the words in the box. Note that *garage* has two possible pronunciations.**

> age average cage camouflage collage cottage courage damage encourage enrage espionage garage *(UK English)* garage *(US English)* heritage image manage massage message stage village

/aːʒ/	/eɪdʒ/	/ɪdʒ/
	age	average

2 🎧 3.5 **Now listen and check your answers.**

3 **If you are working with a partner, read all the *-age* words to each other.**

4 Nature and animals

☐ I know words to describe nature and animals, page 32.

☐ I know how to use adjectives and prepositions, page 32.

☐ I know the spelling of some words with double letters, page 32.

☐ I know the grammar of phrasal verbs, page 33.

☐ I know how to use countable and uncountable determiners, page 33.

☐ I know how to pronounce linking sounds, page 35.

☐ I know how to pronounce /r/, /w/ and /l/, page 37.

EXAM CHECKLIST

☐ I have practised the multiple matching question from the Reading paper, page 30.

☐ I have practised the multiple-choice cloze question from the Use of English paper, page 33.

☐ I have practised how to email for advice in the Writing paper, page 34.

☐ I have practised the multiple matching question from the Listening paper, page 35.

☐ I have practised the word formation question from the Use of English paper, page 36.

☐ I have practised the individual 'long turn' from the Speaking paper, page 36.

Reading

MULTIPLE MATCHING: PAPER 1, PART 3

1 **You are going to read an article about four encounters between people and animals. For questions 1–15, choose from the animals (A–D). The animals may be chosen more than once.**

Which animal

1 was hit by its human victim? ___

2 was created by people? ___

3 lost interest in its victim? ___

4 was hunting in an urban area? ___

5 thought its prey was a different animal? ___

6 travelled across two continents? ___

7 was acting out of curiosity? ___

8 can chase its victims for a long way? ___

9 is normally very difficult to find in the wild? ___

10 put its victim's head in its mouth? ___

11 is creating panic in the media? ___

12 watched its victim after the attack? ___

13 attacked more than one person on the same day? ___

14 attacked a very old person? ___

15 kills its victims by preventing them from breathing? ___

2 **Find these words and phrases (1–10) in the text. Then match the definitions (a–j) to the words and phrases.**

1 exceptional ___   a went into the wrong place by accident

2 a spate ___   b a place where birds and reptiles keep their eggs

3 strayed ___   c a large group of flying insects

4 a swarm ___   d the part of the mouth that moves up and down

5 hives ___   e very unusual

6 seized ___   f places where bees live

7 drown ___   g a series of bad/unfortunate events

8 a nest ___   h die in water when you cannot breathe

9 jaws ___   i a tool often used with a hammer to cut stone

10 a chisel ___   j taken strongly and quickly

ANIMAL ATTACK!

As the spread of humanity gets wider and natural habitats are destroyed, more and more people are coming in contact with wild animals. The vast majority of these encounters pass peacefully, but in exceptional circumstances some unfortunate people have been attacked. We investigate four such encounters.

A Leopards, India

There have been a spate of leopard attacks on people in the Indian state of Maharashtra. In January 2007 three men were attacked by a leopard which had strayed into their town in search of food. The newspapers have been talking of a 'leopard storm' in this region as more attacks of this type take place. The leopards themselves have had to abandon their secretive lives in the depths of the forests because their habitats are being destroyed. Woodland is being cut down to make room for more bungalows, and the big cats are being forced out of the parks in which they live.

B Killer bees, the USA

In a scene from a Hollywood movie come suddenly to life, an elderly woman has been hospitalised after she was attacked by a swarm of killer bees. She was stung all over her body and was only saved when firemen poured water over the woman and her attackers.

The bees were killer bees created by scientists in South America who were trying to breed American honey bees with stronger African bees. The insects escaped from their laboratory in 1957 and migrated north into the USA. So far an estimated one thousand people have been killed after attacks by the swarms. Typically bees attack when there is a threat to their hives and will follow enemies for over a kilometre.

C Crocodiles, Australia

Diver Jeff Tanswell thought his life was over when he was seized by a huge saltwater crocodile while snorkelling over a reef in Queensland, Australia. The animal grabbed him and dragged him down into the deep water. This is normally the prelude to a 'death roll' where crocodiles dive to the depths and spin their prey round until they drown. But Jeff survived.

One explanation for the attack was that it may have been a female trying to protect a nest nearby from a potential danger. However, although Jeff had been unable to put up much resistance, the crocodile gave up the attack and just let him go. Wildlife experts suspect that the fight was over because the crocodile was just interested in what Jeff was. Because crocodiles lack fingers they have to inspect new things with their mouths, which is why it may have bitten the diver in the first place.

D Great white sharks, Australia

Another man lucky to escape a close encounter with a wild animal was Eric Nerhus. While diving for shellfish off Cape Howe, he found himself in sudden jeopardy. A three and half metre great white shark shot towards him through the dark water. It grabbed his head, body and arms in its jaws. Although Eric said it felt like being trapped in a dark cave, miraculously his body was protected by a lead-weight vest. The shark started to shake him, whereupon the diver used his free hand to locate its eye which he stabbed with his diving chisel. As Eric escaped to the surface, the shark circled him until his son was able to drag him back into their boat.

Experts on marine behaviour theorise that in this case Eric was attacked because the shark had mistaken him for a seal and so it released him as soon as he started to put up a fight.

Vocabulary

NATURE AND ANIMALS

1 Complete the words. Write one letter in each space.

1 If you go on safari, you can see w _ _ _ animals such as giraffes, lions and antelope.

2 In India and Thailand they use t _ _ _ elephants to help lift heavy objects.

3 You see very few young pandas in zoos because the animals don't usually b _ _ _ _ in captivity.

4 Animals behave on i _ _ _ _ _ _ _ .

5 Many animal species are now e _ _ _ _ _ _ _ _ _ : they could die out in the next 50 years.

6 Our family has a p _ _ cat called Tiger.

7 Sharks hunt seals as p _ _ _ .

8 You can t _ _ _ _ dogs to help blind people.

9 The natural h _ _ _ _ _ _ of the tiger is the jungles of Asia.

10 We have to do everything possible to save animal species from e _ _ _ _ _ _ _ _ _ _ so that they don't become like the dodo or the dinosaurs.

ADJECTIVES AND PREPOSITIONS

2 Underline the correct preposition.

1 We are leaving at two o'clock, so we need to be aware *for / of* the time.

2 I love cats, but I am allergic *with / to* them.

3 The kids want a dog, but I'm not keen *on / for* the idea.

4 I'm fed up *about / with* the cat: she keeps killing birds and mice.

5 I'm interested *in / for* doing something to help wild animals.

6 Jane Goodall is famous *from / for* her work with chimpanzees.

7 I didn't want to go on the jungle walk because I'm afraid *of / by* snakes.

Spelling

SPOTLIGHT ON SPELLING

Words with double letters
One of the biggest problems with spelling in English is that many words have double letters. As the pronunciation of the word does not tell you if the word is spelt with one letter or two, you often need to learn the spelling of each word individually.

1 Look at the words below which are commonly spelt wrongly. Circle the correct spelling.

1 a necessary
   b neccessary
   c neccesary

2 a acommodation
   b accomodation
   c accommodation

3 a misspel
   b misspell
   c mispell

4 a occasion
   b ocassion
   c occassion

5 a tommorow
   b tomorrow
   c tommorrow

6 a commision
   b comission
   c commission

7 a assistant
   b asisstant
   c assisttant

8 a milionnaire
   b millionaire
   c millionnaire

9 a possessions
   b posessions
   c possesions

10 a inacessible
   b innacesible
   c inaccessible

11 a oportunity
   b opportunity
   c opporttunity

12 a reccomendation
   b reccommendation
   c recommendation

Grammar

PHRASAL VERBS

1 Look at the sentences below. Six of them contain a mistake. Find and correct the mistakes.

1 Mark and Steve get on them well together. They are great friends.

2 I was so poor that I lived rice off. It was all I ate.

3 Some journalists have revealed that big business is destroying wild animal habitats in Africa. I wonder how they found out it.

4 It is an absolute tragedy that so many wonderful species are just dying out.

5 I have some complicated instructions that I want you to carry them out.

6 You shouldn't look down to environmental activists. They are trying to help all of us.

7 I didn't know they were criminals and they stole a lot of money from me. I was completely taken in.

8 One of the most exciting things about Indonesia is that explorers are coming new species across all the time.

COUNTABLE AND UNCOUNTABLE DETERMINERS

2 Choose a suitable word to complete the sentences below. Write one word only in each gap.

1 Only _____ few species of shark are known to attack people.

2 I don't think there is _____ difference between buying a hamster and a guinea pig as a pet.

3 We haven't got _____ pets.

4 The blue whale is very rare. _____ people have had the opportunity to film or photograph one.

5 _____ anyone knows where to find sea snakes in the wild.

6 They were able to speak to a great _____ of people about climate change.

7 There is _____ difference between rats and mice.

8 _____ time I go to Brazil, I see a humming bird.

Use of English

MULTIPLE-CHOICE CLOZE: PAPER 3, PART 1

1 Read the text below and decide which answer (A, B, C or D) best fits each gap. There is an example at the beginning (0).

Michelle Whiteman has **(0)** ...*dedicated*... her life to protecting the orang-utan. For ten months of the year she works in the jungles of Borneo, watching and studying the great apes in their natural **(1)** .... The rest of the time she spends in the UK raising **(2)** .... of the need for help. Like many of the animals in the islands of Indonesia, the orang-utan is in **(3)** .... danger.

The destruction of the jungles is so severe that **(4)** .... to some experts the species may be extinct within ten years. In addition to the destruction of their jungle homes, the animals are also at **(5)** .... due to hunting and the capture of wild animals for the pet trade. Furthermore, their population does not increase rapidly: a female orang-utan has a **(6)** .... baby only once every eight years.

Orang-utans are solitary animals which **(7)** .... almost all of their time in the trees, **(8)** .... for food or sleeping. They can weigh up to 77 kilos, which means they are also the largest tree-living animals in the world.

Michelle learnt about the orang-utans while studying zoology at Bristol University. "When I read about the terrible situation in Indonesia, I could **(9)** .... believe it. There are a great **(10)** .... of new animal species there that could become extinct before we have had a chance to discover them! I knew I **(11)** .... do something, so I came out here. If we don't find a **(12)** .... soon to stop the destruction of their habitat, the orang-utan will simply disappear."

0	A chosen	B selected	C decided	D dedicated
1	A places	B locations	C habitats	D sites
2	A knowledge	B appreciation	C awareness	D realisation
3	A grave	B terrific	C thrilling	D tragic
4	A relating	B furthermore	C further	D according
5	A risk	B trouble	C hazard	D threat
6	A lonely	B one	C single	D unique
7	A take	B spend	C pass	D wait
8	A finding	B locating	C seeking	D searching
9	A hardly	B almost	C just	D absolutely
10	A amount	B group	C number	D lot
11	A must	B had to	C can	D ought
12	A route	B path	C direction	D way

Writing: emailing for advice

COMPULSORY TASK: PAPER 2, PART 1

1 In Part 1 of the Writing test, you may be asked to write an email of advice. Read the exam question below. What information must you include in your reply?

> You have received an email from a friend asking for information about a weekend trip that you had last year.
>
> > Our two children aged 6 and 7 are fascinated with animals and we thought we would take them for a weekend away. I remember that last summer you visited a rescue centre for birds of prey and we are thinking of going there.
> > Could you send me an email to say if you had a good time? Do you think it would be suitable for young children? If the trip is a weekend one, where can we stay?
> > Best wishes
> > Terry
>
> Read the email carefully, and then look at the advertisement for the centre that you visited and the notes that you have added. Then write an email to your friend, saying whether this weekend trip would be suitable or not.

The Western Birds of Prey Rescue Centre

Attend our special weekend courses[1] learning about falcons, hawks and owls.

- Learn how the birds hunt
- Watch the birds being trained
- See the vets treating injured birds rescued from the wild[2]
- Learn about animal conservation
- Activities for all the family[3]

1 You have to stay one night: good cheap bed and breakfast nearby

2 Some of the birds are badly injured – might upset children

3 Play park for children with games and slides, etc. Great!

2 Complete the student's answer to the exam question in exercise 1 with the sentences (a–h). Use the introductory phrases in **bold** to help you.

> Dear Terry
>
> 1 _____
> 2 _____
> 3 _____
> 4 _____
>
> I have to warn you, though, about watching the vets with the injured birds.
>
> 5 _____
> 6 _____
>
> 7 _____
>
> The rooms are modern and very clean and I'd recommend it too.
>
> 8 _____
>
> Best,
> Pete

a Some of the birds were in a very bad condition and my children cried.

b You asked for my advice and **if I were you**, I would definitely take the kids to the Western Birds of Prey Centre.

c One reason was there was a play park there and my kids loved it!

d Thanks for your email.

e **As for** accommodation, we stayed in a good cheap bed and breakfast nearby.

f So, **as far as** I am concerned, the centre is a great place to go for a weekend.

g When we went there, **at first** I was worried that the kids would get bored but actually they enjoyed the whole weekend.

h But, **let's face it**, they have to learn that these animals are in trouble.

3 Now write your own answer to the exam question in exercise 1.

....

....

....

....

....

....

....

....

....

....

....

....

....

....

Listening: special animals

MULTIPLE MATCHING: PAPER 4, PART 3

1 🎧4.1 **You will hear five different people talking about animals that have been important in their lives. For questions 1–5, choose from the list (A–F) the animal that each person is talking about. There is one extra letter which you do not need to use.**

Which animal

A was scared of people?   Speaker ____

B was in the zoo?   Speaker ____

C had been trained to do a job? Speaker ____

D had to be given away?   Speaker ____

E attacked someone?   Speaker ____

F was very rare?   Speaker ____

Pronunciation

1 🎧4.2 **Listen again to these two sentences from the Listening. Can you hear an extra sound which connects (links) the letters underlined?**

1 As it gre**w u**p, it became large**r a**nd larger.

2 You don't often se**e a** kingfisher in the wild.

Linking sounds

Listening to native speakers can be difficult because they do not always say words separately. Instead, when they speak quickly, they use linking sounds to join words together. To become an effective listener, you need to expect to hear these linking sounds.

In the words *grew up*, the linking sound /w/ comes from the final letter of the word *grew*. In the same way, in *larger and* the linking sound /r/ comes from the final letter of the word *larger*.

However, notice that in the words *see a* there is a linking sound /j/, but there is no letter representing this sound in the spelling of the words: there is no *y* or *j*.

2 🎧4.3 **Look at the sentences below and decide which sound is linking the words underlined: /j/, /r/ or /w/? Then listen to check your answers.**

1 My teache**r a**nd I were interviewed on TV.

2 Let's g**o a**nd see the parrots in the park.

3 Andre**w a**sked me if we could have a pet rabbit.

4 We want to se**e a**ll the animals while we're here.

5 The police sa**y a** wild puma has been seen.

6 We sa**w a** giraffe and some lions on safari.

3 Look again at the sentences (1–6) in exercise 2. Which sentences make the linking sound from a letter which is already in one of the words? Which sentences add a linking sound?

4 🎧4.4 **Find the linking sounds in each sentence below. Then listen to check your answers.**

1 Granddad's too old to go for a two-hour walk.

2 Is there another way of working?

3 Here's the tea and coffee for Tina and Sarah.

5 If you are working with a partner, practise together reading the sentences in exercise 4.

Use of English

WORD FORMATION: PAPER 3, PART 3

1 Read the text below. Use the words given in capitals at the end of some of the lines to form a word that fits in the gap in the same line. There is an example at the beginning (0).

After the strange death last week of three sheep on a farm in Somerset, England, the police have begun an **(0)** ...*investigation*... into reports of a big cat in the area. It is not the first time this has happened. Farmer Thomas Sudbury was walking home late last year when he had a **(1)** .... experience. "I heard a noise behind me and when I turned around, I saw a big black cat, as big as a puma," he said. "I was so scared I could hardly **(2)** ...." Although critics say that the story is just a product of Mr Sudbury's **(3)** .... , the farmer defends his story. "That was no **(4)** .... pet cat: it looked dangerous!"

While a few people have been **(5)** .... in getting a photograph of the beast on film, so far nobody has taken a clear picture of the **(6)** .... animal. In the **(7)** .... of the photos, the shape and size of the animal are **(8)** .... vague. However, although no one can say for certain if a big cat is loose in Somerset, local people are **(9)** .... "I don't know what killed my sheep," says farmer Martin Hoggard, "but I know this: the **(10)** .... was big, much bigger than a fox. And it's out there now, roaming the countryside."

INVESTIGATE

TERRIFY

BREATH

IMAGINE

HARM

SUCCESS

MYSTERY
MAJOR

EXTREME

NERVE

ATTACK

Speaking

INDIVIDUAL 'LONG TURN': PAPER 5, PART 2

1 🎧 4.5 Look at the study techniques box above. Julieta is practising before the speaking exam and she has prepared a list of useful phrases. Listen to her describing the pictures on page 37. Which of the phrases in the list does she use?

a Well, let me see. ☐
b Both photos show ... ☐
c In the first photo there's a ... ☐
d The second photo shows ... ☐
e Perhaps ... ☐
f Maybe ... ☐
g In the first one, there's a ... whereas in the second photo, the bottom one, there are ... ☐
h In the first one, there's a ... while in the other one I can see a ... ☐
i Returning to the first picture ... ☐
j Anyway, going back to the first picture ... ☐

2 If you are working with a partner, ask and answer the question below for the photographs.

Compare the two photographs and say which experience is most memorable.

Pronunciation

/r/ and /w/
Many people have problems pronouncing /r/ and /w/.
The difference between these sounds is that when you
say /w/, your lips start closed and then open.

1 🎧 4.6 **Listen and write the word you hear.**

1 _____

2 _____

3 _____

4 _____

5 _____

6 _____

/r/ and /l/
The pronunciation of /r/ and /l/ can also be difficult.
The difference between /r/ and /l/ is that when you say
/l/, your tongue should touch the top of your mouth.

2 🎧 4.7 **Listen and circle the words you hear.**
1 a light
  b right
2 a led
  b red
3 a lock
  b rock
4 a load
  b road

3 🎧 4.8 **Now listen and repeat the words.**
1 light   right   white
2 late   rate   wait
3 lock   rock   wok
4 led   red   wed
5 lay   ray   way
6 law   raw   war

4 **If you are working with a partner, take turns to say one
word from exercise 3. Your partner must point to the
word that you say.**

5 A good story

- ☐ I know words to describe books and film, page 40.
- ☐ I know some gradable and non-gradable adjectives, page 40.
- ☐ I know some verbs of manner, page 40.
- ☐ I know how to use narrative tenses, page 41.
- ☐ I know how to spell some adjectives ending -ous, page 41.
- ☐ I know how to place stress in long words, page 42.

- ☐ I have practised the multiple choice question from the Reading paper, page 38.
- ☐ I have practised the Part 4 dialogue + multiple choice question from the Listening paper, page 42.
- ☐ I have practised the open cloze question from the Use of English paper, page 43.
- ☐ I have practised the multiple-choice cloze question from the Use of English paper, page 43.
- ☐ I have practised writing a story from the Writing paper, page 44.
- ☐ I have practised the collaborative task from the Speaking paper, page 45.

Reading

MULTIPLE CHOICE: PAPER 1, PART 1

1 **You are going to read an article about words that came from fictional characters. For questions 1–8, choose the answer (A, B, C or D) which you think fits best according to the text.**

1 The word 'quixotic'
   A is a compliment.   C can mean one of two things.
   B is a criticism.   D is very old-fashioned.

2 What was Ebenezer Scrooge?
   A A criminal.   C A hero.
   B A very poor man.   D A businessman.

3 What kind of people use the word 'Fagin'?
   A children   C politicians
   B criminals   D journalists

4 What does the writer mean by 'Stevenson also brought two of his characters into everyday speech'?
   A The names of the characters are used by people in their daily lives.
   B The characters spoke very naturally.
   C The characters were named after words people used in their daily lives.
   D The author changed the characters' names to make them more popular.

5 How does the writer feel about genetically modified foods?
   A He is undecided.
   B He opposes them.
   C He thinks they taste horrible.
   D He thinks they are an amazing scientific achievement.

6 What is the effect of the posters of Big Brother?
   A They give people orders.
   B They are used in election campaigns.
   C They make people feel nervous.
   D They advertise a television programme.

7 The word 'Orwellian' is used to describe
   A George Orwell's personality.   C a type of writing.
   B the way a country is organised. D success in writing novels.

8 What does the writer say about the novel *Trilby*?
   A It was a disaster.   C It has become successful recently.
   B Its author was never famous.   D It was very successful when it was written.

Real-life Romeos

When we use the word *Romeo* for a romantic young man, we hardly think of the character from William Shakespeare's play *Romeo and Juliet*. But a sure sign of an author having created a successful character is that the character's name enters the language and becomes a word. Despite only writing in Spanish, Shakespeare's contemporary Cervantes achieved the feat of creating a new word in a different language – English, the adjective *quixotic*. This word comes from the title character of Cervantes' *Don Quixote*. It describes a person who has great imagination and makes incredible plans, but whose plans are unfortunately impossible to achieve.

One author who was particularly successful in seeing his characters enter the language was the novelist Charles Dickens. In modern English a *scrooge* is used to describe someone who is mean and tries to avoid spending money at all. The word comes from the protagonist of Dickens's novella *A Christmas Carol*, Ebenezer Scrooge, who treats the employees in his office poorly and makes them work in terrible conditions. As well as Scrooge, Dickens also had success with Fagin, the villain of *Oliver Twist*. In the novel Fagin controlled a group of child criminals. His name is often used in the press to describe real-life adult leaders of youthful gangs.

The Victorian era (1837–1901) in which Dickens wrote was a major period for the English novel. At the end of the nineteenth century, the Scottish author Robert Louis Stevenson achieved enormous success with his masterpiece *Treasure Island*. Amazingly, Stevenson also brought two of his characters into everyday speech. A *Jekyll and Hyde* character is a person whose personality can quickly change from being kind to being angry, impolite or aggressive. The name comes from the scientist protagonist of *Dr Jekyll and Mr Hyde* whose strange experiments turn him from man to murderous monster, and back again. Stevenson was not alone in seeing success from the field of Gothic Horror. At the age of twenty-one Mary Shelley wrote *Frankenstein*, and the name of her mad scientist is now used as an adjective to describe any kind of science that seems to be out of control: *Frankenstein foods*, for example, for genetically modified ingredients.

It does seem strange that villains enter the language more often than heroes. Sometimes in fact these characters need hardly appear in the original work at all. The television series *Big Brother* is named after the all-powerful dictator who rules the London of the future in George Orwell's novel *Nineteen Eighty-Four*. Big Brother himself is never encountered during the story: we only ever see his face on posters along with the ominous message 'Big Brother is Watching You'. This is why the presence of more and more cameras watching the streets, and greater government controls over the everyday lives of people, has led to the suggestion that we live in a 'Big Brother society'.

Interestingly, Orwell achieved the double feat of creating a character that has entered the language as well as entering the language himself. The word *Orwellian* is used to describe a society which tries to control every aspect of people's lives, as happened in the pages of *Nineteen Eighty-Four*.

Perhaps the strangest thing of all though is that some writers create characters who enter and remain in the language long after the book itself has been forgotten. The character *Svengali* was an evil hypnotist in George du Maurier's novel *Trilby*. The book itself made a massive impact after it was published in 1894 and the character's name became synonymous with manipulative people who try to convince others to do what they say. The word is still used today, especially to describe politicians, despite the fact that the original novel is now almost completely unknown.

"ARE YOU COME FROM DR. JEKYLL?" I ASKED

Vocabulary

BOOKS AND FILM

1 **Complete the puzzle. What is the word in grey?**

1 A very famous book or film which is accepted as being a very important work.

2 One part of a book.

3 The most important bad person in a film or book.

4 The most important female in a film or book.

5 The person who tells the story.

6 A book or film that was invented by a writer, not history or biography, for example.

7 The story of a book or film, what happens.

8 A long-running television programme.

9 The landscape that you see on stage in the theatre or in the background of a film.

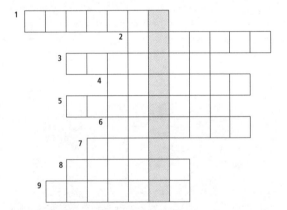

GRADABLE AND NON-GRADABLE ADJECTIVES

2 **Replace the words in bold with one word. Use a suitable non-gradable adjective so that that meaning of the sentence does not change.**

1 I was presenting an award and I read out the wrong person's name. I was **so embarrassed**.

_____

2 The film was **completely stupid**. We couldn't take it seriously.

_____

3 The kids saw a film about ghosts and they were **very frightened**.

_____

4 Frances bought seven DVDs and none of them worked. She was **very angry**!

_____

5 Carlos got a big role in a movie, but the movie studio's money ran out and they couldn't make the film. He was **so disappointed**.

_____

6 They were filming all night and that's why the actors are **really tired**.

_____

7 Olivia has won a local poetry competition. Her parents are **really happy** for her.

_____

VERBS OF MANNER

3 **Complete the words. Write one letter in each space.**

1 Can you drink more quietly? I hate it when you s _ _ _ _ your coffee!

2 He is l _ _ _ _ _ _ because he hurt his leg playing football.

3 When I broke his glasses, he didn't say anything. He just g _ _ _ _ _ at me angrily.

4 He told the girls to stop laughing at him, but they didn't listen and carried on g _ _ _ _ _ _ _ .

5 Everyone was g _ _ _ _ _ _ for breath because there was so much smoke in the room.

6 The tea was hot, so I s _ _ _ _ _ it slowly.

7 We s _ _ _ _ _ _ _ through the woods all afternoon. It was a lovely walk.

8 She's in love with a famous actor. She s _ _ _ _ every time she sees him on TV!

Grammar

NARRATIVE TENSES

1 Read the sentence beginnings (1–6). Match the endings (a–f) to the beginnings to make complete sentences.

1 I told him not to lend me the book because ___

2 That book is really boring. I fell asleep while ___

3 It was a great day for skiing. The sky was clear and ___

4 We decided to wait indoors while ___

5 The doctor didn't recognise the disease because ___

6 It wasn't possible to get an appointment with the doctor because ___

a I was reading it.

b he had never seen the symptoms before.

c it was snowing.

d he was seeing patients all afternoon.

e it had snowed the night before.

f I had read it before.

2 Look at the pictures on the right. They show past events. Complete the sentences using the words in brackets and the past perfect simple, past perfect continuous and past continuous.

1 When I got back to my car, I discovered

_____ (it / disappear).

2 He couldn't leave the stage because

_____ (audience / clap / ten minutes).

3 Gary was really tired in the morning because he

_____ (write / all night).

4 When I heard the bang,

_____ (I / work / garden).

5 I missed my stop because

_____ (I / read / novel).

6 The picture wasn't there –

_____ (it / stole).

Spelling

SPOTLIGHT ON SPELLING

Adjectives ending -ous
Many adjectives end in -ous.
Example: dangerous

When the adjective is made from a noun, sometimes a letter is dropped.
Example: fame ➡ famous

1 Look at the adjectives below. Nine of them contain a mistake. Find and correct the mistakes. Write the correct spelling of the words.

1 furyous _____   7 marvellous _____

2 gorgous _____   8 victoryous _____

3 ridiculous _____   9 unconsious _____

4 cureous _____   10 religous _____

5 viscious _____   11 infectious _____

6 nerveous _____   12 delicous_____

Listening: a ghostwriter

DIALOGUE + MULTIPLE CHOICE: PAPER 4, PART 4

1 🎧5.1 **You will hear an interview with a ghostwriter, George Moore. For questions 1–7, choose the best answer (A, B or C).**

1 Why does George say that ghostwriters write the autobiographies of celebrities?
   A Celebrities are too lazy to write the book.
   B They are fans of the celebrities.
   C Celebrities do not have the time or skill to write the book.

2 What does George say about theatre actors?
   A They don't need a lot of help with the book.
   B They only write about half the book.
   C The ghostwriter writes all of the book for them.

3 Where does George get information about a teenage rock star's early career?
   A from the star's family
   B from national newspapers
   C from local libraries

4 How did George feel about writing the history of music festivals in the 1960s?
   A He preferred it to writing about teenage rock stars.
   B He thought it was boring.
   C He thought it was really difficult.

5 How does George get paid?
   A The star gives him a percentage of his/her earnings from the book.
   B He receives a single payment for his work.
   C He gets royalties.

6 How did George start working as a ghostwriter?
   A His ex-boss gave up a job and George replaced him.
   B A star asked him to help write a book.
   C Through his business contacts.

7 Why does George not worry because his name is not on the cover of the book?
   A because he is embarrassed to be writing about pop music
   B because he gets a lot of money for his work
   C because his books are not as important as encyclopedias and other reference books

Pronunciation

Stress in long words
Placing the stress in new words can be very difficult. There is one guideline that can help you. When a word has more than three syllables, the stress is often on the second syllable from the end of the word.

1 🎧5.2 **Look at the examples from the interview with George Moore. Listen to the pronunciation.**

autobiography

encyclopedia

negotiate

2 🎧5.3 **Which words below have the stress on the second syllable from the end? Which words are exceptions? Listen to check your answers.**

appearances	experienced
appropriate	mysterious
centimetre	necessarily
characteristic	personality
disappearance	professional
disappointment	realistic
embarrassment	retirement
enthusiasm	sympathetic

3 🎧5.3 **Listen again. Where is the stress in the adjectives that end -ic?**

4 🎧5.4 **Now listen to these words of three or more syllables and complete the rule.**

When a word ends in -ion, the stress is on the

_____ syllable from the end.

association	restriction
definition	recognition
communication	suggestion
negotiation	

Use of English

OPEN CLOZE: PAPER 3, PART 2

1 Read the text below and think of the word which best fits each gap. Use only one word in each gap. There is an example at the beginning (0).

Heart of Darkness is **(0)** ....*a*................ dark tale of colonial exploitation set **(1)** .... Africa during the nineteenth century. It was written **(2)** .... Joseph Conrad and published in English in 1902, despite the **(3)** .... that Conrad was born in modern Ukraine, and was of Polish nationality.

Although the book is little more than a hundred pages long, **(4)** .... is a powerful story of the way in which wealthy countries made local people work in terrible conditions. The narrator of **(5)** .... story is a sailor called Marlow **(6)** .... tells the tale while on a boat moored in the Thames. He recounts the story of how he travelled to Africa, excited by maps with empty spaces showing places that Europeans **(7)** .... not yet explored. Marlow takes a job on a boat travelling **(8)** .... a river into the African continent where he encounters an ivory trader, Mr Kurtz, who has become a kind of ruler over the local people.

The events of the novel are based on Conrad's own experience as the captain of a steamboat working in the Congo during the late nineteenth century. Although the African country in the book is **(9)** .... named in the novel, many readers assume that it is the Congo.

Conrad was a major novelist **(10)** .... novels have become even **(11)** .... popular since his death. The book has continued to influence later writers **(12)** .... well as Hollywood films such as *Apocalypse Now*.

MULTIPLE-CHOICE CLOZE: PAPER 3, PART 1

2 Read the text below and decide which answer (A, B, C or D) best fits each gap. There is an example at the beginning (0).

If you want a different perspective on your friends' reading **(0)** .....*habits*............ , why not ask them what was the worst book they ever read? Or what was the last book that they **(1)** .... to finish reading? When I asked a number of my friends this question, I got some surprising **(2)** ....

The first surprise was one of my friends said that they had **(3)** .... on J.R.R Tolkein's *The Lord of the Rings* after only ten pages! I was very disappointed because that is one of my all-time **(4)** .... reads. The same friend said that he had tried to read *Robinson Crusoe* by Daniel Defoe on several **(5)** .... , but had never finished it.

One of my friends said she had always **(6)** .... the modernist novelist Virginia Woolf, but that she had **(7)** .... problems reading her classic fantasy tale *Orlando*. The problem was that the book was difficult to read because of all its descriptions and adjectives. I have to admit that I **(8)** .... the same: I finished the book, but it was **(9)** .... work.

Another interesting response was how many people said that they liked one kind of book when they were younger, but that their taste **(10)** .... as they got older. I remember my brother complaining at school when his teacher **(11)** .... him read *Great Expectations* by Charles Dickens. But when we were having dinner recently, he mentioned to me that now it is **(12)** .... of the books that he likes the most!

0	A <u>habits</u>	B hobbies	C activities	D pastimes
1	A objected	B passed	C failed	D lost
2	A ends	B achievements	C scores	D results
3	A gone away	B put down	C given up	D put away
4	A popular	B favourite	C most	D fine
5	A occasions	B events	C times	D dates
6	A admired	B delighted	C pleased	D preferred
7	A taken	B done	C made	D had
8	A had	B made	C felt	D considered
9	A much	B hard	C heavy	D large
10	A grew	B changed	C distinguished	D turned
11	A said	B told	C let	D made
12	A one	B best	C included	D last

Writing: a short story

OPTIONAL TASK: PAPER 2, PART 2

1 **In Part 2 of the Writing test, you may be asked to write a short story. When examiners look at your answer, they will mark it in two stages. It is a good idea to use two stages yourself when checking your work. The first stage is looking at the structure of the writing. Look at the exam question below and the student's answer, and answer the questions (1–5).**

   1 Does the story have a clear beginning and ending?

   2 Does the story use paragraphs?

   3 Does the story include the given sentence?

   4 Is the story readable?

   5 Is the story between 120 and 180 words?

   > Your teacher has asked you to write a story for the school magazine. The story must include the sentence 'I suddenly realised that I was lost.' Write your story in 120–180 words.

2 **The second stage of the marking is correcting spelling, vocabulary, grammar and punctuation. Look at the story again and do the following:**

   1 Find eight spelling mistakes.

   2 All the verbs in the story are in the past simple. Change these verbs where appropriate to past continuous or past perfect.

   3 Add the punctuation the writer should use for thinking and direct speech.

Bus 149

Five years ago I studied in Finland. One night I went out with some friends and I went to get the last bus home to the vilage where I lived, Kivenlahti. My friends all lived in Helsinki so I was alone, waiting for bus 149. Strangly, there were two buses that night with the number 149. My usual bus was 149X but lots of people already got on that one. The other bus was empty so I thought It'll be much more comftable on a bus with nobody on it and I got on the 149Y. I was tired and feel asleep. Eventually I felt a hand on my shoulder. The bus driver woke me up. He said something wich I didn't understand. I could only say 149 Kivenlahti? But the driver said No, 149X is Kivenlahti. I looked around in panik. I got on the wrong bus and we were in a dark forest covered in snow. The driver told me not to worry and then, in the midle of the night, he drove me home!

3 Now write your own answer to the exam question in exercise 1. Remember to include the given sentence.

....
....
....
....
....
....
....
....
....
....
....
....
....

Speaking

COLLABORATIVE TASK: PAPER 5, PART 3

1 🎧5.5 **In Part 3 of the Speaking test, you have to discuss something with your partner. The subject might be a group of pictures or a written list of possibilities. Listen to two students discussing the question below and tick (✔) the options they choose.**

You need to think of ways of encouraging schoolchildren in your country to read more. Discuss the list of possibilities below and choose the best two ideas.

• put more comics and picture books in city libraries

• introduce an hour of silent reading every day in every school

• invite famous authors to speak to schools

• have a national competition with prizes for the best book review

• give every child a free book

• introduce a book exchange where children can exchange their books for a book from another child

• place posters in classrooms and libraries encouraging children to read

2 🎧5.5 **Correct the sentences (1–6) below. Then listen to the recording again to check your answers.**

1 But there are options which appeal with different people.

2 I don't stand reading in the classroom.

3 It's not obvious choice, is it?

4 Anything that would appeal to me is to invite famous authors to schools.

5 Personal, I think this is difficult because it is expensive for the government.

6 Yes, I'm quite agree.

3 There are a number of phrasal verbs that you can use when you are discussing options in the collaborative task in the Speaking test. Look at the phrasal verbs in bold in the sentences (1–6) below. Match the definitions (a–f) to the phrasal verbs.

1 So these are the options that we have to **go through**. ____

2 Let's **go for** the second idea. ____

3 I'm **weighing up** the possibility of choosing the third picture. ____

4 What exactly is the problem that we are we trying to **sort out**? ____

5 Shall we **move on** to the next picture? ____

6 I think it's time to **sum up** what we have agreed. ____

a fix, correct

b consider the benefits of

c progress

d discuss, examine

e give the conclusions of

f choose, select

4 🎧5.5 **Listen to the discussion again. Try to hear the students using all of the phrasal verbs in exercise 3.**

5 If you are working with a partner, do the exam task in exercise 1 together. In the Speaking test, you will have about three minutes for this part of the test.

Reading

MULTIPLE MATCHING: PAPER 1, PART 3

1 **You are going to read an article about four ancient sites. For questions 1–15, choose from the sites (A–D). The sites may be chosen more than once.**

   Which site

   1 was once a very important urban area? ____

   2 was damaged by a natural disaster? ____

   3 is used as a symbol of its country? ____

   4 is less famous than another site in the same country? ____

   5 has very many visitors? ____

   6 has buildings which were used by more than one religion? ____

   7 can be reached by public transport? ____

   8 was used by people to build their homes? ____

   9 has exhibits of artwork made with little tiles? ____

   10 contains images of animals? ____

   11 was restored by a businessman? ____

   12 is it best to visit early in the morning? ____

   13 was used to transport an important resource? ____

   14 was built by a society with very strong armies? ____

   15 does not have many visitors? ____

2 **Now match the phrases in bold in the text to the definitions (1–10) below.**

   1 some _____

   2 without having to share it with other people, alone _____

   3 the best thing _____

   4 something very special _____

   5 in the end / after some time _____

   6 despite this _____

   7 similar to a thing that comes from _____

   8 not less than _____

   9 nothing is a better example of this _____

   10 which is surprising because it is part of something very special

   _____

LOOKING FOR THE ANCIENT WORLD

A Avebury, England

Stonehenge is one of the first things people want to see when they arrive in the UK. But there is one disadvantage to Stonehenge, which is that you are not allowed to touch the stones. And yet just a short distance away, there is another stone circle, not as well known, where you can walk and touch and explore the real stones: the Avebury stone circle.

Unlike Stonehenge, the Avebury stones are just large rocks which stand upright on the ground. The survival of the ring is **nothing short of** miraculous. The stones were once broken and buried by people who tried to eradicate evidence of the old religions. Later the stones were broken and used as building materials for local residences, as the stone circle surrounds the village of Avebury. **Eventually** the site was rescued by Alexander Keiller, a marmalade manufacturer, who paid for the buried stones to be raised up and for the circle to be restored. And now it can be visited again.

B Tarragona, Spain

The city of Tarragona in Catalonia was the capital city of Roman Spain, when it was known as Tarraco. Today it is a very beautiful city with **a number of** excellent Roman sites. Very near the modern railway station, it is possible to visit the Roman amphitheatre, the city forum (the old marketplace), and a Roman tower, although Tarragona's best ancient site is outside the city walls.

A short bus ride from the city centre will take you to a desolate spot by the roadside. The bus driver will point at you to get off and you will find yourself wandering through hills and trees with no tourist centre, no cafés and bars, and hardly any tourists. And why? To see the ruins of a Roman aqueduct which used to bring water to the city. These ruins are **like something out of** another world. They are covered in weeds and the site is silent. You can walk along the top of the aqueduct marvelling at the view of the valley below. It's a rare treat nowadays: to find an ancient site and to have it **all to yourself**.

C Agrigento, Italy

In ancient times, the island of Sicily was an important part of the Greek world. Cities such as Siracuse were able to win famous battles over Athens and other Greek states. All of this colourful history means that Sicily is **a treat** for history buffs: and **nowhere more so** than Agrigento, the Valley of the Temples.

The sites themselves are scattered over a large area. **The highlight** of the trip is the Tempio della Concordia, a beautiful yellow temple saved from destruction because it was later converted into a Christian church. Other temples were not so lucky. All that remains of the Temple of Jupiter is the base of its columns and rubble after it was destroyed by an earthquake.

One further piece of advice is to drop into the museum on the site, which contains a number of important sculptures, mosaics and artwork.

D Nemrut Daği, Turkey

Turkey is rich with ancient sites, but the mountain of Nemrut Daği is special **even by its standards**. It is home to the massive stone heads which have become one of the iconic images of the country. Nemrut Daği lies in the far south-eastern corner of Turkey, but **even so** the fame of this remote site has meant that today the road to the sculptures is full of tourists.

However, there are still a few moments when you can enjoy the magic of the site with its giant stone heads of ancient gods, eagles and lions. If you arrive at dawn, you can watch the sun rise over the mountain illuminating the monuments.

Vocabulary

PHRASAL VERBS

1 **Look at the sentences below. Six of them contain a mistake. Find and correct the mistakes.**

1 Don't stay in a hotel. We can put you up while you're in London.

2 What time are you checking in your hotel?

3 We can show around you the city and the old town this afternoon.

4 When we get to Vilnius, we're meeting up from some friends.

5 Call me when you arrive and I'll pick you up from the airport.

6 We're setting to at 5pm. That's when we're leaving.

7 We were waiting for Rachel and Robert all afternoon, but they never turned them up.

8 The match is kicking out in five minutes!

2 **Complete the phrasal verbs. Try to predict whether the phrasal verb will be made with *off*, *up* or *back*.**

1 The explorers have started _____ on their journey to the North Pole.

2 If you want to take an FCE course next year, you can sign _____ here.

3 Some teenagers were writing graffiti on the walls. But when they saw the police, they ran _____ .

4 Yvette sent me an email yesterday and I'm writing _____ to her this afternoon.

5 After he left school, Dan joined _____ . He went into the army for seven years.

6 The glasses I had bought were broken, so I took them _____ to the shop.

Grammar

WAYS OF EXPRESSING THE FUTURE

1 **Read the sentences (1–6) below. Match the pictures (a–f) to the sentences.**

1 Don't worry, **I'll get** a taxi. ___

2 **We're going to go** to the beach this afternoon. ___

3 **There's bound to be** a tourist information office in the station. ___

4 What time **does the train leave**? ___

5 We can't meet you for dinner because **we're spending** the evening at the opera. ___

6 I've made some sandwiches because **she's likely to be** hungry after her long journey. ___

2 **Underline the correct option.**

1 According to the timetable, the meeting is *due / bound* to start now.

2 We're likely *to receive / receiving* an answer tomorrow.

3 Sorry, my mobile's ringing. *I'm just answering / I'll just answer* it.

4 Bill's carrying a lot of bags. *Will / Shall* I help him?

5 By the time Marie arrives tomorrow, Urs *will have gone / will be going* home.

6 Dad has to have an early night because he *is driving / will drive* to Manchester tomorrow.

7 Will you *have flown / be flying* to Spain or will you *have gone / be going* there by ferry?

Spelling

British and American English
There are a number of spelling differences between British and American English. Fortunately, most of these spelling differences tend to follow certain simple rules.

1 Look at the two comments from a British and an American speaker, and complete the spelling table.

> **British English:** I heard a rumour that they are going to change the colour of the uniforms in the travel advice centre. I didn't realise that people were complaining about our old uniforms. This means cancelling the orders for uniforms for next year. We also need to look in the clothing catalogue to find a new uniform.
>
> **American English:** I heard a rumor that they are going to change the color of the uniforms in the travel advice center. I didn't realize that people were complaining about our old uniforms. This means canceling the orders for uniforms for next year. We also need to look in the clothing catalog to find a new uniform.

British English	American English
-our, e.g. rumour	_____
_____	-ize, e.g. realize
-re, e.g. centre	_____
_____	-og, e.g. catalog

2 Look at the rule below and the texts in exercise 1. Decide if the rule is true for British or American English.

In _____ English if a verb ends with a single *l*, and the stress is not on the final syllable, the gerund is spelt with a double *ll*: *cancelling*.

3 Look at the words below. Decide if the word is American or British English, as in the example.

1 travelling ___*British English*___
2 odor _____
3 metre _____
4 dialog _____
5 organize _____
6 labour _____
7 specialisation _____
8 signaling _____
9 theater _____
10 litre _____
11 honor _____
12 colour _____
13 analogue _____
14 equalling _____
15 memorize _____

In the FCE exam candidates are permitted to use British English, American English, or other varieties of native speaker English. However, you should try to be consistent in your use of spelling as much as possible.

When you encounter new words that end *-ise*, *-our*, etc. check them in a dictionary to see if there is an acceptable alternative spelling. Try to use the same spelling in all your work while preparing for the final examination.

Listening: travel and visits

EXTRACTS + MULTIPLE CHOICE: PAPER 4, PART 1

1 🎧6.1 **You will hear eight people talking about travel and visits. For questions 1–8, choose the best answer (A, B or C).**

1 You hear a man and woman speaking. What does the woman agree to do?
   A Drive the man in her car.
   B Let the man stay in her house.
   C Go with the man on his journey.

2 You hear a woman talking about her holiday. Why does she complain?
   A She received incorrect information about her hotel.
   B She did not like her hotel.
   C She did not like the beach.

3 You hear a boy talking about his holidays. What was the problem on the train?
   A It was too early.
   B It cost too much.
   C It was full of people.

4 You hear a man talking about his holiday. What did he buy?
   A A guide book.
   B A souvenir.
   C A photograph.

5 You hear a man and a woman talking. Where are they?
   A A car park.
   B An airport.
   C A train station.

6 You hear a man and woman talking. What does the woman want to do?
   A She wants to go sightseeing every day.
   B She wants to save as much money as possible.
   C She wants to arrange the trip herself.

7 You hear a man talking about an excursion. Why was he unable to go?
   A He had a medical problem.
   B The weather was horrible.
   C He was not able to pay for it.

8 You hear a woman talking. What is she describing?
   A Being a tourist.
   B Being a taxi driver.
   C Being a tour guide.

Pronunciation

SPOTLIGHT ON PRONUNCIATION

/dʒ/, /tʃ/ and /j/
The phonetic symbols /dʒ/, /tʃ/ and /j/ explain how to make the sounds.
/dʒ/ is d + z as in *John*.
/tʃ/ is t + sh as in *Czech*.
/j/ is pronounced *y* as in *yes*.

1 **Look at the sentences below. Which phonetic sound is used for the letters in bold?**

1 **J**im is a **j**azz **g**enius. ___
2 **Ch**eryl plays **ch**ess. ___
3 **Y**our **y**ogurt's **y**ellow. ___
4 **J**ane's **j**ust made some **j**ars of **j**am. ___
5 **Ch**arles' **ch**airs are **Ch**inese. ___
6 Mr **Y**oung works at **y**our **u**niversity. ___

2 🎧6.2 **Listen and check your answers. Then listen and repeat.**

3 🎧6.3 **Listen and circle the words you hear.**

chews	use	juice	cheese	jewel	you'll
your	*giraffe*	general	church	*yeah*	
jaw	*chair*	yet	*chin*	judge	jet	*gin*

4 **If you are working with a partner, practise together reading all the words in exercise 3.**

Use of English

OPEN CLOZE: PAPER 3, PART 2

1 Read the text below and think of the word which best fits each gap. Use only one word in each gap. There is an example at the beginning (0).

For travellers on long-haul flights (flights of five hours or more), **(0)** ....*there*............ are two main health problems: jet lag and the risk of DVT (*deep vein thrombosis*). Jet lag is **(1)** .... happens when you travel across time zones. Having jet lag means that your body's biological clock **(2)** .... running at a different time to the time in your destination country. Travellers suffering **(3)** .... jet lag feel tired and have problems sleeping. DVT is a serious medical condition that can be caused **(4)** .... sitting in the same position for a long period of time.

There are a number of things that can **(5)** .... done to prevent jet lag. First, it is better to take a night flight than a daytime flight so that you feel rested when you arrive. Secondly, you should try to drink a lot of water before you fly as well as **(6)** .... your flight. Medical evidence suggests that jet lag is caused by dehydration, so you should also avoid consumption of alcohol. In **(7)** .... to this, also avoid sleeping pills.

A number of health recommendations **(8)** .... been released that show you how to protect yourself against DVT. On long-haul flights, take the opportunity to walk up and down the aisle. There are a number **(9)** .... exercises that can be done without leaving your seat. **(10)** .... your flight includes a stopover in a foreign city, go for a short walk off the plane.

To help relax, wear sensible clothing and comfortable shoes. **(11)** .... your shoes off during the flight. To help you sleep, you **(12)** .... also wear dark glasses or bring your own eyeshades on board.

KEY WORD TRANSFORMATIONS: PAPER 3, PART 4

2 Complete the second sentence so that it has a similar meaning to the first sentence, using the word given. Do not change the word given. You must use between two and five words, including the word given. There is an example at the beginning (0).

0 She is the only one who doesn't want to fly to Morocco.
   APART

   Everyone wants to fly to Morocco

   ....*apart from her*............ .

1 We prefer to go to Switzerland.
   RATHER

   We .... to Switzerland.

2 I think that we should buy the flight tickets now.
   TIME

   It's .... the flight tickets.

3 I advise you to book a hotel before you leave.
   HAD

   You .... a hotel before you leave.

4 One possibility is to go on a walking holiday.
   ALWAYS

   We .... on a walking holiday.

5 I've never been on a plane before.
   FIRST

   This is .... I've been on a plane.

6 How long is the flight from London to Madrid?
   TAKE

   How long .... from London to Madrid?

7 I'll call you the minute I get to Munich.
   AS

   I'll call you .... to Munich.

8 I'd prefer us not to eat dinner at the hotel.
   IF

   I'd prefer it .... dinner at the hotel.

Writing: a report

1 In Part 2 of the Writing test, you may be asked to write a report. Look at the exam question below and answer the questions.

  1 What is the situation?

  2 What is the purpose of the report?

  3 Who is the target reader?

> A language school in your home town has asked you to write a report on the local transport system. The report needs to discuss how to get to your home town from the nearest airport and how to travel around, and to give advice for foreign visitors.

2 Now look at a student's answer to the exam question in exercise 1. Correct the underlined phrases.

TRANSPORT IN MOSCOW
The following report outlining the Moscow transport system. It aim to show how to get around the city.

ARRIVAL
There are two airports: Domodedovo and Sheremetevo. It is better to arrive at Domodedovo because there is a cheap shuttle bus service into the centre. Sheremetevo is further away, but it is still cheap to get into the centre.

THE METRO
The Moscow metro is incredibly beautiful and it is a tourist attraction in itself. One suggestion when travelling by metro is you write down your journey beforehand because some stations have more than one name.

OTHER TRANSPORT
Alternate, you could use the local buses. However, these are often crowded. It is also easy to get lost, so it might be easier to use the underground. Another possibile is the tram system. On the one side this is a good way to see the city, but at the other the trams do not run in the city centre.

CONCLUSION
To sum it up there are many possibilities for travelling around Moscow, but you need to plan your route carefully.

3 Now write your own answer to the exam question in exercise 1.

....

....

....

....

....

....

....

....

....

....

....

....

....

....

....

....

....

....

....

Speaking

COLLABORATIVE TASK: PAPER 5, PART 3

1 Complete the sentences spoken by an FCE exam interlocutor. Write one word in each gap.

1 Now I'd like you to talk about something _____ for about three minutes.

2 I'm just going to _____.

3 I'd like you to _____ that you are in charge of delivering the post to a group of different villages.

4 You have to _____ how to deliver the letters and parcels.

5 First, talk to _____ other about the advantages and disadvantages of each method of transport.

6 Then decide which is the best _____ of delivering the post.

7 You only have about three minutes for this, so once again don't _____ if I stop you.

8 Please speak clearly so that we can _____ you. All right?

2 🎧6.4 **Listen to the interlocutor in Part 3 of the Speaking test. Check your answers to exercise 1.**

3 🎧6.5 **Listen to Claudio and Eleni doing Part 3 of the Speaking test. They are answering the exam question in exercise 1, using the picture below. Which method of transport do they choose?**

4 🎧6.5 **Correct the mistakes in the sentences below. Then listen again to check your answers.**

1 If we chose the plane, we have to build a ... somewhere where it could land.

2 But if we would deliver the post by plane or helicopter, we would need to have a pilot.

3 Well, a pilot is bound want more money than a postman.

4 If money is a problem, we could anyway deliver the post by bike.

5 We must better make up our minds.

6 I think it will be very exciting to deliver the post by speedboat.

7 If we used the truck, it wouldn't can deliver the post to the island village.

5 **If you are working with a partner, ask and answer the exam question in exercise 1.**

7 Technology

LANGUAGE CHECKLIST

- ☐ I know words to describe technology, page 56.
- ☐ I know some three-part phrasal verbs, page 56
- ☐ I know some verbs which are followed by the gerund and infinitive, page 57.
- ☐ I know how to spell nouns ending -ment, page 57.
- ☐ I know how to pronounce /ɪ/ and /iː/, page 59.

EXAM CHECKLIST

- ☐ I have practised the gapped text question from the Reading paper, page 54.
- ☐ I have practised the sentence completion question from the Listening paper, page 58.
- ☐ I have practised the word formation question from the Use of English paper, page 59.
- ☐ I have practised writing a review from the Writing paper, page 60.
- ☐ I have practised the key word transformation question from the Use of English paper, page 61.
- ☐ I have practised the collaborative task from the Speaking paper, page 61.

Reading

GAPPED TEXT: PAPER 1, PART 2

1 **You are going to read an article about professional computer games players. Seven sentences have been removed from the article. Choose from the sentences (A–H) the one which fits each gap (1–7). There is one extra sentence which you do not need to use.**

A Row upon row of fans seated in the giant arena cheered, clapped and stamped their feet as the action unfolded on giant screens above the players.

B He used to play badminton at county level but began gaming after being injured at 15.

C Most gamers only play one game which they practise for up to twelve hours a day.

D By day, Anja Møller studies Nordic languages, but by night she is captain of the Aurora-Gaming Danish women's Counter-Strike team.

E While he cannot match the top gamers in South Korea, the best of whom earn up to £500,000 per year, Liquid is still doing well.

F While gaming has not reached this level of excitement in Europe, it is heading in that direction.

G In front of him, the five members of the UK Four Kings Counter-Strike team shouted warnings and commands to each other.

H It's a small amount in an industry worth £20 billion a year worldwide but a sign of things to come.

2 **Now read the text again and find words that mean the following:**

1 only just (paragraph 1) _____

2 people who fight in a war (paragraph 1) _____

3 walked with big steps (paragraph 3) _____

4 to compete at the same standard (paragraph 3) _____

5 recruited (paragraph 5) _____

6 only just (paragraph 7) _____

7 a place where there is nothing (paragraph 7) _____

8 becoming smaller (paragraph 9) _____

£60,000 A YEAR, AND ALL YOU'VE GOT TO DO IS ZAP THE BAD GUYS

❶ They look as if they are barely out of school, but when their zapping finger hits form, these computer game warriors can earn nearly £60,000 a year. Long gone are the days when playing video games was simply for teenage boys who spent too long in their bedrooms. Today's leading players are professional "gamers" earning a good living from a basic salary, prize money and sponsorship.

❷ In some parts of the world the elite players date models and need bodyguards to protect them from over-eager fans. **(1)** _____ Britain has 13 professional players, some of whom were at the Electronic Sports World Cup in Paris, which finished last night.

❸ In the heat of the competition, coach Ed Harborne paced up and down shouting instructions between the computer screens in front of his young stars. **(2)** _____ They were attempting to hold their own against strong Chinese opponents.

❹ "C'est bien, allez, continuez," called the female coach of the nearby French girls team. **(3)** _____ Approximately 25,000 supporters ignored the sunshine to watch the games.

❺ The 750 players from 53 nations were fighting to win a total of £216,000. **(4)** _____ Marc Mangiacapra, also known as Liquid, put his computer engineering degree on hold when he was signed by the Four Kings team two years ago.

❻ So far this year he has won £10,000 in prize money and spent one month each playing in Finland, China and Denmark. On Wednesday he will fly to Dallas for the World Series of Video Games. **(5)** _____ On top of his £19,000 salary from the team's Intel sponsorship deal, he expects to make around £20,000 in prize money this year, and in his most successful year earned close to £60,000. Last year he won £11,000 in one game. Earlier this year in China, he was chased down the street by autograph hunters and his team was treated to a limousine.

❼ "All my friends think I'm the luckiest person ever, earning much more than them for flying around the world playing games and having fun." James Harding, 23, from Glastonbury, Somerset, is known as 2GD to other gamers. **(6)** _____ In Paris yesterday he narrowly lost to the eventual winner in the quarter finals, earning himself £1,080. He said: "I loved the competitive element of playing badminton and gaming has filled the void my injury left."

❽ "It should be classed as a sport. It requires just as much hand-eye co-ordination as tennis, and you need the same level of strategic and tactical ability as in chess."

❾ Gaming is still a male-dominated activity, but the girls are catching up. **(7)** _____ She said: "Girl gaming is getting much more competitive these days. We are not at the level of the guys yet, but the skill level gap is narrowing every day."

Vocabulary

TECHNOLOGY

1 Complete the puzzle with words for inventors and inventing, and computers and technology. What is the word in grey?

1 This is what you have if you think about something all the time and it makes you a bit mad.

2 This is the part of a computer that you look at.

3 These are problems that can delay the progress of a project.

4 The first page of a website, or the first page you see when you open your web browser.

5 These are part of a webpage that will take you to different websites if you click on them.

6 Making new things or using new ideas.

7 This is an informal word for an inventor's creation or invention.

8 Someone who discovers or develops something for the first time, an early explorer of an area.

9 The first model of a new invention.

10 The part of a computer that you move with your hand.

11 You have this if you are able to think of lots of new, creative ideas.

12 This is an extra document or picture that is connected to another email.

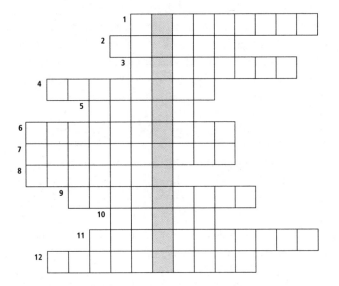

2 <u>Underline</u> the correct part of the phrasal verb.

1 He hacked *into / over* the bank's computer system.

2 Click *at / on* the icon at the top of the page.

3 We've set *off / up* a new website.

4 I can't log *across / into* the system because I've forgotten my password.

5 The printer isn't working – it isn't plugged *in / on*.

6 I'll back the work *down / up* on another computer.

EXTENSION: THREE-PART PHRASAL VERBS

3 Some phrasal verbs come in three parts. These phrasal verbs do not separate. Complete the sentences below with the words in the box.

> forward   from   of   out   to   up   with

1 I'll never understand how inventors come up _____ so many good ideas.

2 We are going to work on the prototype all weekend because otherwise we will run _____ of time.

3 This is the research department and visitors have to keep out _____ these rooms.

4 Modern computer scientists look up _____ the early inventors of computers. They were geniuses.

5 Don't let the other children bully you. You have to stand _____ to them!

6 We're all looking _____ to the technology fair next month.

7 I'm going on holiday to get away _____ it all.

4 Look again at the three-part phrasal verbs in exercise 3. Match them to the definitions (a–g).

a admire, respect _____

b wait for something with excitement

_____

c defend yourself against _____

d not enter _____

e go on holiday, escape from somewhere

_____

f think of _____

g use all of something so that there is no more

_____

Grammar

VERBS FOLLOWED BY THE GERUND AND INFINITIVE

1 Look at the sentences below. Six of them contain a mistake. Find and correct the mistakes.

1 Oh no! I've forgotten telling Mika about the party!

2 I would like see what the world is like in a hundred years' time.

3 Would you prefer to communicate by phone or email?

4 Do you remember to visit the Kremlin when we were in Russia?

5 He started as an assistant engineer and went on to be the chief designer.

6 Sorry, I didn't mean stopping you while you were working.

7 This equipment is out of date. It needs replace.

8 I told them to do some work, but they went on read the newspaper.

2 <u>Underline</u> the correct form of the verb.

1 In the future they will succeed *to develop / in developing* a robot that can think.

2 These robots could be designed *to look after / looking after* patients in hospitals.

3 I expect *to see / seeing* these robots in hospitals in my lifetime.

4 But can we risk *to have / having* robots to do a nurse's job?

5 The government would need *to think / thinking* carefully before they use machines in a medical environment.

6 When I told this theory to my friends, they just laughed at me. I regret *to tell / telling* them now.

Spelling

Nouns with -*ment*
Many nouns in English end with the letters -*ment*. Usually these words are spelt by adding -*ment* to a verb, and the spelling of the verb does not change.
Example: manage ➡ management

1 Find ten nouns ending -*ment* in the wordsearch. Words can be found vertically, horizontally and diagonally.

e	s	p	j	u	d	g	e	m	e	n	t	a
n	a	a	f	g	o	l	z	o	i	b	v	i
c	c	r	y	e	b	q	a	v	u	k	u	z
o	h	j	r	v	n	t	y	e	e	l	l	y
u	i	e	f	a	r	g	u	m	e	n	t	a
r	e	s	u	l	n	k	q	e	t	o	d	d
a	v	q	p	e	e	g	u	n	c	n	f	v
g	e	r	o	n	p	k	e	t	s	s	e	e
e	m	g	o	v	e	r	n	m	e	n	t	r
m	e	b	d	i	b	v	v	o	e	k	e	t
e	n	a	e	r	c	o	d	g	x	n	v	i
n	t	x	d	o	e	n	t	f	p	g	t	s
t	a	w	z	n	p	w	j	w	i	y	o	e
y	f	l	k	m	b	l	e	j	b	e	i	m
p	l	a	c	e	m	e	n	t	s	n	k	e
i	v	o	d	n	y	a	n	g	y	t	c	n
g	l	i	x	t	z	d	w	t	e	x	s	t

2 Look again at your answers to exercise 1 and answer the questions.

1 Which word does not come from a verb?

2 Which word loses one letter when it changes from a verb to a noun?

Listening: Domo

SENTENCE COMPLETION: PAPER 4, PART 2

1 You will hear an interview with Olivia McMath, a technology journalist, about the robot, Domo. Before you listen, think quickly of all the words you might hear on the topic. Which of the words in the box do you think you will hear in an interview about robots?

> IT scientists android assembly line laser pre-programmed breakthrough innovation developers artists prototype secret breakdown potential setbacks danger

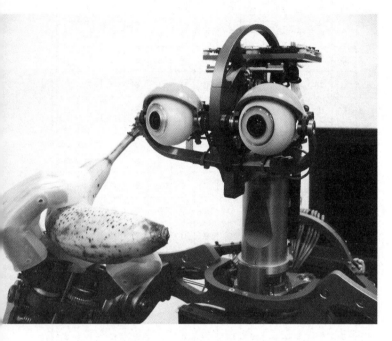

2 🎧7.1 **Now listen to the interview and check your answers.**

SPOTLIGHT ON STUDY TECHNIQUES

Remember that in the Listening test, you will always hear the recording twice. As you work through the listening practice in this book, listen twice before checking your answers. The first time you listen, try to note down as many of the answers as you can without being distracted by the parts you do not understand. You will only find some of the answers when you listen the second time: do not panic the first time around!

3 🎧7.1 **Now listen to the interview again. For questions 1–10, complete the sentences. You will need to write a word or a short phrase in each gap.**

Domo is different from robots on
| | **1** |

Domo can hold things like
| | **2** |

Robots easily break
| | **3** |

Domo's eyes were inspired by
| | **4** |

The robot responds to
| | **5** | controls.

The researchers developed the robot over
| | **6** |

Cog and Kismet were
| | **7** | robots.

The researchers want Domo to aid
| | **8** |

Domo might have a commercial use in
| | **9** |

Money is being provided for the Domo project by
| | **10** |

Pronunciation

/ɪ/ and /iː/
To make an /iː/ sound, open your mouth wider so that you are grinning.

1 🎧 7.2 **Listen and number the pictures 1–6.**

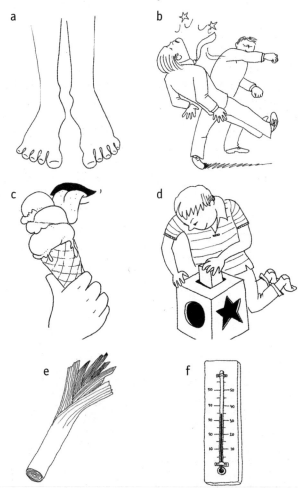

a

b

c

d

e

f

2 **Work with a partner. Say the words in exercise 1 to each other.**

3 🎧 7.3 **Now listen and repeat.**

/ɪ/	/iː/		/ɪ/	/iː/
1 grin	green	5	rid	read
2 pick	peek	6	this	these
3 bit	beat	7	it	eat
4 sit	seat	8	chip	cheap

4 **If you are working with a partner, take turns to say one word from exercise 3. Your partner must point to the word that you say.**

Use of English

WORD FORMATION: PAPER 3, PART 3

1 **Read the text below. Use the words given in capitals at the end of some of the lines to form a word that fits in the gap in the same line. Use the endings in the box. There is an example at the beginning (0).**

-ing	-ion	-er	~~-ment~~	-ing	-ical
-ant	-ity	-al	-ism	-ment	

When I first bought a computer fifteen years ago, I thought turning the machine on was an

(0) ......*achievement*.......... . As far as I was concerned, it was just a glorified typewriter. I had no Internet **ACHIEVE**

(1) .... , no printer, nothing. But after the **CONNECT**

(2) .... revolution of the last few years, I can't believe how my computer has changed my life. **TECHNOLOGY**

When I first bought my computer, the main problem I had was my children having an

(3) .... over who could play a game on it. Now my main **ARGUE**

concern is **(4)** .... Nevertheless, I do use the Internet for **SECURE**

(5) .... and I get all my groceries online. I know there has **SHOP**

been **(6)** .... of the effect online shopping is having on high street shops, but the Internet **CRITICISE**

offers a **(7)** .... choice of books, DVDs and music than I can find in my local stores. **WIDE**

But perhaps the biggest change has been in my working life. My husband is an artist and he now does a lot of

(8) .... using the computer. And for me, I work as a **DRAW**

(9) .... and I now work from home. Fifteen years ago that would have been just a dream, but now it seems completely **CONSULT**

(10) .... to work in my living room. **NATURE**

Writing: a review

OPTIONAL TASK: PAPER 2, PART 2

1 **Complete the student's answer to the exam question below with the phrases (a–h).**

a Personally I found it

b It is worth

c All in all though,

d My favourite film is

e I would advise anyone

f In one scene

g The only downside of the film

h one thing I like about

> Your school magazine has a section called *My favourite film*. Write a **review** of your favourite film, explaining why you like it. Write your answer in 120–180 words.

Revenge of the Sith

1 _____ the last Star Wars film, `The Revenge of the Sith', which was directed by George Lucas. I love science fiction and

2 _____ the film is that it is set on lots of different planets and interesting locations.

3 _____ watching this film just for the special effects. `Revenge of the Sith' uses cutting edge computer graphics.

4 _____, when the characters are fighting over a river of fire, the background looks incredibly lifelike.

The film tells the story of how a young Jedi knight, Anakin Skywalker becomes the evil Darth Vader.

5 _____ really interesting watching this character changing into a villain.

6 _____ was that it was quite violent. I saw the film with my younger sister and she was quite upset by the ending, which has a lot of fighting and violence. 7_____ this was a great movie and 8_____ to go and see it.

2 **Look at the completed review in exercise 1. Find words and phrases which mean:**

1 very modern _____

2 a part of a film which takes place in one location _____

3 realistic _____

4 the bad character in a story, the enemy of the hero _____

5 problem, bad thing _____

6 in total _____

3 **Now write your own answer to the exam question in exercise 1.**

....

....

....

....

....

....

....

....

....

....

....

....

....

....

....

....

....

....

....

....

....

....

Use of English

1 Complete the second sentence so that it has a similar meaning to the first sentence, using the word given. Do not change the word given. You must use between two and five words, including the word given. There is an example at the beginning (0).

0   Your computer might crash, so save all your work.
    CASE

    Save all your work *...in case your computer crashes...* .

1   We forgot to buy a mouse for the new computer.
    REMEMBER

    We .... a mouse for the new computer.

2   They ignored me and continued playing their game.
    WENT

    They ignored me and .... their game.

3   I can't wait to go to the technology fair.
    FORWARD

    I'm really .... the technology fair.

4   I shouldn't have deleted those computer files.
    REGRET

    I .... those computer files.

5   We wanted to fix the printer, but we didn't succeed.
    TRIED

    We .... the printer, but we didn't succeed.

6   Someone should check to see if the website is working.
    NEEDS

    The website .... to see if it is working.

7   Jill hasn't used her phone since she got Skype.
    STOPPED

    Jill .... her phone when she got Skype.

8   Finally, we managed to solve the problem!
    SUCCEEDED

    Finally, we .... the problem.

Speaking

1 7.4 You will hear some students doing the collaborative task in the Speaking test. They have to decide which of the six suggestions below would be most useful for a website that helps to teach people to speak English. Listen and decide which point they are discussing.

Pair 1 ___   Pair 3 ___   Pair 5 ___

Pair 2 ___   Pair 4 ___

---

a   video of people in real situations (in the bank, etc.)
b   online exercises with words to complete
c   an online translation device
d   written models of letters, essays, etc. to print off
e   lists of common errors that people make in English
f   games and songs
g   reading exercises with questions

---

2 7.4 Listen again and complete the sentences with the useful words for exchanging ideas, and expressing and justifying opinions.

1   I think this would be _____ for people learning English. (extract 1)

2   I know what _____, but I don't think you can have a list for every language. (extract 1)

3   I don't _____ this. I mean, if you use the Internet, it's easy to find an article in English. (extract 2)

4   _____ good idea. I never get the opportunity to see English as it's used in real life. (extract 3)

5   Yes, I think _____. (extract 3)

6   For me, _____ one. (extract 4)

7   And we _____ highlight useful words and phrases that students can learn. (extract 4)

8   I don't think this is a good idea _____. (extract 5)

9   This kind _____ never works. (extract 5)

10 Sure. I think it's _____ too. (extract 5)

3 If you are working with a partner, do the exam task in exercise 1 together. In the Speaking test, you will have about three minutes to do the collaborative task.

Reading

MULTIPLE MATCHING: PAPER 1, PART 3

1 **You are going to read an article about four prisons. For questions 1–15, choose from the prisons (A–D). The prisons may be chosen more than once.**

In which prison

1 was there once a supply problem? ___

2 are there places where you can go shopping? ___

3 are prisoners allowed to get takeaways? ___

4 were there restrictions on washing? ___

5 can you play racket sports? ___

6 are cells traded as property? ___

7 is there a tranquil environment? ___

8 is excellent cuisine served? ___

9 can sports skills improve the lives of prisoners? ___

10 could prisoners have alcoholic drinks? ___

11 do some people meet a wife or husband? ___

12 is there a big divide between the living conditions of different prisoners? ___

13 do foreigners prefer to spend their time? ___

14 is there nowhere to borrow books? ___

15 do people want to become prisoners at the jail? ___

2 **Now match the words in bold in the text to the definitions (1–8) below.**

1 many _____

2 a building and organisation like a school, a prison or a hospital

_____

3 made to do something that you do not want to do

_____

4 the government and the organisations that it controls, such as the police, the army, etc.

_____

5 absolutely enormous

_____

6 inside _____

7 in a very bad condition (especially for a building)

_____

8 money you can pay so that you can wait for trial in your home and not in prison

_____

Prison tales

This week we profile four rather unusual prisons and prison systems.

A Bolivia

On arriving at the San Pedro prison in La Paz, Bolivia, you could be forgiven for thinking you weren't in jail at all. The jail seems like a city **within** a city. The prisoners have a market and restaurants, and children are running around the streets. It seems almost surreal, but this is a jail: everything is surrounded by huge walls, and all the entrances and exits are guarded.

Uniquely at San Pedro, the world of commerce rules the prison world. Inmates have to pay for their cells, which means that they need to work to earn money. There's just one problem: they still have to spend their time in jail! There are even wealthy areas of the prison where cells can be traded for as much as £1,500. Not everyone lives in this luxury and other prisoners are **forced to** share small cells elsewhere in the prison complex.

You might wonder where people get the money to support this sort of lifestyle, but in fact, it is not that much different from life outside. For example, there is a football pitch in the prison and games are played by **numerous** teams. A top player can be signed up by a team with more money, which is a ticket to living in the nicer end of 'town'.

B India

Once the prison at Parappana Agrahara in Bangalore was **an institution** with serious problems. In a country with intense heat and high population, the prison suffered for many years from a serious water shortage. The prison needed almost 30,000 gallons every day, which was an unsustainable rate of consumption. It affected everyone at the prison, and forced the authorities to reduce the amount of water available for bathing.

That was some years ago and now the prison is enjoying a resurgence in popularity from its own inmates! The prison cooking has been taken over by the International Society of Krishna Consciousness and the prisoners are delighted with the delicious meals that are being served. Some prisoners are even neglecting to apply for **bail** and opting to remain locked up. "When we are getting tasty, nutritious food three times a day, why should we go out and commit crimes?" one burglar inquired. There are even reports of criminals wanting to get in!

C Spain

Popular prisons are not the sole preserve of Asia, however. In his excellent book *Ghosts of Spain*, the author Giles Tremlett describes Spanish jails in a similarly positive way.

"Spanish jails are remarkably modern, well equipped and tolerant places," he writes. "Some boast glass-backed squash courts, swimming pools and theatres. Most of the British prisoners in them do not apply to serve their time back home in Britain's **run-down**, aggressive Victorian-built prisons."

Most surprising of all is the fact that prisons are not separated into male and female prisons. Some prisoners even meet their future spouses while serving time for their crimes.

D Switzerland

The more comfortable prison is nothing new, however. In 1970 the writer Paul Erdman was arrested after the bank he was running went out of business with **colossal** debts. He was incarcerated in a three-hundred-year-old dungeon in the Swiss city of Basel, but was lucky to avoid the terrible conditions of eighteenth century justice.

Instead he found himself living in near luxury. The dungeon was much improved. Prison life included room service which brought him his evening dinner along with wines of the finest vintage. This service was not delivered by **the state** as Erdman had enough money in his own bank account to pay for this food to be delivered to him from local restaurants.

Untroubled by the usual conflicts and noise of prison life, Erdman passed the time writing his first novel, having brought along a typewriter to his cell. In many ways it was the deficiency of the jail that caused his career change. The prison lacked a library, preventing him from doing research. This meant Erdman decided to work on a novel instead of non-fiction and soon became a best-selling novelist once he was released.

Vocabulary

CRIME AND PUNISHMENT

1 **Complete the crossword.**

Across

1 This the crime of going too fast in your car.

6 The people and lawyers in a trial who accuse someone and try to send them to prison.

8 A punishment where you have to pay money because you did something wrong.

9 A person who damages or destroys property.

11 A period of time when a criminal must avoid committing crimes. If they fail, they go to prison.

Down

1 A person who steals from shops.

2 A special kind of policeman who investigates complicated crimes.

3 A person who steals.

4 Making illegal copies of money, documents or a signature.

5 The people who watch a trial and decide if the person is guilty or innocent. In Britain there are twelve of these people.

7 Instead of going to prison, a criminal may have to work in his/her local area helping people or doing cleaning, etc. This punishment is called community _____ .

10 This is the crime of setting things on fire, especially buildings, cars or property.

Grammar

RELATIVE CLAUSES

1 **Combine the two sentences with a relative clause to make a single sentence, as in the example.**

1 Sherlock Holmes was the detective. He solved the crime.

Sherlock Holmes was the detective who solved the crime.

2 This is the hotel. The murderer was caught here.

_____

3 The police want to speak to the man. His car was parked outside the bank during the robbery.

_____

4 Three people were working in the jewellery store on Wednesday. Several watches and pairs of sunglasses were stolen then.

_____

5 The police interviewed five people. They had reported the vandalism in the railway station.

_____

6 No one knew the reason. The crime had taken place.

_____

7 These are the keys. The keys were stolen last night at 11pm.

_____

2 Non-defining relative clauses add extra information to a sentence. Unlike defining relative clauses, they are separated from the main sentence with commas. Add commas to the sentences, if necessary.

1 Martina Kruger is the person that asked to speak to you.

2 The police released the man who then sold his story to the newspapers.

3 My father who you met last year is now writing a detective novel.

4 Our head office which is being decorated at the moment is on the top floor of this building.

5 The police have found the place where the murder happened.

6 Matt Damon starred in *The Bourne Ultimatum* which was directed by Paul Greengrass.

3 Look at the sentences below. Five of them contain a mistake. Find and correct the mistakes.

1 This is the building where was built by Sir Norman Foster.

2 That is the man who dog is outside.

3 The reporters interviewed the man that was accused of murder.

4 This is the book which you gave me.

5 Denise is the woman what comes from France.

6 Do you know the name of the man whom is working here tomorrow?

7 I know the reason why you helped me.

8 I think November 19th is the day which we are having the party.

4 Complete the sentences with a preposition to make more formal relative clauses.

1 This is a list of the addresses of all the people _____ whom the invitations should be sent.

2 11 July is the date _____ which the trial will begin.

3 We have selected the building _____ which the ceremony will be held.

4 Do you know _____ which reason these documents are required?

Spelling

Negative adjectives
The negative of many adjectives is spelt with the prefix *un-*.
Example: comfortable ➡ uncomfortable

However, there are other adjectives which use a prefix starting with *in-*.
Example: effective ➡ ineffective

Some negative adjectives are made by adding *i-* and doubling the first consonant. These words may start with *l*, *m*, *p* or *r* and you need to learn them in each case.
Example: legal ➡ illegal

Many adjectives that begin with *p* use a prefix starting with *im-*.
Example: possible ➡ impossible

1 Look at the adjectives below. Write the negative adjective.

1 responsible _____

2 mature _____

3 accurate _____

4 logical _____

5 relevant _____

6 moral _____

7 regular _____

8 probable _____

9 appropriate _____

10 literate _____

11 precise _____

12 mortal _____

13 resistible _____

14 capable _____

15 polite _____

Listening: victims of crime

MULTIPLE MATCHING: PAPER 4, PART 3

1 When you do the multiple matching task, look at the options and identify the key words. Try to think of related words that you might hear in the recording. These related words might help you to match the options. You are going to listen to some extracts about victims of crime. Before you listen, try to match the key words in the box to the crimes (1–6) below. Write the words next to the crimes.

> a bag   a bank statement   to break   to break in
> to clone   a credit card   the fire brigade
> the front door   to hit   holiday   a knife   matches
> the number   to scratch   a shelf   a store   a till
> a wallet   a window

1 arson _____

2 shoplifting _____

3 vandalism _____

4 mugging _____

5 forgery _____

6 burglary _____

2 🎧8.1 **Now do the listening task. You will hear five people talking about being victims of crime. For questions 1–5, choose from the list (A–F) the crime that each person was a victim of. There is one extra letter which you do not need to use.**

Which speaker

A was a victim of arson?   Speaker ____

B was a victim of shoplifting?   Speaker ____

C was a victim of vandalism?   Speaker ____

D was a victim of mugging?   Speaker ____

E was a victim of forgery?   Speaker ____

F was a victim of burglary?   Speaker ____

Pronunciation

SPOTLIGHT ON PRONUNCIATION

Nouns and verbs with changing pronunciation (1)
Some words are stressed differently, depending on whether the word is a noun or a verb. This only affects a small number of words, fortunately. Errors here rarely cause misunderstanding.

1 **Look at the sentences below. What kind of word is the word in bold in each sentence?**

1 a I have bought Joe a **present** for his birthday. ____

   b Who is going to **present** the report? ____

2 a The plates were cheap because they were **rejects** from the factory. ____

   b The problem with Dieter is that he **rejects** everyone else's suggestions. ____

3 a I'm going to **conduct** the orchestra at a concert next week. ____

   b All members of the club have to obey our code of **conduct**. ____

4 a I was shocked that the police had no **record** of the crime. ____

   b You can't use the video because I'm going to **record** something on TV. ____

5 a We only stock fresh **produce** in the store. ____

   b If you accuse someone of a crime, you need to **produce** some evidence. ____

6 a Here is all the equipment you need to **project** your presentation from your computer. ____

   b Karen is working on a very difficult **project** at the moment. ____

2 🎧8.2 **Now listen and underline the stress on the words in bold, as in the first sentence.**

Use of English

OPEN CLOZE: PAPER 3, PART 2

1 Read the text below and think of the word which best fits each gap. Use only one word in each gap. There is an example at the beginning (0).

Middlesbrough **(0)** ....*has*.......... become the first town in Britain **(1)** .... introduce talking CCTV cameras. Faced with problems like littering, drunkenness and antisocial behaviour, the city mayor started placing loudspeakers next **(2)** .... security cameras last year. Now, **(3)** .... people are breaking the law, they will hear a voice warning **(4)** .... that they are being watched. This affects all sorts of petty offences, including riding a bicycle through **(5)** .... pedestrianised zone.

If you are foolish enough to ignore the law inside **(6)** .... system's zone, you **(7)** .... be very quickly told to change your behaviour. For example, people **(8)** .... throw litter on the streets will hear themselves being described and an instruction to pick up their rubbish and throw it away **(9)** .... the correct place.

This system is the brainchild **(10)** .... the local mayor, Ray Mallon, an ex-policeman who **(11)** .... known as Robocop for his hard stance against law-breaking. Of course, as this is England, the voices are very polite. They use 'please' and 'thank you', **(12)** .... the women are addressed as 'madam' and the men as 'sir'.

MULTIPLE-CHOICE CLOZE: PAPER 3, PART 1

2 Read the text below and decide which answer (A, B, C or D) best fits each gap. There is an example at the beginning (0).

The police have announced that **(0)** ......*crime*........ figures in the capital have increased yet again. A police **(1)** .... warned that small offences were increasing and warned the public to be on their guard against attacks in the streets, such as **(2)** ....

The police did report a crackdown on offenders after they made a number of **(3)** .... of gangs of thieves who work on the underground network. This attracted a great deal of **(4)** .... attention and the photographs of the suspects appeared in all major newspapers. The police have also encouraged local storekeepers to install security cameras to reduce the amount of **(5)** .... throughout the city.

Nevertheless, it is the organised gangs that remain public **(6)** .... number one. They have been responsible for graffiti, vandalism and violent attacks on the major housing estates north of the city. Many elderly people **(7)** .... from intimidation from the gangs and some are afraid even to leave their own homes. The police have **(8)** .... for witnesses who may be able to give evidence against these people. The police commissioner has **(9)** .... that this situation cannot continue. "We cannot **(10)** .... these hooligans ruin the lives of everyone else in the community," she said yesterday. "But whether we can catch the leaders of the gangs **(11)** .... on us getting information from the public." She also emphasised the increased **(12)** .... to the city's essential tourist industry if future conditions do not improve.

0	A	illegal	B	suspect	C	police	D crime
1	A	announcer	B	presenter	C	spokesperson	D speaker
2	A	burglary	B	mugging	C	arson	D forgery
3	A	arrests	B	stops	C	escapes	D catches
4	A	journalist	B	media	C	presentation	D report
5	A	blackmailing	B	hacking	C	shoplifting	D kidnapping
6	A	opponent	B	protestor	C	enemy	D fear
7	A	afflict	B	suffer	C	affect	D injure
8	A	demanded	B	complained	C	applied	D appealed
9	A	stated	B	talked	C	refused	D considered
10	A	permit	B	accept	C	let	D allow
11	A	requires	B	needs	C	follows	D depends
12	A	rise	B	threat	C	opposition	D destruction

Writing: an article

OPTIONAL TASK: PAPER 2, PART 2

1 In Part 2 of the Writing test, you may be asked to write an article. Complete the student's answer to the exam question below with the phrases (a–i).

a So why not
b A second way
c In conclusion
d So it is clear to see
e Take, for example,
f There are three main things
g There is no doubt that
h Finally
i Firstly

Read this advertisement from a website. Write an article for the website.

We are looking for suggestions for three ways that local people can get involved to help improve our city and make it a nicer place to live in. Write your answer in 120–180 words.

GET INVOLVED!

1 __g__ our city needs improvement.
2 __e__ the litter and the graffiti which are everywhere. Many public places have also been damaged by vandalism. 3 __d__ that we need to do something to encourage people to help improve our city.

4 __f__ that we can do.
5 __i__ , it is difficult to stop people littering. 6 __a__ start groups to pick up the litter? If we keep the streets clean, people will think carefully before dropping rubbish.
7 __b__ is to ask people to plant more trees in the parks. People will want to get involved if they are helping the environment. If the city is a nice place to live, it will discourage vandalism.
8 __h__ , we need to set up special spaces for graffiti. Then graffiti artists can paint in these special places and not on public buildings.

9 __c__ , if we want to live in a nice city, we all have to do something to make our environment pleasant to live in.

When you are writing an article, an essay or a report, there are a number of standard phrases that you can use to structure your answer. For example, phrases a–i in exercise 1 could be used in many different articles. When you are doing written work before the exam, write out a list of possible phrases that you could use in your article. Write this list before you write the article itself and then try to add the phrases as you write. This will help you to use and remember useful phrases for structuring your writing.

2 Now write your own answer to the exam question in exercise 1. Use this plan:

Paragraph 1: introduction and explanation of the problem

Paragraph 2: three solutions and explanations of the solutions

Paragraph 3: conclusion

Speaking

COLLABORATIVE TASK: PAPER 5, PART 3

1 🎧8.3 **Sometimes in the Speaking test you might work in a group of three rather than two. It is even more important to use phrases to show that you are listening. Listen to five extracts of Philippe, Claudio and Julieta discussing the exam question and pictures below, and decide which picture they are talking about.**

Extract 1 ___   Extract 4 ___

Extract 2 ___   Extract 5 ___

Extract 3 ___

Look at the illustrations which show different ways of dealing with crime and bad behaviour. Discuss which of them is the most effective and which of them is the most important.

2 🎧8.3 **Listen again and write the words that Claudio (C), Julieta (J), and Philippe (P) use to respond to suggestions, and to show that they are listening.**

1 **C** The problem is that you hear these alarms all the time.

   J _____.

2 **C** You think, 'Oh, there's another alarm. How noisy!'

   J I'm _____ on that.

3 **P** I think that drivers don't care if they drive very fast.

   C _____.

   P You know, the drivers, they don't really care, so you have to do something else. To ...

   J _____. You have to force them to drive with more care.

   P Yes. _____. To force.

4 **J** In my country this is very common.

   C _____, Julieta?

   J _____. Every time you buy with your credit card, they ask to see your identity card. It's normal.

   P _____.

5 **J** The police don't know who you are, who anyone is.

   C _____, but I don't think that they are very useful.

6 **C** This is a very quick way to tell people 'look out'.

   P _____ you mean, but I really don't agree. The photo is terrible. This could be anybody.

   C _____, but it is important to say to people, 'Be careful'.

   J _____, so do we think this is effective or not?

7 **J** And also you can cover your face so nobody sees you.

   P _____. Anyway, the pictures you get from these cameras are often not very clear.

   C _____. But sometimes they are useful after a crime. The police have caught lots of criminals by using these cameras.

   J _____.

3 **If you are working with a partner, do the exam task in exercise 1 together. Try to use the words and phrases from exercise 2.**

LANGUAGE CHECKLIST

☐ I know words to describe food and drink, page 72.

☐ I know how to pronounce some words with silent letters, page 72.

☐ I know how to use *used to* and *would*, page 73.

☐ I know how to spell adjectives ending -*y*, page 73.

☐ I know some phrasal verbs with *up*, page 75.

EXAM CHECKLIST

☐ I have practised the gapped text question from the Reading paper, page 70.

☐ I have practised writing an essay from the Writing paper, page 74.

☐ I have practised the multiple matching question from the Listening paper, page 75.

☐ I have practised the key word transformation question from the Use of English paper, page 76.

☐ I have practised the open cloze question from the Use of English paper, page 76.

☐ I have practised the collaborative task from the Speaking paper, page 77.

Reading

GAPPED TEXT: PAPER 1, PART 2

1 **You are going to read an article about the history of food. Seven sentences have been removed from the article. Choose from the sentences (A–H) the one which fits each gap (1–7). There is one extra sentence which you do not need to use.**

A This is because the traffic was not all one-way.

B Elsewhere, in Ecuador, there is evidence that chillis have been used in cooking for over 6,000 years.

C At first the local people were shocked and believed that the animal and its rider were the same creature.

D This impacted our diet and our languages.

E Instead they were grown for decoration.

F Supermarket shelves are full of every imaginable type of fruit and vegetable.

G The avocado was known to the Maya, one of the ancient peoples of Mexico.

H It was known in ancient times: Alexander the Great had encountered the fruit while he was travelling in India.

2 **Now read the text again and find words or phrases that mean the following:**

1 a popular piece of jargon (paragraph 2) _____

2 come from (paragraph 2) _____

3 a large quantity of (paragraph 3) _____

4 in the beginning (paragraph 4) _____

5 is the largest participant in (paragraph 6) _____

6 to change an animal species from wild to tame (paragraph 7) _____

The first food revolution

① Can you imagine goulash, the national dish of Hungary, without its spicy paprika? Or Italian cooking without the tomato? These foods are a huge part of each country's national cuisine. So it comes as rather a shock to know that both countries have been using these ingredients for little more than 600 years. This is because both paprika and the tomato came to Europe from the New World, after the arrival of Columbus in the Americas in 1492.

② One of the most popular buzzwords of the moment is *globalisation*: people are coming closer together because of improved communication and international business. This modern trend is in fact far from new. After the first encounter of Europeans and native Americans, there was an enormous movement of food from the Old World to the New World, and vice-versa. **(1)** _____ The words *tomato*, *avocado* and *chocolate* all originate from the civilisations of the New World, such as the Aztecs.

③ Agriculture in the 'New' World was very old indeed. Peoples such as the Maya and Aztecs in modern Mexico had developed a wide range of interesting foodstuffs. For example, the Spanish conquistadors were astonished to see the Aztec ruler Montezuma drinking chocolate. They soon exported this drink to Europe. **(2)** _____ The spice would be mixed with corn, which was also grown on ancient farms.

④ Like all new things, there was suspicion of the discoveries made by the European explorers. Originally, both the turkey and the tomato were not used as food in some parts of Europe. **(3)** _____ The turkey was kept for its beautiful feathers and the tomato as a plant for gardens. In the past, experts believed the tomato was a similar plant to *belladonna* and so many people believed that it was dangerous to eat. There is some truth in this, as the leaves and roots of the plant are actually poisonous.

⑤ The huge movement of foods which took place after 1492 has become known as The Columbian Exchange. **(4)** _____ In addition to new crops moving to Europe and Asia, Old World crops were planted across North and South America.

⑥ One example is the banana. **(5)** _____ Once it moved to the Caribbean islands, it soon became an enormously important crop throughout the area. In the same way, coffee was discovered in Africa and then transported to South America. We now have a situation where the world's largest producer of the drink is Brazil, which dominates world production.

⑦ The arrival of the horse into the Americas also had dramatic effects. **(6)** _____ Quickly, they learned how to domesticate and use the animals themselves. In North America, the horse revolutionised the native American's way of life. On horseback, the local tribes were able to hunt the wild buffalo, which were then common across the continent.

⑧ From the Columbian Exchange we can see that globalisation is not a new process, but rather the result of centuries of cultural exchange. In our modern world we are now able to buy and grow all of these food products with ease. **(7)** _____ This makes it difficult to imagine a world where a tomato was looked at with fear and a horse was something magical. This is one of the greatest losses of our era: that we are no longer excited by the extraordinary world around us.

Vocabulary

FOOD AND DRINK

1 Look at the pictures. Write the verb for each way of preparing food.

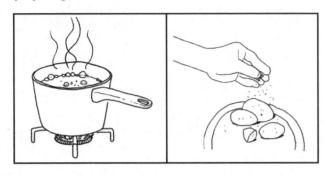

1 _____   2 _____

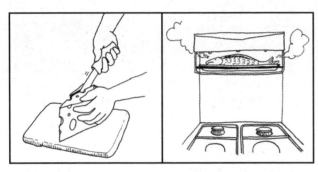

3 _____   4 _____

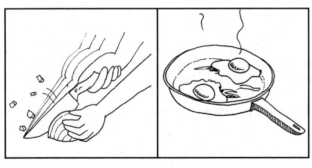

5 _____   6 _____

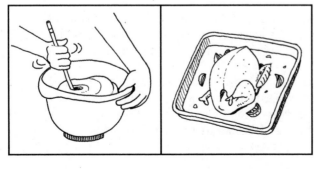

7 _____   8 _____

2 Complete the words. Write one letter in each space.

1 When I went to India, I was in heaven because I love curries and s _ _ _ _ food.

2 I don't like eating crisps because I don't like s _ _ _ _ food.

3 I prefer my steak w _ _ _- _ _ _ _ . I don't want any blood in it.

4 I'd prefer to get a d _ _ champagne than to get a sweet one.

5 Would you like still or s _ _ _ _ _ _ _ _ water?

6 Sushi is usually made with rice and r _ _ fish.

7 Lemons taste s _ _ _ .

8 The food was really b _ _ _ _ . It didn't taste of anything.

Pronunciation

Silent letters
English words frequently contain silent letters. Be careful that you do not pronounce these letters when you say the words.
Example: iron ➡ i̶ron /ɑɪən/

1 🎧9.1 **Cross out the silent letters in each word, as in the example above. Then listen to check your answers.**

answer	island	sandwich
calm	knight	sword
castle	knitting	vegetable
chocolate	palm	Wednesday
cupboard	pneumonia	whole
guardian	psychiatrist	yacht
guess	salmon	

2 If you are working with a partner, read all the words to each other. Remember not to pronounce the silent letters.

Grammar

USED TO AND *WOULD*

1 <u>Underline</u> the correct form of *used to*.

1 When I was a child, I *used to love / got used to loving* watching my mother making biscuits.

2 I've been living in this country for 20 years, but I still *can't be used to / can't get used to* the appalling weather!

3 They *used to / were used to* wrap fish and chips in newspaper, but they don't do that any more.

4 When we first moved to this country, we didn't like all the hot food. But we *are used to / get used to* it now.

5 Many foreigners don't like the idea of eating rice for breakfast. But, after living here in Korea for over ten years, I *have been used to / have got used to* it!

6 The kids have fallen asleep. They *used not to eat / aren't used to eating* this late.

2 In four of the sentences below, it is not possible to use *used to*. Decide which sentences are incorrect. Then rewrite the incorrect sentences, replacing *used to* with the past simple.

1 My father used to work for the post office for five years.

_____

2 My mother used to drive a motorbike.

_____

3 I used to study at Bristol University from 1993 to 1996.

_____

4 He used to be an English teacher.

_____

5 Bill Clinton used to be president of the USA for eight years.

_____

6 We used to travel across Asia from January to June 2003.

_____

3 Look at the sentences below. All the sentences are correct. However, if it is also possible to replace *used to* with *would*, rewrite the sentence.

1 Gabriele used to own a toy kitchen when she was a little girl.

2 My family always used to eat lunch together on Sundays.

3 We always used to go on holiday to the same seaside village.

4 I used to like sweets when I was younger, but I can't stand them now.

5 I used to know how to make a really nice fish pie, but I've forgotten the recipe now.

Spelling

SPOTLIGHT ON SPELLING

Adjectives ending -y
Many English adjectives are made by adding -y to the end of a noun.
Example: salt ➡ salty

Spelling problems occur when the noun ends in -e. In this case the final -e is usually dropped and replaced by -y.
Example: grime ➡ grimy ~~grimey~~

1 Find ten adjectives ending -y in the wordsearch. Words can be found vertically, horizontally and diagonally.

p	m	y	n	o	i	s	y	i	c
g	s	t	o	n	y	u	y	t	o
k	g	a	r	l	i	c	k	y	l
w	a	s	h	a	b	c	b	d	k
e	p	t	p	a	s	m	o	k	y
j	i	y	g	i	f	q	n	p	o
z	u	g	h	x	c	k	y	i	r
a	t	i	u	r	r	y	a	i	p
g	t	i	c	y	b	o	j	o	q
o	v	m	s	y	d	n	o	s	y

2 Which adjective in the wordsearch comes from a noun that does not end -e? What extra letter is added to this adjective before the -y ending?

73

Writing: an essay

1 Look at the five extracts from students' answers to the exam question below. Which extracts say that fast food restaurants are good for society? Which extracts say that fast food restaurants are bad for society?

> Your teacher has asked you to write an essay with the title: Are fast food restaurants bad for society? Write your *essay*. Write your answer in 120–180 words.

1

It is said that people today have unhealthy diets because of fast food restaurants, but it is not certain that this is the case. Most people only go to a fast food restaurant for a special treat. There is no problem eating fast food if you only do this occasionally. For many families, they only go to fast food restaurants for children's parties or special occasions. So fast food restaurants cannot be held responsible for unhealthy diets. In fact they are excellent places for families to go to.

2

It is clear that fast food restaurants are having a terrible effect on our cities and towns. It is impossible to go into the city centre without seeing rubbish from fast food restaurants everywhere. The main problem is that they use too much packaging and people just throw this on the streets.

3

There is some truth in the statement that fast food restaurants are bad for society. If people only go to fast food restaurants, then traditional restaurants might close. This is because they have more expensive prices and because people prefer fast food. It is important therefore that people eat in both fast food restaurants and restaurants which serve their national cuisine.

2 Match the underlined phrases in the extracts to the definitions below.

1 You can't disagree that this is

_____

2 Obviously _____

3 What happens next is

_____

4 People say _____

5 this is really what happens

_____

6 So what people should do is

_____

7 After thinking about both sides of the argument, it appears _____

8 The biggest thing that is wrong is

_____

9 I more or less believe it when people say

_____

10 The answer can change because people use different definitions of _____

4

It depends on what is meant by society. Fast food restaurants are very important for young people. There are not many places where they can go out with their friends. Other restaurants are too expensive. For teenagers and young people, fast food restaurants are places where we can meet and spend time. That must be good for society.

5

On balance it seems that fast food restaurants are having a negative effect on society. When people start eating fast food, they get used to eating lots of sugar and salt. This results in people changing their diets and eating with more salt and sugar at home, which is very unhealthy.

3 Now write your own answer to the exam question in exercise 1. Write the whole essay.

....

....

....

....

....

....

....

....

....

....

....

....

....

....

....

....

....

....

....

Listening: favourite dish

MULTIPLE MATCHING: PAPER 4, PART 3

1 🎧 9.2 **You will hear five different people talking about the dish they most enjoy cooking. For questions 1–5, choose from the list (A–F). Use the letters only once. There is one extra letter which you do not need to use.**

Which speaker

A does not eat any animal products?   Speaker ____

B cooks fish?   Speaker ____

C thinks their country's cuisine is
different in other countries?   Speaker ____

D uses ingredients that other people
normally throw away?   Speaker ____

E uses only raw vegetables?   Speaker ____

F does not cook their dish at home?   Speaker ____

Vocabulary

EXTENSION: PHRASAL VERBS WITH *UP*

1 *Up* **has many different meanings in phrasal verbs. Look at the phrasal verbs in bold in the sentences (1–5) below. Match the definitions (a–e) to the phrasal verbs.**

1 People don't eat lunch on Sundays together any more because the traditional family is **breaking up**. ____

2 You need to **chop** all the vegetables **up** and put them in a saucepan. ____

3 I always add extra chilli to **spice** it **up**. ____

4 People have been eating this for hundreds of years and I think it's important to **keep** the old traditions **up**. ____

5 Although the food tastes different, they always **eat** everything **up**. ____

a into little pieces

b going

c more

d all, completely

e into separate parts

2 **Now complete the sentences with the correct form of the phrasal verbs in exercise 1.**

1 You've been doing some really good work.

_____ it _____!

2 It tastes really bland. What can I add to

_____ it _____?

3 The team played together for years, but now it is

_____ because lots of players are leaving.

4 That meat is too big for the cats to eat. You need to

_____ it _____.

5 I was worried that no one would like the dinner I

prepared, but they _____ everything

_____.

Use of English

KEY WORD TRANSFORMATIONS: PAPER 3, PART 4

1 **Complete the second sentence so that it has a similar meaning to the first sentence, using the word given. Do not change the word given. You must use between two and five words, including the word given. There is an example at the beginning (0).**

0 It's not worth going on a diet if you don't do any exercise.
   POINT

   There ....*is no point going*........... on a diet if you don't do any exercise.

1 Can you look after the children this afternoon?
   CARE

   Can you .... the children this afternoon?

2 I still have problems with driving on the left.
   USED

   I haven't .... on the left yet.

3 We didn't think about his inexperience before we gave him the job.
   ACCOUNT

   We didn't .... before we gave him the job.

4 Let's delay the decision until next week.
   OFF

   Let's .... the decision until next week.

5 Your mother is upset because you don't think about the work she does for you.
   GRANTED

   Your mother is upset because you
   ....

6 My grandmother would spend all day long baking cakes.
   USED

   My grandmother .... all day long baking cakes.

7 How is Martina doing at university?
   ON

   How .... at university?

8 I'd prefer to eat at home.
   WE

   I'd rather .... at home.

When learning new verbs, also take note of the prepositions that follow them. Many questions in the FCE exam concentrate on verb-preposition collocations.

After finishing a Use of English exercise in this book, look at all the questions and write down any verb–preposition collocations that you find. For example, in exercise 1, you can see the collocation:
go + on + a diet.

SPOTLIGHT ON STUDY TECHNIQUES

OPEN CLOZE: PAPER 3, PART 2

2 **Read the text below and think of the word which best fits each gap. Use only one word in each gap. There is an example at the beginning (0).**

What is a normal price to pay for lunch? I **(0)** ....*still*.......... remember the most expensive lunch of my life. It was in **(1)** .... hotel in Paris and I was entertaining a business customer. Between the two of us we spent €75 – and that was **(2)** .... even drinking any wine!

But **(3)** .... a country house hotel in the UK, chefs **(4)** .... recently produced a sandwich that **(5)** .... its own costs £100 (€150)! The sandwich is made from corn-fed chicken, Italian ham and a topping of white truffles. It is the latter that really sends **(6)** .... cost soaring!

The white truffle, a wild fungus **(7)** .... is traditionally found with the help of pigs or dogs, sells at outrageous prices. The Alba truffle of South-Eastern France can sell for as **(8)** .... as £2,500 a kilo! This delicacy is the most expensive ingredient in Europe, but not quite the world.

This is because **(9)** .... prize must belong to the lychee, a fruit that is prized **(10)** .... Asian cuisine. In 2002 a Chinese businessman paid £45,270 **(11)** .... a single fruit from a 400-year-old tree! It was **(12)** .... valuable because the fruit of the tree was once eaten by the Qing emperors of China.

Speaking

COLLABORATIVE TASK: PAPER 5, PART 3

1 Read the sentences (1–7) below. Match the functions (a–g) to the sentences.

1 Where shall we start? ___

2 Well, what would you suggest? ___

3 Let's turn to the next picture. ___

4 So are you suggesting that we choose this one? ___

5 I hear what you're saying, but I think this one might cause some problems. ___

6 Are there any pictures that we haven't talked about yet? ___

a asking for your partner's opinion

b changing the topic

c checking that you have completed the task

d beginning the discussion

e asking someone to confirm a decision

f adding a warning

2 🎧 9.3 Listen to two students, Philippe and Julieta, answering the exam question below. Who says each phrase (1–6) in exercise 1? Write P for Philippe and J for Julieta.

Phrase 1 ___

Phrase 2 ___

Phrase 3 ___

Phrase 4 ___

Phrase 5 ___

Phrase 6 ___

> Imagine that you are looking after a group of children aged five to seven for the day and you have to prepare lunch for them. Decide together which things in the picture you would prepare and tell each other why.

3 If you are working with a partner, answer the exam question. When you are speaking, try to use the phrases in exercise 1 and tick (✓) each one after you have used it.

10 Is it real?

LANGUAGE CHECKLIST

☐ I know words to describe objects, page 80.

☐ I know some phrasal verbs with *down* and *off*, page 80.

☐ I know how to use modal verbs for guessing, speculating and deducing, page 81.

☐ I know how to spell words with *ei* and *ie*, page 83.

☐ I know how to use intonation in question tags, page 85.

EXAM CHECKLIST

☐ I have practised the multiple choice question from the Reading paper, page 78.

☐ I have practised writing an email from the Writing paper, page 82.

☐ I have practised the sentence completion question from the Listening paper, page 83.

☐ I have practised the key word transformation question from the Use of English paper, page 84.

☐ I have practised the multiple-choice cloze question from the Use of English paper, page 84.

☐ I have practised the individual 'long turn' from the Speaking paper, page 85.

Reading

MULTIPLE CHOICE: PAPER 1, PART 1

1 **You are going to read an article about a dinosaur. For questions 1–8, choose the answer (A, B, C or D) which you think fits best according to the text.**

1 The idea that the extinction of the dinosaurs was caused by an asteroid
   A is the most modern theory.
   B is the most improbable theory.
   C is the most probable theory.
   D is one of the oldest theories.

2 In the 1980s scientists travelled to the Congo because they were
   A paid to go by the newspapers.
   B looking for dinosaur bones.
   C interested in seeing Mokele-Mbembe.
   D invited there by the local people.

3 The writer of the 1913 German report
   A believed that it was possible that Mokele-Mbembe existed.
   B had seen Mokele-Mbembe.
   C thought the reports from the local people were false.
   D believed that Mokele-Mbembe was actually another African animal.

4 When local people were asked to identify Mokele-Mbembe from pictures,
   A they did not recognise any of the pictures.
   B they thought it was similar to a camel.
   C they thought it looked like two or three of the animals.
   D they thought it looked like an extinct animal.

5 What physical evidence of Mokele-Mbembe has been claimed to exist?
   A its nest
   B its tail
   C its footprints
   D its teethmarks found on other animals

6 What does the writer mean by "There are indeed conflicting reports about what Mokele-Mbembe looks like".
   A None of the reports are trustworthy.
   B The reports give different information.
   C Each report attacks the findings of another report.
   D The reports are confusing to read.

7 What does the writer think about Mokele-Mbembe?
   A He thinks it is a fictional creation of the local people.
   B He thinks it is definitely a living dinosaur.
   C He thinks it was originally a trick created by foreigners.
   D He thinks that there is enough real evidence to believe in it.

8 Cryptozoologists
   A only study modern sources.
   B work in secret.
   C try to see if monsters really exist.
   D do not believe in modern science.

Dinosaurs in Africa

Several million years ago, the dinosaurs were wiped out in a major extinction event. Huge numbers of species simply disappeared from the face of the planet. There have been numerous explanations for their sudden disappearance, although the most likely explanation is that they were devastated when an asteroid hit the earth, with cataclysmic results. But what if not all the dinosaurs had perished? What if they had survived over millions of years, and are still alive today?

In the 1980s there was a surge of media interest following reports of a mysterious creature living in the forests of the Congo. This beast was known to the local population as Mokele-Mbembe, which means 'the one who stops rivers' and it was described as a long-necked herbivore that lived in rivers and was rarely seen. When scientists and explorers travelled to the region to investigate these extraordinary claims, they were astonished to learn that Mokele-Mbembe was believed to be a sort of brontosaurus: a living dinosaur!

What is interesting about the Mokele-Mbembe story is that the sightings go back a very long way. When Europeans were first charting the area, they came upon reports of monsters in the jungle, and they mentioned these sightings in their official reports, albeit with plenty of caution. One of the most famous records comes from a German report of 1913, which wrote of Mokele-Mbembe that "The animal is said to be of a brownish-gray color with a smooth skin, its size is approximately that of an elephant; at least that of a hippopotamus. It is said to have a long and very flexible neck … A few spoke about a long, muscular tail like that of an alligator. … its diet is said to be entirely vegetable. This feature disagrees with a possible explanation as a myth."

Twentieth-century scientists investigated the claims. They spoke to local people and showed them books full of images of animals that were both local to the area and from much further away. According to their reports, when the local people saw animals such as camels, which were unknown in the region, they explained that these creatures did not exist nearby. However, they frequently pointed to the image of the brontosaurus as the creature known as Mokele-Mbembe.

There are many sceptics. The creature has never been photographed and although possible 'dinosaur' tracks have been discovered, there is no definite evidence that these were not a hoax. There are indeed conflicting reports about what Mokele-Mbembe looks like, with some people reporting a horn that other witnesses did not mention. It seems probable that despite the conclusions of the German report, the living dinosaur is really just a legendary monster that has only existed in folk tales for centuries.

Interestingly, the search for Mokele-Mbembe has become part of a new field of research, known as *cryptozoology*. This word comes from the Latin *crypto-* meaning 'secret' or 'hidden', and *zoology*, the study of animals. Such people investigate the possibility that apparently mythological creatures are really alive today, or once existed in the past. Their aim is to bring the study of monsters into the real world of science by publishing as much evidence as they can relating to mysterious creatures. Of course, success relies on actually finding the monsters to research!

Vocabulary

DESCRIBING OBJECTS

1 Complete the descriptions of the pictures with an adjective describing shape.

1 Most coins are _____ (although some British coins are not).

2 Look out for the _____ warning notices.

3 Katja lives in the room with the _____ window.

4 I bought a _____ block of wood because I'm going to make a table.

2 Look at the sentences below. Six of them contain a mistake. Find and correct the mistakes.

1 The police have received reports of sphere objects in the sky.

2 What is the wide of the football pitch?

3 We'd like to know your high and weight.

4 Young children can get scared when they are in the deep end of the swimming pool.

5 I was surprised by the soft of the material. It felt lovely and smooth.

6 I saw this coloured summer dress and I really wanted to buy it. It was all the colours of the rainbow.

7 Do you know the long of the garden?

8 Their house has a gorgeous wooden floor.

3 Look at the phrasal verbs in **bold** in the sentences (1–6) below. Then match the pictures (a–f) to the sentences.

1 The wind **blew** the papers **off** my desk. ___

2 The wind **blew** all the trees **down**. ___

3 Karen **fell off** her bike. ___

4 The picture **fell down**. ___

5 Fred **threw** the toys **off** the table. ___

6 Dad **threw** his tools **down** in frustration. ___

4 **Underline** the correct form of the verb.

1 Johnny broke his leg when he came *off / down* his horse in the competition.

2 I took a packet from the bottom of the pile and everything came *off / down* at once.

3 You'll be able to put everything in the suitcase if you push all the clothes *off / down*.

4 Mark is crying because Danny pushed him *off / down* his chair.

5 The top is too tight on this jar. It's impossible to get it *off / down*.

6 Sandra's got quite a bad fever. The doctor said that she has to take paracetamol to get her temperature *off / down*.

7 I put some peanuts in my hand and the birds flew *off / down* to eat them.

8 The cat was running after the birds. But when they saw him, they flew *off / down*.

Grammar

MODAL VERBS FOR GUESSING, SPECULATING AND DEDUCING

1 **Put the words from the box into the sentences below. Add one word to each sentence.**

| be   can't   could   have   must   not |

1 You should read his email right away! It be important – we don't know.

2 He have been in a hurry because he ran out of the room.

3 I know she spoke French, but she might be from France because we also have students here from Quebec.

4 It may not been the postman. We get a lot of people here delivering junk mail.

5 You have seen Diana at the station: she's in Lithuania at the moment!

6 He says he's a detective, so he must from the police.

2 **Eric and Jack were camping when they heard a noise and saw something moving in the forests. Complete their sentences using the words in brackets and *can't, must* and *might*.**

E What was that noise?

J It ¹_____ (be) a plane. I'm sure that was it.

E No, it ²_____ (be) a plane because the noise came from over there.

J Where?

E There, in the bushes.

J Rover ³_____ (make) the noise when he was looking for something. That dog is always looking for rabbits or cats.

E No, look. Rover's asleep over there. What's that light in the tent?

J My mobile.

E Maybe that's the answer? Someone

⁴_____ (sent) you a text message and then the noise woke us up. Check.

J No. There's no message on my phone. The light's on, but I don't know why. Something else

⁵_____ (happen).

E Hey, look at our bags! Our food is all over the floor.

J That explains it. Some animal

⁶_____ (found) our food and then it woke us up when it was eating. It

⁷_____ (run) away when we woke up and started talking.

E I hope it wasn't a bear that did the damage.

J Don't be ridiculous. A bear ⁸_____ (do) that! There aren't any in these forests. It

⁹_____ (be) a fox or something like that.

Writing: an email

COMPULSORY TASK: PAPER 2, PART 1

1 **When taking the Writing test, it is essential to answer the exam question correctly. Look at the exam question below and decide which of the subjects (1–8) you must include in your answer.**

1 what ghosts they talk about

2 what old buildings you visit

3 the ages of the other people on the tour

4 your personal opinion of the tour

5 whereabouts in London the tour is

6 how to get tickets

7 the cost of the tour

8 when the tour takes place

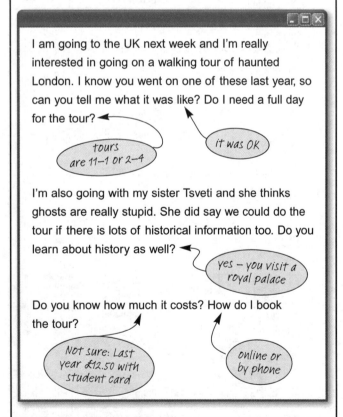

You have received an email from your friend Yasen. Read the email and the notes you have made. Then write an email in 120–150 words using all your notes. You must use grammatically correct sentences with accurate spelling and punctuation in a style appropriate to the situation.

I am going to the UK next week and I'm really interested in going on a walking tour of haunted London. I know you went on one of these last year, so can you tell me what it was like? Do I need a full day for the tour?

tours are 11–1 or 2–4

it was OK

I'm also going with my sister Tsveti and she thinks ghosts are really stupid. She did say we could do the tour if there is lots of historical information too. Do you learn about history as well?

yes – you visit a royal palace

Do you know how much it costs? How do I book the tour?

Not sure: Last year £12.50 with student card

online or by phone

2 **Complete the student's answer to the exam question in exercise 1 with the sentences (a–h).**

Hi Yasen

1 _____

2 _____

3 _____

4 _____

There are two walking tours every day.

5 _____

6 _____

But I do remember that last year it was £12.50 with a student card discount (so don't forget your card!).

7 _____

8 _____

Speak soon,

Diana.

---

a I did this last year and I thought it was OK but nothing amazing.

b Now here's some information about the price and times and everything.

c There's one in the morning and one in the afternoon (11–1 and 2–4). I did the morning one.

d Does this answer all your questions? I hope it's helpful!

e In your mail you asked about the walking tour of haunted London.

f I hope you're well – and thanks for your email!

g The bad news is that I don't know the price.

h That's expensive, but I still think your sister will like it because you see lots of old buildings and you even get to go in a royal palace. That's the best bit!

3 **Look again at the answer in exercise 2. The writer has forgotten to include one piece of information. What did she forget?**

4 Now write your own answer to the exam question in exercise 1.

....
....
....
....
....
....
....
....
....
....
....
....
....
....
....

Spelling

1 The words in this group all follow the rule. Complete the words with *ei* or *ie*.

1 fr _ _ nd

2 exper _ _ nce

3 rec _ _ pt

4 rev _ _ w

5 perc _ _ ve

6 dec _ _ ve

7 ch _ _ f

8 inconc _ _ vable

2 There are also a number of exceptions. All of the words below break the rule in exercise 1. Complete the words with *ei* or *ie*.

1 n _ _ ther

2 anc _ _ nt

3 effic _ _ nt

4 n _ _ ghbour

5 for _ _ gn

6 profic _ _ nt

7 w _ _ rd

8 prot _ _ n

9 spec _ _ s

10 h _ _ ght

11 sc _ _ nce

Listening: a ghost hunter

SENTENCE COMPLETION: PAPER 4, PART 2

1 🎧10.1 You will hear David Hick talking about his experience as a ghost hunter when he was a student. For questions 1–10, complete the sentences. You will need to write a word or a short phrase in each gap.

2 Before checking your answers in the back of the book, check the spelling of the words that contain *ei* or *ie*.

David was an [_____ 1] ghost hunter.

He was studying [_____ 2]

He was told a ghost story by his [_____ 3]

The person who told the ghost story had been staying in a [_____ 4]

Suddenly the [_____ 5] of her room just opened.

David investigated it with [_____ 6]

When they stayed in the same room, they saw [_____ 7]

David's website was called [_____ 8]

People could leave [_____ 9] on the website.

All the messages they received came from [_____ 10]

Use of English

KEY WORD TRANSFORMATIONS: PAPER 3, PART 4

1 Complete the second sentence so that it has a similar meaning to the first sentence, using the word given. Do not change the word given. You must use between two and five words, including the word given. There is an example at the beginning (0).

0 She started investigating UFOs when she was forty-two years old.
   AGE

   She started investigating UFOs
   ....*at the age of*.............. forty-two.

1 I think this is OK. It doesn't appear to be wrong.
   SEEM

   I think this is OK. It .... it is wrong.

2 It looks as if there has been a problem.
   SEEMS

   It .... there has been a problem.

3 Maybe Mike forgot that we were going out tonight.
   MIGHT

   Mike .... that we were going out tonight.

4 You rarely see reports of UFOs in the newspapers.
   RARE

   It .... reports of UFOs in the newspapers.

5 Can you explain your answer?
   REASON

   Can you .... your answer?

6 I don't know what happened last night.
   IDEA

   I .... what happened last night.

7 Denise was the only one who saw the strange lights.
   APART

   No one saw the strange lights
   .... Denise.

8 We shouldn't tell them our story because they won't believe us.
   POINT

   There's .... them our story because they won't believe us.

MULTIPLE-CHOICE CLOZE: PAPER 3, PART 1

2 Read the text below and decide which answer (A, B, C or D) best fits each gap. There is an example at the beginning (0).

UFO **(0)** ......*simply*........ means *Unidentified Flying Object*: it refers to any object in the sky that you cannot explain. There have been **(1)** .... numbers of UFO reports from the late 1940s onwards, when a craze swept across the USA. People really started to believe that UFOs were **(2)** .... craft from alien planets.

Much of this interest was **(3)** .... by the growth of science fiction. Movies from the 1950s such as *Invasion of the Body Snatchers* (1956) were full of aliens. However, this was not a new **(4)** .... In 1938 a radio broadcast by Orson Welles included news reports of alien attacks: many people believed that what they were **(5)** .... was true!

The public's **(6)** .... were fuelled by events such as the Roswell Incident in 1947. **(7)** .... to most reports of the accident, some kind of vehicle crashed in the desert. At first the US military **(8)** .... to journalists by saying it was a UFO. Then later the official story changed and it was explained **(9)** .... a weather balloon. Since then there have been countless rumours of what really happened. In 1995 a film was **(10)** .... produced which claimed to show the scientific examination of the spaceship's alien crew!

Although many in the scientific **(11)** .... may doubt the existence of extraterrestrial life, there are still experts who **(12)** .... reports of UFO sightings. Indeed, many professional pilots have seen strange fast-moving objects in the sky. So perhaps there really is something out there after all.

0	A almost	B quite	C simply	D likely
1	A enlarged	B developing	C increasing	D expanded
2	A presently	B actually	C completely	D increasingly
3	A sparked off	B run off	C moved off	D flown off
4	A phenomenon	B manifestation	C demonstration	D exhibition
5	A listening	B attending	C hearing	D presenting
6	A panic	B fears	C worries	D concern
7	A Concerning	B According	C Deciding	D Including
8	A answered	B spoke	C defended	D responded
9	A to	B as	C by	D like
10	A even	B so	C such	D surely
11	A group	B laboratory	C company	D community
12	A decide	B enter	C harvest	D gather

Speaking

INDIVIDUAL 'LONG TURN': PAPER 5, PART 2

1 🎧 10.2 **Listen to the start of Part 2 of the Speaking test. What question does the student, Claudio, ask the interlocutor?**

2 🎧 10.3 **Now listen to Claudio talking about the photos below. Complete the descriptions of the pictures with the words he uses.**

> OK. Both photos show magic tricks. In the
> ¹ _____ we have a magician and a girl,
> and she is above the floor. This is ² _____
> levitation, isn't it? It looks ³ _____ he is
> on the stage in a theatre or somewhere
> ⁴ _____. Now, in the second picture we
> have another magician and he's doing a card trick, and
> everybody looks amazed. ⁵ _____ is which
> trick is the most entertaining. Well, the first picture
> ⁶ _____ looks entertaining, but
> ⁷ _____ that the magician is on stage and
> the audience just sits and watches. For me it's
> ⁸ _____ boring. I ⁹ _____
> prefer the second picture. This is a
> ¹⁰ _____ entertaining because the
> magician is very near and you can see what he is doing.
> You can try to see the 'trick'. I think that's definitely the
> better of ¹¹ _____.

3 **Claudio gives a very strong opinion when he answers the question. Look again at the words he used in exercise 2. Which words does he use to show that he feels strongly about his answers?**

4 **If you are working with a partner, answer the interlocutor's question for the photographs. The question is in listening script 10.2 on page 163.**

Pronunciation

Intonation in question tags
In English, intonation of question tags goes up if the tag is a real question.

Example: Thomas won the competition yesterday, **didn't he?** I hope he did because he's telling everyone.

The intonation goes down if the tag is used to check information that the speaker believes is true.
Example: This is called levitation, **isn't it?**

1 🎧 10.4 **Listen to the two tags.**

2 🎧 10.5 **Listen to the sentences below said twice. Write C if the speaker is checking information and Q if the speaker is asking a real question.**

1 a Sydney isn't the capital of Australia, is it? ____
  b Sydney isn't the capital of Australia, is it? ____

2 a You haven't seen Brett recently, have you? ____
  b You haven't seen Brett recently, have you? ____

3 a Matthew will be at the party, won't he? ____
  b Matthew will be at the party, won't he? ____

4 a I'm not working tomorrow, am I? ____
  b I'm not working tomorrow, am I? ____

5 a They were Irish, weren't they? ____
  b They were Irish, weren't they? ____

6 a We hadn't heard the news before, had we? ____
  b We hadn't heard the news before, had we? ____

3 **If you are working with a partner, practise saying the sentences and question tags in exercises 1 and 2.**

Reading

MULTIPLE MATCHING: PAPER 1, PART 3

1 **Buying something immediately without thinking about it for a long time is called making an impulse buy. You are going to read an article about four people who made an impulse buy. For questions 1–15, choose from the people (A–D). The people may be chosen more than once.**

Which person

1 made their impulse buy in their own country? ___

2 got help transporting their impulse buy? ___

3 was disappointed by the impulse buy? ___

4 originally planned to give the impulse buy to someone else? ___

5 frequently makes impulse buys? ___

6 doesn't usually make impulse buys? ___

7 was encouraged to make the impulse buy by a member of their family? ___

8 thought their impulse buy looked alien? ___

9 uses the impulse buy to remember a holiday? ___

10 had had an accident? ___

11 was taken by a shopkeeper to another shop? ___

12 went to a shop that didn't look very new? ___

13 was visiting family abroad? ___

14 does not need to know everything about a product before buying? ___

15 saw the purchase on the Internet? ___

2 **Look again at the article and find one phrase from each speaker which means _immediately_ or _without waiting_.**

3 **Find these phrasal verbs (1–6) in the text. Then match the definitions (a–f) to the phrasal verbs.**

1 I snapped one up ___

2 it really brings that trip back ___

3 The bike was completely written off. ___

4 I decided to sleep on it. ___

5 I like to think things through ___

6 I ran across this stall of fruit ___

a to destroy something, especially a vehicle

b to think about something overnight

c to buy/take something very quickly

d to consider something carefully

e to find by chance/accident

f to remind you of something

IMPULSE buy!

Today we talk to four people from around the world who tell us about a time when they made an impulse buy.

A Sabine, USA

My parents were both from Leipzig, but they moved to the USA in the early 1950s. I'd always wanted to visit their home country, but for many years it was impossible. I was thirty when the Berlin Wall came down and I desperately wanted to see an uncle in East Germany that I had never met.

Some time before I went there, one of my friends, Melissa, had asked me to bring her a present back. And while I was in Berlin, I saw a piece of the Berlin Wall. I thought it was perfect and I snapped one up on the spot. But when I got back, Melissa told me she already had a piece because her brother had been to Germany a couple of months earlier. So I kept it for myself as a souvenir. I'm pleased I did because it really brings that trip back to me and the emotional experience of meeting my uncle and staying with his family, who we had lost contact with for forty years.

B Dirk, Holland

I used to ride a motorbike. It was a big one too, 500cc, but I stopped riding it after I had a crash. The bike was completely written off. After that I learned to drive a car. But in my heart of hearts, I always wanted to be back on that bike!

About a year ago, I was online and just browsing when I found that someone was selling a bike just like my old one, and they lived about ten minutes away on the other side of Rotterdam. I would have bought it instantly, but I am married now and I thought my wife would never let me buy it. So I decided to sleep on it. But the next morning all I could think of was that machine. In the end my wife asked what was wrong and I told her. We went online together and we agreed to buy the bike. In fact, she told me it had always been her dream to ride on a motorbike too, so we got it together!

C Amandine, France

I'm not what you might call a shopaholic and I like to think things through before I make a purchase. But last year I was on holiday in Turkey and I went into a carpet shop. The shop owner was very polite and he offered me some tea. At the end I said I didn't really want to buy a rug or anything because what I was really interested in was furniture. The shopkeeper said he owned another shop across the street, so he led me over the road to that one.

At first the place seemed a bit run-down, but inside it was one of the most beautiful shops I have ever seen and at the back I saw this carved table. It was stunning. I had to have it and I agreed a price right then and there. After I bought it, I then realised that I would never get it on the plane back to Lyon, but he arranged shipping and everything too.

D Walter, Switzerland

I think in general I am quite an adventurous person and I especially like to eat new food. One of the first things I do when I arrive in a new country is go to the market to buy something completely new. I remember eating some cooking in Vietnam that was the most delicious meal I have ever had in my life, but I still don't know what it was called or what the ingredients were. That's the way it is when you travel.

The last time I was abroad, I ran across this stall of fruit. One of the fruits looked extraordinary, like it had dropped out of space. In the middle it was very pink with black seeds and the outside was green but with sort of leaves. I was very excited and I bought it just like that. Unfortunately, although it looked very exciting, it was actually pretty bland and I don't think I even finished it.

Vocabulary

SHOPPING AND CONSUMERISM

1 Complete the puzzle. What is the word in grey?

1 A reduction in the normal price.

2 The amount of money you have available, or the amount of money that you allow yourself to spend.

3 Famous names of products or companies, like Nike or Coca-Cola.

4 When you decide to spend a lot of money, you splash _____.

5 When something is on sale for a very good price, or if it is part of a promotion like 'buy one, get one free', it is on special _____.

6 When you do something for no particular reason, you do it on a _____.

7 An agreement between a buyer and seller.

8 Something that you buy for a very low price.

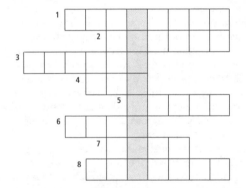

PHRASAL VERBS FOR SHOPPING

2 Choose a suitable word to complete the sentences below. Write one word only in each gap.

1 It's a good idea to pay _____ your credit card bills at the end of every month.

2 You can buy the same laptop cheaper if you go to town and shop _____ for the best price.

3 I hardly get any money in my job and I have five children. I don't know how I'm going to get _____.

4 Tim's been saving his money _____ because he wants to buy a surfboard.

5 We had a five-course meal with drinks and coffee, and in the end the bill came _____ €1,200!

6 I'm expecting a large tax bill at the end of the year, so I have set _____ some money to pay for it.

Grammar

CONDITIONALS

1 Look at the sentences below. Five of them contain a mistake. Find and correct the mistakes.

1 I wish I study harder when I was at university.

2 If I have a million euros, I would buy a yacht and sail around the Mediterranean.

3 If it will rain tomorrow, you'll need to take an umbrella.

4 If the shop hadn't been closed, we would have bought Rob's present today.

5 If my boss didn't leave, I would still be working for the company.

6 We won't have any more of these computer problems if we get the latest software.

7 If you would work in the shop, you would be able to buy watches, rings and jewellery at half price.

2 Put the words from the box into the sentences below. Add one word to each sentence.

had   long   provided   should   unless   were   will

1 If the shop still has those nice earrings, I buy them.

2 I would get the DVDs online if I you. They're cheaper.

3 If I known that you can only cook this dessert in a microwave, I wouldn't have bought it.

4 Customers can return products to the store that they are not damaged in any way.

5 I'll go to the shop as as you do the washing up.

6 I see Eric, I'll ask him to call you.

7 Don't buy anything you really want to.

3 Look at the sentences. Choose the best conditional (a or b) to describe each sentence.

1 I saw a very nice jacket when I was on holiday in New York last year, but I didn't want to pay $500.
   a I would have bought it if it had been less expensive.
   b I would buy it if it were less expensive.

2 The weather says it might rain this afternoon, but don't worry – we can still play tennis.
   a If it's wet, we'll always play on one of the indoor courts.
   b If it's wet, we always play on one of the indoor courts.

3 I really want to improve my English.
   a If I spent a year living in Britain, it would get a lot better.
   b If I spend a year living in Britain, it gets a lot better.

4 There was a huge argument and I told my boss that I thought he was an idiot.
   a If I hadn't been so angry, I wouldn't have said it.
   b If I weren't so angry, I wouldn't say it.

5 I love my husband, but I sometimes dream about living a different life.
   a If I'm not married, I will travel around the world.
   b If I weren't married, I would travel around the world.

6 I'm going to look for a new TV this afternoon.
   a If I find a cheap one, I'll buy it.
   b If I find a cheap one, I buy it.

Spelling

Two words, one sound
There are a number of words in English that sound the same and are written in a very similar way. However, if you make a small spelling mistake, you will change the meaning of the word.
Example: We've **already** finished.
         Are we **all ready** to go?

1 Look at the words in **bold** in the sentences (1–13). Then match the full forms and meanings (a–m) to the words in bold.

1 **You're** not going to believe this! ___

2 I think **they're** leaving at three. ___

3 **Maybe** Alexis knows what to do. ___

4 The shop is open **every day**. ___

5 **It's** a really nice day today. ___

6 The sales team want to know what time **their** taxi arrives. ___

7 Does anyone know **whose** pen this is? ___

8 I saw **your** brother at the airport in Rome. ___

9 It **may be** possible to buy a cheap oven in the sales. ___

10 The department store has cut **its** prices by 50 per cent. ___

11 Mobile phones are now a part of **everyday** life. ___

12 Do you know **who's** coming to dinner tonight? ___

13 That looks like an interesting shop over **there**. ___

a who is
b of whom
c it is
d of it
e possibly
f might be
g of you
h you are
i of them
j not here
k they are
l normal, usual
m all the time

Listening: spending money

1 🎧11.1 **You will hear eight people talking about money. For questions 1–8, choose the best answer (A, B or C).**

1 You hear a woman talking about her holiday plans. Why is she frustrated?

A Her children do not want to go.

B She cannot buy other things.

C She has to stay with someone that she doesn't like.

2 You hear a girl talking about her job. How does she feel about the shop?

A She thinks she receives good money.

B She has a problem with the shop discount.

C She would not buy anything in the shop herself.

3 You hear a man talking about a night out. How much money did he spend?

A too much

B more than everybody else

C none

4 You hear a man talking about shopping at the supermarket. What happened when he had to pay?

A He paid the full cost of the shopping.

B He decided not to pay for any of the shopping.

C He decided not to buy some of the shopping.

5 You hear a woman talking about clothes shopping. Why did she buy the top?

A She needs nice clothes for her work.

B She is addicted to shopping.

C She bought it on a whim.

6 You hear a woman talking about her husband. What kind of things does he buy?

A He buys lots of things that he doesn't need.

B He only buys essential items.

C He only does the food shopping.

7 You hear a boy describing how he spends his pocket money. What does he spend his money on?

A toys

B comics

C snacks

8 You hear a woman talking about her financial plans. What does she say about her pension?

A She hasn't made a decision about it yet.

B She is going to take her friends' advice.

C She has a very good pension in her current job.

Pronunciation

Sentence stress

If you change the word that is stressed in a sentence, you can change the sentence's meaning.

Example: I don't want an ice cream!

Stressing *I* might suggest someone else does want an ice cream.

Stressing *ice cream* might suggest that there is something else you want.

1 🎧11.2 **Read and listen to seven versions of the same sentence (1–7) below. The stressed word is in capital letters. Match the reasons why the words were stressed (a–g) to the sentences.**

1 MY brother is the only person here who speaks Russian fluently. ___

2 My BROTHER is the only person here who speaks Russian fluently. ___

3 My brother IS the only person here who speaks Russian fluently. ___

4 My brother is the ONLY person here who speaks Russian fluently. ___

5 My brother is the only person HERE who speaks Russian fluently. ___

6 My brother is the only person here who speaks RUSSIAN fluently. ___

7 My brother is the only person here who speaks Russian FLUENTLY. ___

a Some people can speak other languages very well, but not Russian.

b There are people in other places who can speak Russian fluently.

c Not my sister, for example.

d Some people can speak Russian, but only my brother speaks it fluently.

e Not someone else's brother.

f There isn't anybody else.

g Believe me – this is true.

2 🎧11.3 **Look at the sentence below. How many different places could you put the sentence stress? Listen and check your answer.**

We don't want to watch the concert tomorrow.

3 **If you are working with a partner, practise together saying the sentences in exercises 1 and 2.**

Use of English

KEY WORD TRANSFORMATIONS: PAPER 3, PART 4

1 Complete the second sentence so that it has a similar meaning to the first sentence, using the word given. Do not change the word given. You must use between two and five words, including the word given. There is an example at the beginning (0).

0 Your responsibility is to look after the money.
RESPONSIBLE

You ...*are responsible for looking*... after the money.

1 I'm sorry that I didn't help Peter.
WISH

I .... Peter.

2 When did you borrow the money from the bank?
LEND

When .... the money?

3 Can I tell Ildiko the news?
MIND

Do .... Ildiko the news?

4 I regret telling them that I was ill.
WISH

I .... them I was ill.

5 I can't go on holiday with my friends because I don't have enough money.
GO

If I had more money, I .... on holiday with my friends.

6 The total of the bill is €456.
COMES

The bill .... €456.

7 If you don't phone, we'll meet outside the cinema.
UNLESS

We'll meet outside the cinema ....

8 I advise you not to go by train.
WERE

I wouldn't go by train ....

MULTIPLE-CHOICE CLOZE: PAPER 3, PART 1

2 Read the text below and decide which answer (A, B, C or D) best fits each gap. There is an example at the beginning (0).

Just twenty years ago who would have **(0)** ...*suspected*... that Russia would **(1)** .... a place to buy designer goods? Back then it was a country suffering from a **(2)** .... of major products with a limited **(3)** .... of everyday items like bread and milk. Nowadays, everything has changed.

One place to see the greatest change is the GUM department store in Red Square, the heart of Moscow. Once this was **(4)** .... only for long queues of customers waiting outside empty shops, but now it is a shopping centre full of designer labels, jewellery and stylish cafés. With the money that rising oil prices are **(5)** .... to Russia, the demand for luxury products is **(6)** .... all the time.

But it is a mistake to think things were always worse in the past. When I first went to Russia, caviar was incredibly cheap. But it is getting more and more expensive owing to the falling **(7)** .... of sturgeon, the fish that produces the caviar eggs.

For a different kind of shopping, the Izmaylovo Market on the **(8)** .... of Moscow is popular with tourists and locals alike. It **(9)** .... the best location to pick up souvenirs from the country's fascinating past. Military uniforms, Soviet badges and posters are all readily **(10)** .... For locals, it is a **(11)** .... shopping spot to pick up bargains on belts, clothes and shoes.

One final warning: don't **(12)** .... the cost of a visit to the capital. Prices in Moscow are high and hotel accommodation especially will make a big hole in your budget.

	A	B	C	D
0	<u>suspected</u>	revealed	learned	mistrusted
1	become	change	adapt	evolve
2	hole	minority	collapse	lack
3	distribution	supply	sale	transport
4	thought	considered	known	recognised
5	bringing in	leading in	travelling in	sending in
6	raising	increasing	enlarging	towering
7	counts	animals	groups	numbers
8	ends	outsides	limits	outskirts
9	continues	remains	keeps	survives
10	found	sale	available	bought
11	popular	required	preferable	selected
12	underperform	undertake	underestimate	undermine

Writing: an essay giving arguments 'for and against'

OPTIONAL TASK: PAPER 2, PART 2

1 **Complete the student's answer to the exam question below with the phrases (a–g).**

a On the other

b Nevertheless

c So on balance

d You could also argue that

e So the question is

f While it is true

g On the one

> Should the government stop large stores opening on Sundays? Write an **essay** giving arguments 'for and against'. Write your answer in 120–180 words.

---

¹_____ that most large stores are open on Sundays, not all small shops are able to stay open all weekend.

²_____, if people want to go shopping on Sundays, they should be able to. And if small shops decide to stay open seven days a week, they will make more money. ³_____ this will create new jobs – as small shops will need to employ more staff.

What are the arguments for and against Sunday opening? ⁴_____ hand this is useful for working people, who do not have time to go shopping Monday to Friday. ⁵_____ hand if big shops open on Sundays, some people might do all their shopping then, and only go to the big stores.

⁶_____ whether we allow big stores to open and possibly damage the business of smaller stores. Large stores have more staff, so they can stay open on Sundays when small businesses are usually closed. This would be a disaster for smaller shops.

⁷_____ I feel that larger stores should close on Sundays to protect smaller, local businesses.

---

2 **Now write your own answer to the exam question in exercise 1.**

....

....

....

....

....

....

....

....

....

....

....

....

....

....

....

....

....

....

....

Speaking

1 🎧11.4 **Look at the pictures which show people shopping. Decide whether the words and phrases below could be used for picture 1 or picture 2 – or both. Then listen to four different students on the recording to check your answers.**

	Picture 1	Picture 2
department store		
to try		
spices		
a special deal		
included in the price		
a guarantee		
to taste		
sacks		
special features		
shop assistant		
merchant		
to haggle		

Picture 1

Picture 2

2 🎧11.4 **Look at the two photos. Correct each sentence (1–8) below. Then listen again to check your answers.**

1 What the pictures have by common is that they show customers talking to salesmen.

2 Both the salesman seem to be very friendly.

3 These pictures show very similarity situations.

4 One thing what is the same in the pictures is that the customers are really going to buy something.

5 We can see the same thing happens: the customers are asking questions.

6 In every picture the salesman looks very friendly.

7 There isn't a big different here: we can see people thinking about buying something.

8 The pictures show a same sort of thing.

SPOTLIGHT ON STUDY TECHNIQUES

When preparing for the Speaking test, make sure you learn some useful phrases for discussing the differences and similarities between pictures, as well as phrases for giving your own opinion. You do not need to learn every phrase, but do learn at least one phrase for every situation. When you are practising for the Speaking test, try to use these phrases as much as possible.

3 **If you are working with a partner, answer this exam question for the photographs.**

Here are your photographs. Talk about the pictures for a minute. Say what the pictures show and mention ways in which they are similar or different. Say how you would feel about shopping in these two places.

12 Forces of nature

LANGUAGE CHECKLIST

☐ I know words to describe weather and disasters, page 96.

☐ I know how to use transitive and intransitive verbs, page 96.

☐ I know how to use clauses of contrast and concession, page 97.

☐ I know how to use the articles *a* and *the*, page 97.

☐ I know how to spell the plurals of nouns ending -*o*, page 97.

☐ I know how to pronounce the definite article (*the*), page 98.

EXAM CHECKLIST

☐ I have practised the gapped text question from the Reading paper, page 94.

☐ I have practised the Part 4 dialogue + multiple choice question from the Listening paper, page 98.

☐ I have practised the word formation question from the Use of English paper, page 99.

☐ I have practised the multiple-choice cloze question from the Use of English paper, page 99.

☐ I have practised writing an essay from the Writing paper, page 100.

☐ I have practised the collaborative task from the Speaking paper, page 101.

Reading

GAPPED TEXT: PAPER 1, PART 2

1 **You are going to read an article about the history of Easter Island. Seven sentences have been removed from the article. Choose from the sentences (A–H) the one which fits each gap (1–7). There is one extra sentence which you do not need to use.**

A The trees had been vital in making canoes to go fishing.

B Many of the heads were found in the island's quarry, unfinished and discarded.

C Nowadays interest in the fate of the island has surged once more.

D So how was it that a once green land became almost entirely deforested?

E Devastating ecological damage by rats has been recorded on other locations in the Pacific area.

F This was because they needed wood to act as rollers in transporting the giant statues.

G Rather he places the blame on another culprit: a plague of rats.

H The rumours of cannibalism have especially been questioned.

2 **Find these words and phrases (1–8) in the text. Then match the definitions (a–h) to the words and phrases.**

1 remote ___	a the process where trees and plants disappear
2 soil ___	b the things that trees and plants grow out of
3 cannibalism ___	c without knowing
4 deforestation ___	d far away from other places
5 unwittingly ___	e to support something
6 to overrun ___	f the ground, the earth
7 seeds ___	g people eating other human beings
8 to back something up ___	h to grow in numbers until an area is completely full

SPOTLIGHT ON STUDY TECHNIQUES

The best way to improve your reading and vocabulary is to read as much as possible in English. Many English language websites have extensive articles about many different issues, so it is often easy to find articles that you are interested in. The BBC website, www.bbc.com, includes articles on science, entertainment, history, geography and many other issues. Try to read one web article every day.

EASTER ISLAND CATASTROPHE

Two thousand miles away from Chile, Easter Island is one of the most remote spots on Earth and yet it has fascinated visitors ever since
5   the first Europeans arrived on Easter Day, 1772. The reason at first was the mysterious giant heads that pepper the island, staring mysteriously out to sea. **(1)** _____

10 This time it has come from new theories that the collapse of human society on the island provides a warning to the modern world of ecological disaster waiting to
15 happen.

Even when the first Europeans arrived on Easter Island, they found it almost empty of trees. Yet later scientific analysis has revealed that it
20 was once covered in palm forests. **(2)** _____ In his recent history of ancient people surviving in harsh conditions, *Collapse*, the American author Jared Diamond argues that the Easter Islanders themselves were responsible for much of the devastation.

25 According to Diamond, the statues that so amazed those first European visitors played a part in the disaster. The population of the island began competing in constructing the stone heads and in doing so they cut down more and more of the forests. **(3)** _____

Once the forest had been cut down, serious problems emerged in the local society.

(4) _____ They also kept water in the soil: with little rain on the island, this was vital to
30 help crops grow. With agriculture and food supplies devastated, the result was war and starvation, and there is even a suggestion of cannibalism on the island.

But this is far from the only theory. **(5)** _____ The only real evidence for this comes from ancient stories and it is possible that Europeans exaggerated the tales of horror to help destroy the islanders' original religion.

35 In the last few years an alternative theory has been proposed. This is the work of Dr Terry Hunt of the University of Hawaii. Like all historians of the area, Dr Hunt agrees that serious deforestation took place on Easter Island, but he does not blame the local population. **(6)** _____
Possibly unwittingly transported by the original Polynesians, the rodents would have
40 hidden in their canoes and then escaped onto the island. With no natural predators, a rat population can increase at incredible speed. Within a few years, millions of the animals would have overrun the island, eating everything in sight.

They did this not by eating the trees themselves but by eating the seeds. Instead of people cutting down the forests, the rats would have prevented any new plants from growing. This
45 theory has strong evidence to back it up. **(7)** _____

Whatever did cause the final collapse of the ecosystem on Easter Island, it is clear that something terrible did happen on that small piece of rock, lying alone in the Pacific Ocean.

Vocabulary

WEATHER AND DISASTERS

1 **Look at the pictures and complete the words, as in the example.**

1 m _e t e o r i t e_

2 d _ _ _ _ _ _

3 e _ _ _ _ _ _ _ _ _

4 f _ _ _ _

5 t _ _ _ _ _ _

6 v _ _ _ _ _ _ _ e _ _ _ _ _ _ _

7 f _ _ _ _ _

8 t _ _ _ _ w _ _ _

2 **Complete the crossword.**

Across

1 An argument about something unimportant is a _____ in a teacup.

5 Light, continuous rain.

7 A prediction of the weather.

Down

2 The sound you hear when you see lightning.

3 Very strong wind.

4 The weather conditions that a place usually has.

6 A light kind of fog.

TRANSITIVE AND INTRANSITIVE VERBS

3 **Complete the sentences with the words in the box.**

> devastated   died   disappeared   raised   rose
> was destroyed   was killed   was lost

1 He _____ of old age. I went to the funeral.

2 The environmental campaigners _____ some serious issues at the meeting.

3 The temperature _____ by 10°C.

4 The doctors think the man _____ by an electric shock.

5 The tornadoes _____ farmland and crops for miles around.

6 Our house _____ by the earthquake.

7 The contract _____ by my lawyer. He left it on a train.

8 After the rain came, the snowman _____.

Grammar

CONTRAST AND CONCESSION

1 Complete the sentences with the words in the box.

> although despite even fact
> knowing nevertheless

1 Despite not _____ any Turkish, Dominic travelled all over Turkey.

2 _____ the rain, we had a really good holiday in Britain.

3 He was wearing a winter coat, _____ though it was warm and sunny.

4 Despite the _____ that there was a terrible gale, we decided to drive to my grandmother's house.

5 _____ there was a lot of drizzle, no one was carrying an umbrella.

6 We read that the weather was awful in December. _____, we decided to go on holiday there because it was the only time we were able to go.

THE ARTICLES *A* AND *THE*

2 <u>Underline</u> the correct option. Ø means no article.

1 There was *a / the / Ø* cat in the kitchen. I had never seen it before.

2 *A / The / Ø* Aztecs came from Mexico.

3 My father is *a / the / Ø* businessman.

4 My favourite way of travelling across Spain is by *a / the / Ø* train.

5 What is *a / the / Ø* lowest temperature that has been recorded here?

6 We are expecting a visit by *a / the / Ø* president of the USA.

7 Did you read in the newspaper about the man who was struck by *a / the / Ø* lightning?

8 I don't know *a / the / Ø* reason why Karen didn't come to your party.

Spelling

Plurals of nouns ending in -o
When nouns end in -*o*, there are three ways of making the plural. You can add -*s* as in regular nouns.
Example: kilo ➡ kilos

Other nouns can only be spelt -*es*.
Example: torpedo ➡ torpedoes

But most nouns can either be spelt -*s* or -*es*. Both options are correct.
Example: mosquito ➡ mosquitos/mosquitoes

1 Complete the table with the words in the box. Three words go in each column.

> mango potato radio tomato hero
> domino video volcano studio

-os	-oes	-os/-oes
avocados	tornadoes	flamingos/flamingoes

Listening: San Francisco earthquake

DIALOGUE + MULTIPLE CHOICE, PAPER 4, PART 4

1 🎧12.1 **You will hear an interview with an expert on earthquakes in San Francisco, Denise Wei. For questions 1–7, choose the best answer (A, B or C).**

1 Why were people surprised by the 1906 earthquake?
   A People thought there was only a very small earthquake risk.
   B At that time, nobody knew about the San Andreas Fault.
   C People thought earthquakes would only happen in other parts of California.

2 What did Liz Hickok use to make a model of the city?
   A food
   B ice
   C computer video images

3 Why did Liz Hickok make her model of San Francisco?
   A To eat it.
   B It was a work of art.
   C To make a scientific study of earthquake effects.

4 How did people react when roads and bridges were destroyed in the 1986 earthquake?
   A They expected the level of damage.
   B They thought the damage should have been much worse.
   C They expected much less damage.

5 Why were there low casualties in 1986?
   A The experts had warned everybody about the earthquake.
   B Because many people were working in their offices.
   C Because there was a major sports event on.

6 What does the Big One refer to?
   A a future earthquake
   B the 1906 earthquake
   C the 1986 earthquake

7 How likely is another earthquake in San Francisco in the next 25 years?
   A It is very unlikely.
   B It is quite probable.
   C It is almost certain.

Pronunciation

The definite article (the)
The definite article, *the*, can be pronounced in two ways: /ðə/ and /ðiː/. We use /ðə/ before consonant sounds. We use /ðiː/ before vowel sounds.

1 🎧12.2 **Listen and decide if the pronunciation of *the* in these sentences is /ðə/ or /ðiː/.**

1 Do you know the answer to the question? _____

2 Have you got to the end of the book? _____

3 Do you want the orange or the banana? _____

However, many words that begin with a consonant may actually start with a vowel sound. In the same way, many words that begin with a vowel may actually start with a consonant sound.
Examples: honest ➡ /ɒnɪst/
          unique ➡ /juniːk/

2 🎧12.3 **Decide if the pronunciation is /ðə/ or /ðiː/ in these phrases. Then listen to check your answers.**

1 the hour   /ðə/   /ðiː/
2 the university   /ðə/   /ðiː/
3 the one   /ðə/   /ðiː/
4 the uniform   /ðə/   /ðiː/
5 the honour   /ðə/   /ðiː/
6 the European   /ðə/   /ðiː/

Use of English

WORD FORMATION: PAPER 3, PART 3

1 Use the word given in capitals at the end of each sentence to form a word that fits in the gap. The word in each pair of sentences is formed the same way. There is an example at the beginning (0).

0 a I don't feel _optimistic_ about the future of our planet. **OPTIMISM**

   b Why are you always so _pessimistic_ ? **PESSIMISM**

1 a Big .... needs to get involved in environmental protection. **BUSY**

   b Many people in the Third World suffer from a disease called river .... **BLIND**

2 a Global warming could have .... consequences. **CATASTROPHE**

   b I'm feeling really .... today. **ENERGY**

3 a The water supply in this country is not .... **DRINK**

   b The film was fun, but it wasn't very .... **BELIEVE**

4 a He was in hospital for a week, but he has made a complete .... now. **RECOVER**

   b I really admire the .... of environmental campaigners. **BRAVE**

5 a There was a volcanic eruption which left very few .... **SURVIVE**

   b Françoise is going to be a .... on the march tomorrow. **DEMONSTRATE**

MULTIPLE-CHOICE CLOZE: PAPER 3, PART 1

2 Read the text below and decide which answer (A, B, C or D) best fits each gap. There is an example at the beginning (0).

As global temperatures continue to (0) ...._rise_.......... , environmental problems (1) .... more and more distress for people caught up in sudden catastrophe. Summers in Europe are getting longer and hotter, and the heatwaves that result can have serious effects with many (2) .... people being hospitalised or even dying from the intense temperatures.

Along with the dangers of the heatwave, a further problem affects many Mediterranean countries: forest fires. In hot weather, fires (3) .... in the countryside causing terrifying destruction to homes, properties and lives. But what is most alarming of all is that many of these fires are not (4) .... : they are the product (5) .... arson.

In Greece it has been (6) .... that people have deliberately started fires. Investigators looking into the destruction (7) .... that they were started as a way of clearing land of natural forests. In Spain in 2007, the Canary Islands were seriously affected by fires that grew with incredible (8) .... It appears that these fires began after being deliberately (9) .... alight. The fires grew due to strong winds, making fighting the blaze an almost impossible (10) .... As a result, the government was forced to order the closure of motorways and evacuate thousands of people from their homes.

(11) .... of this damage has come in spite of the best efforts of the government to educate the public about the dangers of fires in summer. The Canary Island fires came soon after the Spanish government had put up posters making people (12) .... of the dangers of fires to the environment.

	A	B	C	D
0	life	arise	<u>rise</u>	raise
1	become	do	cause	result
2	antique	aged	ancient	elderly
3	break out	cut out	burn down	get away
4	natural	environmental	ecological	organic
5	from	by	over	of
6	reported	told	described	explained
7	decide	suspect	reveal	demand
8	haste	rapid	speed	quick
9	made	took	brought	set
10	trouble	task	work	stage
11	Little	Every	Many	Much
12	understand	comprehend	learn	aware

Writing: an essay

OPTIONAL TASK: PAPER 2, PART 2

1 **Complete the student's answer to the exam question with the words below.**

> these places   even though   this   their   They
> In this case   this problem   this   it   Instead

> Your teacher has asked you to write an essay explaining how people can be encouraged to recycle more. Write your **essay**. Write your answer in 120–180 words.

Recycle more!

People are not recycling as much as they could because they often do not know where or how to recycle.

One way of solving [1]_____ is giving infomation to show people where they can recycle. Often [2]_____ are easy to find, but some products like bateries need to be recycled in a speshul place. Notices need to be put up to show where [3]_____ can be done.

It is also important to remember that many eldrely people have trouble moving hevy objects. [4]_____ cannot always carry bottles or cans to a recycling area. [5]_____ older people should be helped by local councils who can collect rubbish from [6]_____ homes.

Finaly, [7]_____ many people recycle at home, they do not recycle when they are out. [8]_____ people often throw rubbish like drink cans away in normal litter bins. To prevent [9]_____, more places need to have litter bins avalable where rubbish is seperated into cans, glass, etc.

In conclusion, people will always recycle when [10]_____ is easy for them to do.

2 **Look again at the student's answer. Can you find eight spelling mistakes?**

3 **Now write your own answer to the exam question in exercise 1.**

....
....
....
....
....
....
....
....
....
....
....
....
....
....
....
....
....

Speaking

COLLABORATIVE TASK: PAPER 5, PART 3

1 **You are going to discuss ways of raising money to help endangered species. Read the descriptions of five activities (a–e). Match the pictures (1–5) to the activities.**

  a Getting signatures on a petition which you will send to the government to ask them to do something. ___

  b Holding an event where people buy tickets and all money goes to charity. ___

  c Running a stall to sell things to the public: all profits go to charity. ___

  d Doing a sponsored event to raise money: you do something difficult and people pay you money depending on how successful you are. ___

  e Going round door to door asking people for money or support. ___

2 🎧12.4 **You will hear four pairs of students doing the collaborative task in the Speaking test. They have to decide which of the five suggestions in the pictures below would be the best way of helping endangered species. Listen and decide which picture each pair is discussing.**

  Pair 1 ___

  Pair 2 ___

  Pair 3 ___

  Pair 4 ___

3 🎧12.4 **Correct each sentence (1–8) below. They are all ways of rejecting a possibility or saying that a possibility may not work. Then listen to the recording again to check your answers.**

  1 I don't think this is a good idea to all.

  2 This doesn't work by me.

  3 I don't see the point to do this.

  4 This is not effective solution to the problem.

  5 In this cause I don't think this is the best option.

  6 I don't think it's a bad idea, but I think some of the other one are better.

  7 Does this really work? I don't sure.

  8 How if nobody comes to the event?

4 **If you are working with a partner, do the exam task in exercise 1 together. In the Speaking test, you will have about three minutes for this part of the test.**

13 In the news

Reading

MULTIPLE CHOICE: PAPER 1, PART 1

1 You are going to read an article about newspapers. For questions 1–8, choose the answer (A, B, C or D) which you think fits best according to the text.

1 How does the writer feel about free newspapers?
   A She likes reading them.   C She thinks there are too many.
   B She never reads them.   D She loves the wide choice.

2 What does 'it' in line 17 refer to?
   A the habit of buying newspapers   C getting news for free
   B the growth of online news sites D Wikipedia's news site, Wikinews

3 Why may the number of newspaper buyers increase in the future?
   A Younger people will start buying them.
   B There will be more older people.
   C People will be attracted by the adverts.
   D People will get bored with free newspapers.

4 Why are companies not putting as many adverts in newspapers that people buy?
   A They are too expensive.
   B Their readers do not have much money.
   C They think their target customers do not read these newspapers.
   D The number of readers will fall in the future.

5 What does the writer mean by "the free papers are more daring than their traditional counterparts"?
   A The free newspapers take more risks with the position of their adverts.
   B The free newspapers are more careful.
   C The free newspapers put more frightening news stories on their covers.
   D The free newspapers are confusing to read.

6 Why did *The Times* change its format?
   A To have larger pages.   C Their readers requested it.
   B Their advertisers demanded it. D To make it easier to read.

7 What was the result of *The Times* changing its format?
   A It was a success.   C It made no difference.
   B It was a disaster.   D No one knows the result yet.

8 How are traditional newspaper companies reacting to the Internet?
   A They are ignoring it.
   B They are advertising more online.
   C They are buying successful Internet sites.
   D They are selling their newspapers to online companies.

The death of the newspaper?

We are drowning in a sea of newspapers. No sooner does the morning commuter step outside the front door than a small army of people descends, forcing a newspaper into their hands. It is happening across Europe, where bars and cafés have piles of competing titles stacked up in their shops. The newspaper 20 Minutes, founded in Sweden, has enjoyed huge success and now boasts five million daily readers across the continent. Metro manages to distribute a million copies in the UK alone. This growth is all the more mysterious considering that the traditional newspaper, paid for by its readers, appears to be dying.

Newspaper readers are ageing fast. Many younger people have grown up with the Internet and are used to getting their news for free. These people prefer to get their news from other sources, which means that they have never got into the newspaper habit. Indeed, with so many sites offering a news service, it seems unlikely to become a part of their lives in the future. Even the company that runs Wikipedia, the free online encyclopedia, offers a special news service: Wikinews, and new news sites are springing up every day.

Meanwhile older people continue to buy a newspaper: over sixty per cent of Americans between the ages of 45 and 54 are regular newspaper readers. Interestingly, there are actually more people living longer and so statistically the number of newspaper readers may actually get larger over the next few years as more people enter this age bracket.

But this alone will not ensure the traditional newspaper's survival because newspapers have never received all of their funding from their readers alone. Advertising plays a huge part in newspaper profits. It is true that older people are more prosperous than ever before, but this makes no difference it seems to the advertisers, who are seeking a younger audience for their products.

Money is flowing away from traditional newspapers into the free newspapers. This is because free newspapers are read by people on their way to work: the dynamic, younger market that advertisers want to reach. Knowing this, the free papers are more daring than their traditional counterparts. They frequently come with a wrap-around cover that displays one large advert, with the real cover appearing inside. One free newspaper in Spain even produced a fake cover whose headline proclaimed 'an alien invasion' as a way of promoting a computer game!

So as websites and free newspapers prosper, will the traditional newspaper disappear? It is still too early to say.

First of all, newspapers are fighting back. In 2004 The Times newspaper of London turned its back on two centuries of history by changing its size, moving from a broadsheet to a smaller tabloid format. It might seem like a gimmick, but it does have a practical purpose: the tabloid size made the newspaper more practical for passengers to read on busy trains and buses, and the change had an immediate impact. Sales of The Times shot up after the changeover.

As well as changing themselves, the newspaper companies are getting involved in the new media. The business empires that own newspapers and magazines have an enormous amount of experience in the media market and they are not sitting idly by while You Tube and Facebook snap up all their customers. In 2005 the newspaper tycoon Rupert Murdoch purchased the social networking site MySpace and other companies have their eye on competing sites. So it seems that although newspapers might appear to be on their last legs, they are ending up taking over the websites, not the other way around.

Vocabulary

NEWS AND NEWSPAPERS

1 **Complete the crossword.**

Across

1 News about diet, preventing disease, doing exercise.

2 A newspaper or magazine that comes out every seven days.

6 A newspaper article that describes someone's life after they have died.

7 Someone who writes for a newspaper.

9 The title of a newspaper article.

10 An informal word for news about celebrities, movies, pop music, etc.

11 Someone who writes for a newspaper from a particular place, for example, the Moscow _____.

Down

1 Your star sign: Leo, Aquarius, Scorpio, etc.

3 An article that gives the opinion of the newspaper.

4 People who try to take personal or shocking photographs of famous people.

5 News about government.

8 This will tell you if it will be rainy, sunny, etc.

PHRASAL VERBS

2 <u>Underline</u> **the correct option.**

1 The situation looks good. Our wages are *going / coming* up by 5 per cent next month.

2 The politicians had a furious argument and they *took / broke* off the talks with the protesters.

3 I was going to enter the tennis competition, but I hurt my arm and I had to pull *out / away*.

4 On the third day of the golf tournament Tiger Woods pulled *out / ahead* of the other players and started to lead the competition.

5 Tara was going out with her boyfriend for years, but then they broke *up / over* last week.

6 Sam and Ian were good friends for years, but they fell *off / out* about a month ago. Now they're not talking to each other at all.

7 The mayor tried to cover *up / over* the fact that he had stolen money, but a journalist discovered what had happened.

8 We told everyone that this information was secret! How did it *flood / leak* out to the press?

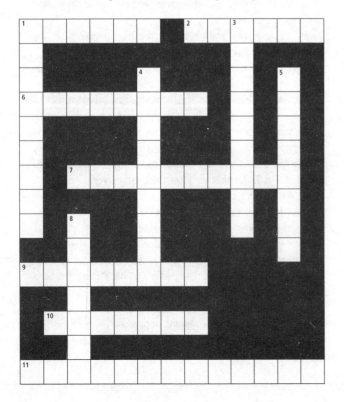

Grammar

REPORTED SPEECH

1 Write the sentences in reported speech.

1 Cathy: "We're not making any progress!"

   Cathy said that we weren't making any progress.

2 Rich: "I didn't see Tina."

   _____

3 Maria: "Are you going to buy a newspaper?"

   _____

4 Schoolteacher: "It'll be a nice day tomorrow."

   _____

5 Policeman: "No one can go in the building."

   _____

6 Katy asked: "Has Simon heard the news?"

   _____

7 Joe: "They have been asking me questions."

   _____

REPORTING VERBS

2 Put the words from the box into the sentences below. Add one word to each sentence.

for   he   him   to   us   we   who

1 When we left, our parents warned not to speak to people who seem too friendly.

2 Gemma advised me compare prices on the Internet.

3 His sister reminded to post the letter.

4 He didn't apologize arriving late.

5 When the teacher spoke to Jim and me, he suggested do an exam preparation course.

6 They criticized the people didn't do the work.

7 I recommended ask for some help from our teacher.

SPOTLIGHT ON STUDY TECHNIQUES

When learning new collocations, it is important to see as many examples of the structure as possible. You can do this by doing the exercises in a grammar book. Alternatively, go on the Internet and place a structure in speech marks in your search engine (Google, Yahoo, etc.), such as "recommended that". This will give you examples of the structure in real English sentences.

Spelling

SPOTLIGHT ON SPELLING

Adjectives with -able and -ible
Two different spellings of adjectives have come from Latin into English: -*able* and -*ible*. Note that the pronunciation of both endings is the same: /əbl/.
Examples: available   sensible

Be careful with verbs that end in -e. These may make the adjective -*able* either by keeping or dropping the -e.
Examples: excuse ➡ excusable   notice ➡ noticeable

There are no simple rules to follow, so you need to be careful with spelling.

1 Look at the adjectives below and circle the correct spelling.

1 a breakable   b breakible

2 a adaptable   b adaptible

3 a edable   b edible

4 a visable   b visible

5 a flexable   b flexible

6 a inevitable   b inevitible

7 a capable   b capible

8 a invincable   b invincible

9 a countable   b countible

10 a predictable   b predictible

2 Complete the table with the verbs in the box. Three words go in each column.

advise   believe   change
knowledge   manage   note

-able	-eable
excusable	*noticeable*

Listening: a journalist

SENTENCE COMPLETION: PAPER 4, PART 2

1 🎧 13.1 **You will hear an interview with a journalist, Linda Bridgestone, about her early career. For questions 1–10, complete the sentences. You will need to write a word or a short phrase in each gap.**

When she was younger, Linda wanted to be Britain's first female [_____ **1**]

She became a journalist because she was interested in [_____ **2**]

She was the editor of the [_____ **3**]

She was paid [_____ **4**] on her work experience.

While she was doing her work experience, Linda felt like the [_____ **5**]

Her first job was typing [_____ **6**]

She misspelt [_____ **7**] Sherborne.

She and another journalist went to interview [_____ **8**]

The other journalist did not go into work because he had to go to [_____ **9**]

Linda's first paid job was on [_____ **10**]

Pronunciation

SPOTLIGHT ON PRONUNCIATION

Place names

In the interview in *Listening*, Linda Bridgestone said that she had problems spelling *Sherborne*. Many place names in the English language have a very different pronunciation to their spelling. It is important to learn the correct spelling of the more common places in English-speaking countries.

1 🎧 13.2 **Listen to the place names below and circle the correct pronunciation.**

		a	b
1	Norwich	/nɔːrwɪtʃ/	/nɒrɪtʃ/
2	Greenwich	/griːnwɪtʃ/	/grenɪtʃ/
3	Leicester Square	/lɪsestə skweə/	/lestə skweə/
4	Gloucester	/glɒstə/	/glaʊsestə/
5	The Thames	/ðə θeɪmz/	/ðə temz/
6	Birmingham	/bɜːmɪŋəm/	/bɜːmɪŋhæm/
7	Nottingham	/nɒtɪŋam/	/nɒtɪŋəm/
8	Edinburgh	/edɪnbrə/	/edɪnbɜːg/
9	Melbourne	/melbɔːn/	/melbən/
10	Brisbane	/brɪsbən/	/brɪsbeɪn/
11	Connecticut	/kənektɪkʊt/	/kənetɪkət/
12	Eire	/eərə/	/eəriː/

2 **If you are working with a partner, practise saying the words in exercise 1.**

Use of English

OPEN CLOZE: PAPER 3, PART 2

1 Read the text below and think of the word which best fits each gap. Use only one word in each gap. There is an example at the beginning (0).

They built straight roads **(0)** ...*that*... still exist today and huge cities and temples. One other thing that the Romans did was to invent the newspaper. The *Acta Diurna*, which means 'events of the day', was founded **(1)** .... Julius Caesar. It was **(2)** .... newssheet, written by hand. The *Acta Diurna* was available in the capital city and all over the Roman Empire. Astonishingly the *Acta Diurna* survived **(3)** .... some three centuries, as long as many of the oldest newspapers today. Many of the ancient writers used the *Acta Diurna* **(4)** .... the basis for their historical works. Through them we are **(5)** .... to read about daily life in Ancient Rome as written in their **(6)** .... words.

The purpose of the *Acta Diurna* was to publish official news about Roman political life and the empire's inevitable victories in war. However, like most newspapers before and since, **(7)** .... also included lots of other general interest sections which were probably **(8)** .... more popular, including sports reports (gladiator fights) and predictions of the future – using omens! No doubt the obituaries section was particularly busy during the reign **(9)** .... the murderous emperor Caligula.

Needless **(10)** .... say, not all the news was printed in the *Acta Diurna*. Under the emperors **(11)** .... succeeded Caesar, democracy in Rome collapsed. And while the *Acta Diurna* printed the main news, a secret newssheet was prepared in **(12)** .... the records of government business were kept. This was known by a different name: the *Acta Publica*.

MULTIPLE-CHOICE CLOZE: PAPER 3, PART 1

2 Read the text below and decide which answer (A, B, C or D) best fits each gap. There is an example at the beginning (0).

For many young people journalism seems to be a career full of **(0)** ...*excitement*...... and adventure. However, if you are thinking of **(1)** .... journalism, it is important to ask yourself whether this is really for you. This is because there is another side to the world of the journalist.

Today news is everywhere: news **(2)** .... are providing 24 hour **(3)** .... online while readers are clamouring for the latest headlines. However, it now seems that working as a journalist is more dangerous than ever. The BBC reported that 168 journalists were killed in 2006, which is the most ever recorded. It is well **(4)** .... that many of them were deliberately murdered to stop their stories reaching the public and it is essential to do more to bring their killers to justice. **(5)** .... , journalists are also at **(6)** .... risk of physical attacks, intimidation and being **(7)** .... hostage.

Press photographers too must travel to some of the most violent and lawless places in the **(8)** .... and their lives are very different from the celebrity-chasing antics of the **(9)** .... To get the picture that tells a thousand words, they have to get closer to the action than anyone else. Sometimes it is impossible to **(10)** .... placing themselves in danger. One can only **(11)** .... the courage of these men and women and it is worth remembering their bravery when flicking through the various **(12)** .... in the morning paper.

	A	B	C	D
0	A exploration	B imagination	C excitement	D reality
1	A bringing up	B taking up	C making up	D going up
2	A sites	B headlines	C agents	D places
3	A downloads	B print outs	C updates	D alerts
4	A decided	B spoken	C known	D thought
5	A Furthermore	B As well as	C Because	D However
6	A considerable	B expanded	C countless	D sizable
7	A kidnapped	B imprisoned	C captured	D taken
8	A planet	B earth	C world	D globe
9	A cameramen	B snappers	C paparazzi	D printers
10	A avoid	B skip	C deny	D protest
11	A notice	B celebrate	C enjoy	D admire
12	A supplements	B additions	C departments	D columns

Writing: punctuation

COMPULSORY TASK: PAPER 2, PART 1

1 **You need to be very careful in checking your punctuation. There are mistakes in all these sentences (1–6). Match the teacher's comments (a–f) to the sentences.**

1 I saw Mike, he was running to the station. ___

2 There is a canadian student in the class who speaks english and french. ___

3 The person, that they are looking for, isn't here. ___

4 I worked in Switzerland for six month's. ___

5 „Can anyone see my pen?" he asked. ___

6 It cost me €1.999,99! ___

a Do not put commas around a defining relative clause.

b Do not make a noun plural by adding an apostrophe.

c Numbers are written with a comma to show thousands and a full stop to show decimals.

d Do not join two separate sentences with a comma. Write them as separate sentences or use a conjunction (*and*, *when*, *but*, etc.).

e Speech marks are always written above the words at the beginning and ending of the statement.

f Nationality adjectives and languages are written with a capital letter (ABC, etc.).

2 **Correct the sentences in exercise 1.**

SPOTLIGHT ON PUNCTUATION

Apostrophes
We use '*s* to show possession by one owner.
Examples: the soldier's orders (= one soldier)
the boss's seat   the man's office

We use an apostrophe after the plural ending *s* to show possession by more than one owner.
Examples: the soldiers' orders (= more than one soldier)
the bosses' seats

We also use '*s* with irregular plural nouns.
Examples: the men's office   the children's games

If someone's name ends in *s*, you can either simply add an apostrophe or '*s*.
Example: Anders' house / Anders's house

---

3 **Correct the apostrophes in the sentences below. There are two correct sentences.**

1 I think that's Gary's wifes car.

2 Eight students answers were right.

3 Tina's brother's go to the same school as me.

4 Where can I find ladies' shoes?

5 I couldn't find Charles phone anywhere.

6 We were surprised by peoples' response to the questionnaire.

7 The children's homework is really difficult.

8 Everybodys answer is wrong.

4 **In Part 1 of the Writing test, you may be asked to write an email. Look at the student's email below. It has no punctuation. Punctuate the email correctly and organise it in three separate paragraphs.**

---

hi anders

im really pleased that youre coming to london to study english i think that you will have a great time when you are over here in your last email you asked me to help you find some accommodation the good news is that you will be able to stay in james room while you are here because he is going to madrid to learn spanish over the summer the bad news is that you will have to leave the room in september when he comes back but it will be easy to find somewhere else then you also asked me how to get to the house from heathrow airport the best way is to get a travelcard which you can buy at the station it costs £670 i was planning to meet you at the airport but unfortunately on that day my university puts up a notice with all the students exam results and i need to go and see it anyway im really looking forward to seeing you in a fortnight

speak soon

tony

Speaking

TOPIC DISCUSSION: PAPER 5, PART 4

1 At the end of the Speaking test, the interlocutor will ask you some general questions. These questions are usually on the same general topic that you talked about in Part 3. Read the interlocutor's questions (1–6) on the right. Match the students' answers (a–f) to the questions.

2 🎧13.3 Now listen to six people answering the questions. Check your answers in exercise 1.

3 🎧13.3 Listen again. Complete the answers (a–f) in exercise 1 with phrases that are useful when answering general discussion questions.

4 If you are working with a partner, ask and answer the exam questions in exercise 1.

1 What do you think is the best way of getting news? ___

2 Do you often read newspapers or watch the news on TV? ___

3 Is it important for people to watch the news? ___

4 What are the advantages and disadvantages of getting news over the Internet? ___

5 Do you like reading about celebrities in newspapers and magazines? ___

6 What part of the newspaper is most interesting to you? ___

a _____ I think if there is a big story, then it's important that the public know what's going on: if there is a weather problem or something like that. But often there isn't really any big news, so it's not necessary to find out what's going on all the time.

b _____ I read a free newspaper if there's one in the station. And I sometimes watch the news when I'm cooking because we have a TV in the kitchen. But I don't think I'm very interested in the news.

c _____ it's the crossword. I love doing it in my coffee break when I'm at work. Sometimes I work on it all day and I always have to buy the next day's newspaper to see what answers I didn't get.

d _____ I can't get enough gossip to be honest. I think everyone really likes to read about that sort of thing. I buy two or three gossip magazines each week. I think I'm a bit addicted!

e _____ Er … it's a very quick way of getting information, of course, and you can get a lot of different opinions too. I think it's good as long as you use the sites from serious newspapers or news services. Otherwise you don't know who wrote the news that you're reading.

f _____ I have to say the radio. On TV they don't really have enough time to discuss all the complicated issues. On the radio they have a lot of time to talk and you can hear experts speak.

14 Fashion

LANGUAGE CHECKLIST

- [ ] I know words to describe fashion, page 112.
- [ ] I know some phrasal verbs for using with clothes, page 112.
- [ ] I know how to use the passive, page 112.
- [ ] I know how to use *have something done*, page 113.
- [ ] I know how to spell some homophones, page 114.
- [ ] I know how to pronounce some homographs, page 117.

EXAM CHECKLIST

- [ ] I have practised the multiple choice question from the Reading paper, page 110.
- [ ] I have practised the Part 1 extracts + multiple choice question from the Listening paper, page 113.
- [ ] I have practised the topic discussion from the Speaking paper, page 114.
- [ ] I have practised the key word transformation question from the Use of English paper, page 115.
- [ ] I have practised the word formation question from the Use of English paper, page 115.
- [ ] I have practised writing a description from the Writing paper, page 116.

Reading

MULTIPLE CHOICE: PAPER 1, PART 1

1 **You are going to read an article about the latest handbag craze. For questions 1–8, choose the answer (A, B, C or D) which you think fits best according to the text.**

1 How does the writer feel about women's obsession with handbags?
   A He thinks men need to carry them too.
   B He thinks they contain a lot of non-essential objects.
   C He thinks they are too expensive.
   D He thinks it's a short-term craze.

2 Whose influence is encouraging women to spend more on handbags?
   A their husbands and boyfriends   C famous people
   B their colleagues at work   D large corporations

3 What is the problem with the Dior Gaucho bag?
   A There are not enough of them on sale.
   B It is the most expensive bag on the market.
   C It is not popular any more.
   D You have to be a member of a special club to buy one.

4 Most handbag sales in the UK are
   A only from a few famous shops.
   B generated only by a small number of designers.
   C only made in one season of the year.
   D from selling bags that look like more famous ones.

5 How does Tamara Mellon feel about handbags?
   A Any handbag will look good.
   B You have to match your clothes very carefully with your handbag.
   C What you wear on your feet is as important as your handbag.
   D Handbags aren't really very important.

6 What does 'it' in line 50 refer to?
   A the typical handbag   C a report on handbag ownership
   B annual sales of handbags   D the number of handbags people have

7 What do women's handbags typically contain?
   A some cosmetic items   C no objects that are useful for work
   B mainly cheap objects   D nothing relating to their home

8 What do many women feel about the value of their handbag contents?
   A They underestimate it.   C They aren't able to guess how much it is.
   B They overestimate it.   D They know exactly how much it is.

HOW HANDBAGS BECAME A GIRL'S BEST FRIEND

BY DAVID DERBYSHIRE

Of all the subjects that divide men and women, it is probably the female love of accessories – and handbags in particular – that baffles men the most. For women, a handbag is a statement of personality and attitude. It
5 is an indicator of status, a weapon in a crowd and a home on the move.

For men, it seems to be little more than an expensive device for carrying around unwanted receipts and other useless items. It is certainly no substitute for a
10 really good trouser pocket.

The gap between the sexes looks likely to grow deeper with a study suggesting that women's love affair with handbags has reached a new level of intensity. Between 2000 and last year sales of handbags in the
15 UK soared by 146 per cent to a record £350 million.

Claire Birks, the author of the study, believes that the phenomenal growth is being fuelled in part by the must-have celebrity handbag. "The rising number of working women has played a key role in this market as
20 they not only have the money but also the need for stylish, well-accessorised outfits and handbags. It is now commonplace for women to have a wide variety of bags for a whole host of occasions – from smart evenings out to a night in the pub and from a day in
25 the office to a day's shopping."

Top of the range designer bags with price labels of £1,000 are not uncommon and their popularity has never been greater. Any woman wanting one of this season's must-have handbags, the Dior Gaucho,
30 should be prepared to fork out £815 and join a month-long waiting list.

It takes just a glimpse of a new Gucci or Chloé bag on the arm of Kate Moss or Paris Hilton in Heat magazine for that model to fly off the shelves at
35 Selfridges and Harrods. But while designer brands have played a part, the rising sales have mostly been driven by cheaper imported handbags and own-label imitation designs. Supermarkets are also branching out into the lucrative accessories market.

Tamara Mellon, the owner of the Jimmy Choo 40 label, said she had seen a major change in the accessory market. "It doesn't matter what you are wearing – if you have good shoes and a good bag, you will look right," she said. "Handbags are a status symbol, the perfect accessory to dress up your day and your outfit. 45 For women of all ages and from all walks of life, acquiring a handbag is an enjoyable experience."

Last year a study found that 60 per cent of women own at least 10 handbags, while three per cent have at least 25. In addition to this, it also suggests that the 50 demand for handbags has yet to be sated.

"There is no reason to believe that sales will not continue to increase over the next five years," Miss Birks said.

While men may remain baffled by the attraction of 55 handbags, some light has been shed on what they contain. A survey of 1,700 women carried out by Prudential discovered that alongside the old train tickets, receipts and pens, the average handbag contains around £550 worth of personal possessions. 60 Typically, they include a mobile phone, a purse, a hairbrush, perfume, a make-up bag, a leather diary or personal organizer, and house and car keys. In summer months, a pair of sunglasses usually joins the collection. Most women questioned assumed that 65 their handbags and contents were worth only £150.

Vocabulary

FASHION

1 **Complete the puzzle. What is the word in grey?**

1 To lose colour and become paler.

2 A time when everybody is excited about doing or buying the same thing.

3 Something which is very fashionable, especially among young people.

4 Another word for *fashionable*.

5 Things which are fashionable for a short time.

6 When two colours or styles look awful together, they _____.

7 Something that used to be fashionable and is now fashionable again.

8 This is what people have when they stand out from a crowd and are exciting to look at.

9 This is an adjective that describes someone who dresses very well and looks good.

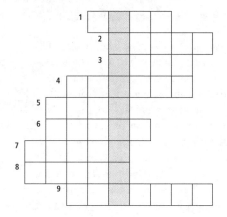

PHRASAL VERBS FOR USING WITH CLOTHES

2 **Underline the correct word.**

1 Could you *hang / hung* these clothes up in the wardrobe for me?

2 If the trousers are too long, I can *send / turn* them up for you.

3 If you would like to *place / try* the suit on, there is a fitting room behind you.

4 I'm getting a bit fat. I can't *do / make* up these trousers any more.

5 It's getting hot. I think I'll *put / take* my coat off.

6 This is your costume for the play, but I think we need to *let / make* the jacket out a bit so that it will fit you.

7 It's a black-tie event, so we're going to *dress / wear* up for the occasion.

8 These trousers are too large. Can you *take / put* them in for me?

Grammar

THE PASSIVE

1 **Look at the sentences below. Six of them contain a mistake. Find and correct the mistakes.**

1 The city destroyed by a volcanic eruption.

2 I couldn't believe that he was being question by the police.

3 They hadn't been told about the fashion show.

4 Many synthetic fibres, like nylon and polyester, are use in clothes manufacture.

5 *The Name of the Rose* was written for Umberto Eco.

6 The window had been opened from a screwdriver.

7 The washing machine has been ruined my new shirt!

HAVE SOMETHING DONE

2 Look at the pictures. Complete the sentences using the words in brackets and the correct form of *have something done*.

1 Before they joined the army, the soldiers

_____ (their heads / shave).

2 Annie _____ yesterday (her windows / clean).

3 My grandmother always _____ (her shopping / deliver).

4 The house looks terrible, but we

_____ next week (the walls / paint).

5 My computer broke down last year and I

_____ (it / repair). It cost €200.

6 Grandad isn't here because he is at the optician's.

He _____ (his eyes / test).

Listening: clothes and fashion

EXTRACTS + MULTIPLE CHOICE: PAPER 4, PART 1

1 🎧14.1 **You will hear eight people talking about clothes and fashion. For questions 1–8, choose the best answer (A, B or C).**

1 You hear a woman talking about a present she bought for her husband. Why did he not wear the shorts?

A He thought they were not fashionable.

B He did not like the colour.

C He did not like the design.

2 You hear a father talking to his son. Why does he tell the son to change his clothes?

A The colours clash.

B He is wearing the wrong clothes for the weather.

C He does not look smart enough.

3 You hear a daughter talking to her mother. Why does the daughter want to have the dress?

A She wants to wear it in a play.

B It is now back in fashion.

C She needs some new clothes.

4 You hear a man talking about buying a shirt. Why did he buy the wrong size?

A He was not able to try it on.

B He ordered it on the Internet and the size was wrong.

C He didn't look at the label.

5 You hear a woman shopping with a friend. Why does her friend convince her to buy the necklace?

A It has a classic look.

B It matches her new earrings.

C It looks good on her.

6 You hear a mother talking to her son. Why does she stop him throwing the shirt away?

A She can repair it.

B It was very expensive.

C It is almost new.

7 You hear a man talking about a clothes shop. What does he complain about?

A Their clothes are boring.

B Their clothes are not good quality.

C Their clothes are expensive.

8 You hear two people talking about clothes. Where are they?

A at a party

B at work

C at a wedding

Spelling

Homophones
Homophones are words with the same sound but a different spelling, for example, *pour* and *poor*. Check the spelling of these words carefully in your written work.

1 Complete the sentences from the *Listening* with one of the pairs of homophones in the box.

> complements   compliments   die   dye   flour
> flower   genes   jeans   heals   heels   hole
> whole   sight   site

1 There was a big _____ on the back of the shorts.

2 You can't wear _____ to a wedding.

3 You can't get a tie-_____ dress like that any more.

4 There's a _____ which has some really great clothes.

5 It really _____ the colour of your eyes.

6 There's a _____ in it, and I've had it over a year.

7 I shouldn't have worn these high _____ – they are killing me!

2 Now complete each of these sentences with the other homophones from the box.

1 You should wear sunglasses on the beach to protect your _____ from the sun.

2 I used the wrong sort of _____ when I was making bread, and it tasted horrible.

3 She has wonderful hair. I guess she's just got good _____.

4 The shop is closing down and their _____ range of clothes is on sale.

5 I got so many _____ from people who told me I looked nice in that dress you bought me.

6 Don't go swimming in the sea until that cut on your arm _____. It's still bleeding at the moment.

7 I think I would _____ of embarrassment if I had to wear something like that!

Speaking

TOPIC DISCUSSION: PAPER 5, PART 4

1 🎧14.2 Listen to two students discussing the exam question below. Why do they disagree about the answer?

> Do you think young people spend too much money on clothes and fashion?

2 🎧14.2 Listen again. Complete the phrases that Claudio and Eleni use to disagree with and challenge each other's opinion.

1 But _____ that sometimes you have to go to the expensive shops?

2 But do you really need the brand name? _____, if clothes look good, the name is not important.

3 What _____ that if you want to look good, you need to buy quality clothes, designer clothes, big brands.

4 Yes, _____ speaking about young people.

5 I _____. But if your friends have the best clothes, you want them too.

6 All _____, I think there are better things to spend your money on when you're young.

7 I _____ so. But I still think they spend too much money on clothes.

3 Look at the extract from the conversation and choose the best definition (a–b) of *Not necessarily*.

a That is never true. The situation is impossible.

b That is not always true. There are other possibilities.

Eleni	So their parents have to spend money on these clothes.
Claudio	Not necessarily. Many of my friends have jobs, and they study and work. So they can buy their own clothes.

4 If you are working with a partner, discuss the exam question in exercise 1 together.

Use of English

KEY WORD TRANSFORMATIONS: PAPER 3, PART 4

1 Complete the second sentence so that it has a similar meaning to the first sentence, using the word given. Do not change the word given. You must use between two and five words, including the word given. There is an example at the beginning (0).

0 My shoe has got a hole in it.
   THERE

   ....*There is a hole in*.......... my shoe.

1 He had to wear a uniform.
   MADE

   They .... a uniform.

2 The teacher said I couldn't leave early.
   LET

   The teacher didn't .... early.

3 We are not permitted to wear jewellery.
   ALLOW

   They don't .... jewellery.

4 Someone should water the plants.
   NEED

   The plants ....

5 We have to give these tickets to Jane immediately.
   GIVEN

   Jane .... these tickets immediately.

6 I have a hire car because they are repairing mine.
   HAVING

   I have a hire car because I
   ....

7 Someone cleans Steve's house once a week.
   CLEANED

   Steve .... once a week.

8 Two famous artists were designing the new clothes.
   DESIGNED

   The new clothes .... two famous artists.

SPOTLIGHT ON STUDY TECHNIQUES

When preparing for the key word transformation question, try to make a note of all the words given in **bold** at the start of each question. Do this for every exercise that you look at. Then group the key words and see what different possible answers they can have.
For example: **have**
have might be used in:
have something done
the present perfect (*have done*)
have to
or the third conditional (*would have done*).
Making lists like this will help you anticipate answers in the exam.

WORD FORMATION: PAPER 3, PART 3

2 Use the word given in capitals at the end of each sentence to form a word that fits in the gap. The word in each pair of sentences is formed the same way. There is an example at the beginning (0).

0 a You will get a wide ....*variety*............... of different customers. **VARY**

   b He gave me back my wallet with all my money and credit cards, and I thanked him for his
   ....*honesty*........... . **HONEST**

1 a I cannot believe that there is still famine and
   .... in the world. **HUNGRY**

   b There was a lot of .... because of the price of the team's new football shirts. **ANGRY**

2 a This haircut is really .... at the moment. **FASHION**

   b After they had heard the bad news, they looked
   .... **MISERY**

3 a These jeans were .... last year, but they've gone out of fashion already. **TREND**

   b These trousers have a special pocket for my mobile phone, which is really ....
   HAND

4 a What is the .... of the carpet?
   WIDE

   b We are going to study this subject in
   .... **DEEP**

5 a Everyone should know about the
   .... of many workers in this industry. They work in terrible conditions. **EXPLOIT**

   b You need a lot of .... to be a successful clothes designer. **IMAGINE**

Writing: a description

1   In Part 2 of the Writing test, you may be asked to write a description of people or places. Look at the exam question below and the extracts from two students' answers. Which student is writing about a village? Which student is writing about a town?

> You have recently rented a room in a new town or village. You have decided to write a letter to a friend describing the place and the people you are living with. Write your letter. Do not write any addresses. Write your answer in 120–180 words.

1

> The house is a really traditional little place close to the sea and everyone knows everyone. In general people are very welcoming and they say hello to you in the street. There is a little shop nearby which is covered in ivy, and sells things like newspapers and milk. All around us is countryside and little farms, and I spend a lot of time walking down the country lanes.

2

> The room is in a house in the suburbs with a garden and a view of the river. There are large numbers of red-brick houses all around, however, and most of them all look very similar. There is a shopping centre nearby and we're very close to the railway station, which is really convenient for me. One problem is that it's quite noisy especially in the morning as you can hear all the commuters driving to work.

2   Look at the pictures (A–F) and match them to phrases describing places in the extracts in exercise 1.

3 Before you start writing a description, it is a good idea to think of as many words as you can to use in your answer. Read the sentences (1–6) and think of other words to replace those in **bold**.

1 She was **a little bit fat**. _____plump_____

2 She was an elderly lady with lots of **lines in her face**. _____

3 She was **too thin and it looked unhealthy**.

_____

4 She had lots of **red marks on her face** because she had been out in the sun. _____

5 Her hair was **very untidy**. _____

6 Her hair was **not its natural colour**.

_____

4 Now write your own answer to the exam question in exercise 1. Use words and phrases from exercise 2. Use words from exercise 3 to describe your new landlord/landlady – the person who owns the house where you rent a room. Write your answer in 120–180 words.

....
....
....
....
....
....
....
....
....
....
....
....
....
....
....
....
....
....

Pronunciation

Homographs
There are many words in English that are spelt in an identical way, although the words actually have a different meaning and a different pronunciation.
Examples: close = near ➡ /kləʊs/
The hotel isn't close to the beach.
close = shut ➡ /kləʊz/
Close the door please.

1 Look at the sentences below. In each group of sentences, one word in **bold** is pronounced differently to the other two. Circle the word which is pronounced differently.

1 a He always wears a **bow** tie.
  b You use a **bow** in archery.
  c Give a **bow** at the end of the performance.

2 a We employed a guide to **lead** us through the forests.
  b They use **lead** to protect the body from radiation when they take X-rays.
  c Where is the dog's **lead**?

3 a Don't worry – this job will only take a **minute**.
  b There is a **minute** difference between the results: a difference of 0.001%.
  c Who is going to **minute** what is said in the meeting?

4 a Everyone disagreed and there was a terrible **row**!
  b There is a **row** of chairs on the stage.
  c I don't know how to **row** a boat.

5 a The road **winds** through the valley.
  b The clock is very accurate because an engineer **winds** it every day.
  c It was a real hurricane, with **winds** of 150 kph.

2 🎧14.3 **Listen and check your answers.**

3 If you are working with a partner, practise saying the words in exercise 1.

15 New traditions

Reading

GAPPED TEXT: PAPER 1, PART 2

1 **You are going to read an article about the Mongolian emperor Ghengis Khan. Seven sentences have been removed from the article. Choose from the sentences (A–H) the one which fits each gap (1–7). There is one extra sentence which you do not need to use.**

A But the reverence in which he is held by mainstream Mongolians comes as a shock to visitors.

B During this event Mongolian men and boys compete in the three "manly sports" of wrestling, archery and horse-racing.

C Historians also point to the introduction to the West of inventions such as gunpowder and paper that his empire made possible.

D Throughout his lifetime he extended his rule to the south and west.

E The Mongolian president was formerly a student at Leeds University in the UK.

F This is because of disputes over building contracts.

G This is presumed to be Genghis himself.

H In a radical reshaping of Genghis's popular reputation, historians are increasingly taking the Mongolian side.

2 **Find these words and phrases (1–8) in the text. Then match the definitions (a–h) to the words and phrases.**

1 clan ____	a	ignored, did not notice
2 rituals ____	b	a large area with open grass and no forests
3 overlooked ____	c	using a large number of something
4 an advocate ____	d	religious ceremonies
5 the steppe ____	e	give energy to
6 hordes ____	f	a supporter
7 reinvigorate ____	g	a large family group
8 mass ____	h	a large group of people

GENGHIS KHAN IS BACK –
WITH A NEW IMAGE

The Mongolian capital has been covered with images of its former leader, Genghis Khan, for the anniversary of his unification of the nation in 1206. A crowd of onlookers including visiting royalty gathered in the city for the event. At the climax of celebrations in Ulan Bator yesterday, soldiers in traditional uniform heralded the unveiling of an enormous statue of the Great Khan in the main Sukhbaatar Square. The monument contains earth and stones from the holy and historic places in Mongolia associated with his rule.

Ghenghis Khan was born in 1162, the son of a murdered clan chief. After a childhood spent mostly on the run from family enemies, he was elected the tribes' Great Khan in 1189. **(1)** _____ Finally his reign came to an end when he fell from his horse and died in 1227.

Genghis has always had a cult of admirers. **(2)** _____ After all, in the West his name is associated with bloodshed and terror.

To those who still think of themselves as his people, he is a unifying symbol. "People know his military side, but they do not know his philosophy," said Nomch P Davaanyam, a 30th-generation descendant who is trying to revive the sky-worshipping rituals Genghis performed.

Mr Davaanyam is not alone in his assessment. **(3)** _____ "The West was blinded by his conquests," said Jack Weatherford, the American author of _Genghis Khan and the Making of the Modern World_. "They overlooked his great impact on law and commerce. He outlawed the kidnapping of women, guaranteed diplomatic immunity to ambassadors and granted religious freedom to all people." **(4)** _____ "He was an advocate of free trade and a flat tax system," Mongolian President Enkhbayar told a gathering of journalists. "He changed the whole world."

Unfortunately, the monument of Genghis Khan remains half-finished. **(5)** _____ Mr Enkhbayar unveiled it beneath scaffolding.

The ceremony was timed to match the beginning of the annual festival of Naadam. **(6)** _____ Visitors can also watch _Genghis Khan – the Rock Opera_ in the state theatre. On the steppe outside Ulan Bator, 500 members of the armed forces are re-enacting the campaigns of the Khan's hordes.

Despite the money being spent on the monument and the celebrations, most Mongolians seem to appreciate the effort to reinvigorate the memory of Ghengis Khan. Tumurbat Altanmur, 16, said: "I think he was very cruel and tough. But without cruelty his kingdom would not have stood."

Recent studies based on mass DNA testing have suggested that 16 million men living in Eurasia are descended from one person in the early 13th century. **(7)** _____ President Enkhbayar said: "That shows he is not just Mongolia's; he is the world's."

Vocabulary

CULTURE AND HERITAGE

1 Complete the crossword.

Across

1 A formal event such as a wedding or a funeral.

3 A painting or drawing of a person.

7 A painting or drawing of nature or the countryside.

9 These are places where the public can look at paintings and other works of art.

Down

1 A tradition, such as eating a particular food to celebrate a special day.

2 A work of art or a structure that is built to remember people who have died.

4 A special event or day when everybody in a place or country has a party and celebrates together.

5 A public building where you can see important objects, especially from history.

6 An artwork made of stone or metal that represents a person or animal, for example *David* by Michelangelo.

8 Tourist _____ are places where tourists can see famous and important buildings.

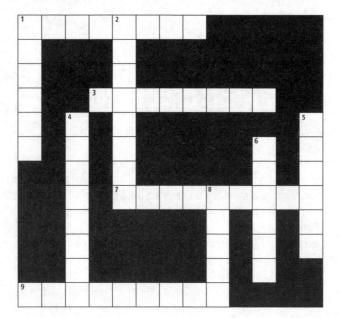

PHRASAL VERBS

2 Choose a suitable word to complete the phrasal verbs below. Write one word only in each gap.

1 I set _____ to be a serious artist, but my whole career has been drawing comics.

2 They tried to pass the painting _____ as a genuine Picasso, but an expert realised it was a fake.

3 Have you found a babysitter yet to look _____ the children?

4 I hadn't seen my nephew for five years and then he turned _____ at my front door one day. It was completely unexpected.

5 The factory is turning _____ 100 cars a week.

6 The family had had the painting for 50 years before they found _____ that it was by Raphael. They were all amazed.

7 He's going _____ a bad time at the moment. He failed an important exam and he's lost his job.

8 Have you ever heard Tony when he's taking _____ the boss? His impression is hysterical!

9 He spent €500,000 on a fake vase. He was completely taken _____ by the fraudsters.

Grammar

INVERSION

1 **Put the words from the box into the sentences below. Add one word to each sentence.**

also	had	hardly	longer	not	only	than

1 No sooner he given her the answer than she started to laugh.
2 Not did he break the window, but he also lost the house keys!
3 Had they sent the email than they realised they had made a terrible mistake.
4 No does the government ask people to apply for this form by going to their offices.
5 No sooner had he left the room the whole class started arguing.
6 Only had he not done his homework, but he also hadn't brought any of his books to school.
7 Not only did they cancel the flight, but they refused to pay us our money back!

2 **Look at the sentences below. Four of them contain a mistake. Find and correct the mistakes. All the sentences should contain an example of inversion.**

1 Hardly had David started shouting than walked Maria out of the room.
2 Not only had he made a fake picture, but he had also made seven fake statues!
3 No sooner arrived the police than he admitted he was responsible for the fraud.
4 No longer does he make forgeries.
5 Not only broke she the vase, but she also broke the mirror.
6 No sooner had he told the newspapers about the crime than he received ten requests for an interview.
7 Hardly I arrived at work than the telephone started ringing.
8 No longer are they looking for the lost works of art.

Spelling

SPOTLIGHT ON SPELLING

Words with similar spelling
There are a number of words which get spelt incorrectly because they look like another common word. Remember to check the spelling of these words carefully, especially if you are working on the computer because a spellchecker cannot always identify these mistakes.

1 **Underline the correct word.**

1 a I can't eat butter, cheese, yogurt or any other *dairy / diary* products.
   b I think I can meet you on Tuesday. Let me check my *dairy / diary*.

2 a Can you look after my keys? I don't want to *loose / lose* them.
   b I don't like tight jumpers. I prefer them to be a bit *loose / lose*.

3 a He's on *trail / trial* for murder.
   b If you go to Peru, you can walk along the Inca *Trail / Trial*.

4 a People have started *exciting / exiting* the cinema.
   b That was a really *exciting / exiting* film.

5 a She went to the Sahara on a trip to take some photos of the *desert / dessert*.
   b We'd both like the strawberries and cream for *desert / dessert*.

6 a You have to *choose / chose* one of the options.
   b He *choose / chose* the red one because he didn't like the green one.

7 a The government have given us their *assurance / insurance* that the country is prepared for the bad weather.
   b I was really ill on holiday and I had to go to a local hospital. Luckily, I had travel *assurance / insurance* and that paid for the treatment.

8 a The newspaper said that the play is *quiet / quite* good.
   b Will you be *quiet / quite*! I'm trying to sleep!

Listening: works of art

MULTIPLE MATCHING: PAPER 4, PART 3

1 🎧 15.1 **You will hear five people talking about works of art that are important for them. For questions 1–5, choose from the list (A–F) the work of art that each person is talking about. Use the letters once only. There is one extra letter which you do not need to use.**

Which work of art

A was discovered underground?   Speaker ____

B was not by a famous artist?   Speaker ____

C was recently moved?   Speaker ____

D is an abstract work of art?   Speaker ____

E was based by the artist on his own body? Speaker ____

F is not as famous as it should be?   Speaker ____

SPOTLIGHT ON STUDY TECHNIQUES

Listening is one of the most difficult skills to practise if you do not live in an English-speaking country. It is also difficult to listen to English-language films and television programmes. If you get English-language films on DVD, it is a good idea to watch the film in your own language first and then to watch the original version in English. This will help you to understand the story and characters, making it easier to concentrate on the English language when you watch the second time around.

Pronunciation

1 🎧 15.1 **Listen again to the extracts in exercise 1 and complete the sentences with adverbs.**

1 _____, it's not there any more.

2 _____, the experts think that it will be easier to preserve there.

3 _____, most of the tourists who come to London don't know it's there.

4 _____, there is only one Michelangelo sculpture in the UK.

5 It's not easy to find even when you're in the museum, _____.

6 _____, it still has the original glass eyes that bronze statues used to have.

7 _____, it's a miracle that the sculpture survives at all.

8 _____, it's by Antony Gormley, who is one of Britain's most important living artists.

9 You know, _____, Picasso liked children's art.

2 **Where do the speakers make pauses in sentences 1–9 in exercise 1?**

3 🎧 15.2 **Now mark the pauses in these sentences using the symbol /, as in the example. Then listen and check your answers.**

1 Luckily,/ the portrait wasn't damaged.

2 He didn't tell anyone the bad news, surprisingly.

3 They did not ask the cost of the painting, however, because they weren't interested in buying it.

4 This is a very dangerous expedition. Nevertheless, I want to be involved in it.

5 Basically, they weren't really interested in art.

6 Actually, I have a degree in History of Art.

4 **If you are working with a partner, practise saying the sentences in exercises 1 and 3.**

SPOTLIGHT ON PRONUNCIATION

Adverbs in conversation
Adverbs such as *actually, however, unfortunately* add to the whole meaning of a sentence. When they are used in speaking, it is usual to separate them from the rest of the sentence with a short pause before or after the adverb.

Use of English

KEY WORD TRANSFORMATIONS: PAPER 3, PART 4

1 Complete the second sentence so that it has a similar meaning to the first sentence, using the word given. Do not change the word given. You must use between two and five words, including the word given. There is an example at the beginning (0).

0 Can you explain why you decided to hold the exhibition in Liverpool?
REASON

Can you ......*give the reason for*...... why you decided to hold the exhibition in Liverpool?

1 You can borrow my bike.
MIND

I .... you borrow my bike.

2 You have to make a decision!
MIND

You have to .... !

3 Could you work on Saturday this week?
MIND

Do .... on Saturday this week?

4 The moment I told them what happened, they phoned the police.
SOONER

No .... them what happened than they phoned the police.

5 He arrived two hours late and he forgot the books!
ONLY

Not .... arrive two hours late, but he also forgot the books!

6 He completely fooled me: I believed everything he said.
IN

He completely .... : I believed everything he said.

7 Poor Mike! He's having a terrible time at the moment.
THROUGH

Poor Mike! He's .... a terrible time at the moment.

8 I want everyone to be involved in the school play.
PART

I want everyone to .... the school play.

WORD FORMATION: PAPER 3, PART 3

2 Read the text below. Use the words given in capitals at the end of some of the lines to form a word that fits in the gap in the same line. There is an example at the beginning (0).

In 2003 the Dutch **(0)** ....*artist*..........	**ART**
Vermeer was the subject of the film *Girl with a Pearl Earring*, which showed a fictional	
(1) .... between the	**RELATION**
painter and his maid. Since then, Vermeer's work has become more and more popular for	
his **(2)** .... ability to	**REMARK**
capture light and colour. However, Vermeer died in 1675 when he was only 43 and he left only 35 paintings behind. The fact that he painted so little has led to	
(3) .... cases of fraudsters	**FAMOUS**
making counterfeit versions of his works. These have been sold for huge prices, and only afterwards the	
(4) .... was made that	**DISCOVER**
they were fakes.	
The cost of a new exhibition means it is now **(5)** .... that all of the	**LIKELY**
real 35 pictures will ever appear together in one place. Because of this, a new museum in Vermeer's home town has	
(6) .... opened, which	**RECENT**
aims to show all of the artist's works – in the form of reproductions. The Vermeer Center (VermeerCentrum) in the artist's home city of Delft has produced an	
(7) .... re-creation of	**IMPRESS**
Vermeer's world, including projections of all of his works on the walls.	
Also in the **(8)** .... there	**BUILD**
are models of the houses where Vermeer worked and the equipment that he used. There is also information on the	
(9) .... background to his	**HISTORY**
work and a 3D animation which provides an	
(10) .... of the	**EXPLAIN**
complicated process used by Vermeer in creating his small number of masterpieces.	

Writing: a magazine article

1 **Look at the exam question below and the student's answer. Complete the text with the phrases (a–f).**

a afterwards

b at first

c before

d eventually

e first of all

f the end

g once

> A student magazine is running a series of articles on the theme of a festival. Write an **article** about a festival you have been to, explaining what you liked about it. Write your answer in 120–180 words.

Last year I was studying in Cologne in Germany and I experienced Carnival. The whole city goes crazy. ¹_____ I was quite shocked, but I soon started enjoying it.

²_____ we put on fancy dress. ³_____ going out, the men also all put on ties. I didn't know why until a girl cut my tie off – and she was a stranger! It's a tradition on women's day.

There were crowds everywhere. ⁴_____ we got into a restaurant, we saw that there were no tables and chairs. There wasn't room for people and furniture! We stayed there for a while and ⁵_____ we went to a friend's house because we'd been invited to his party.

Everyone was singing carnival songs. I didn't know any of the words in the beginning, but ⁶_____ I learned them and I was singing with everybody else. In ⁷_____ I got home very late after a fabulous day. I really enjoyed the procession through the city too, which came at the end of the celebrations.

2 **Look at the sentences below. They all contain a mistake. Find and correct the mistakes.**

1 We all put on fancy clothes: I was dressed as a pirate.

2 There was crowded everywhere: it was difficult to move.

3 The best part of carnival is when a huge manifestation walks though the main street of the city.

4 Several people have been invited at our party tomorrow.

5 It's a traditional in Carnival that women can cut off men's ties.

6 The whole city makes crazy during Carnival.

3 **Now write your own answer to the exam question in exercise 1. Use words and phrases from exercise 2.**

....

....

....

....

....

....

....

....

....

....

....

Speaking

INDIVIDUAL 'LONG TURN': PAPER 5, PART 2

1 🎧15.3 **Listen to two different students talking about similarities between the pictures below. Decide which question (a–c) the interlocutor asked them.**

Student 1 ____

Student 2 ____

---
a Say which of these activities you would enjoy most.

b Say how you think the people are feeling in these photographs.

c Say what sort of person would enjoy these activities.
---

2 🎧15.3 **Complete the sentences the students used to describe the pictures. Write one word in each gap. Then listen again to check your answers.**

1 Well, _____ me see.

2 In the _____ a girl is looking at some abstract art, I think it is, and er ... in the _____ a man is looking at some very small pictures.

3 _____ the second picture, I think perhaps this is more for party people.

4 They are celebrating something, _____ in the other photo the people are looking at art.

5 So _____ photos show people doing something in their free time.

6 But _____ back to the other picture, I think this looks like a lot of fun.

3 **If you are working with a partner, answer the exam questions in exercise 1 together.**

Reading

MULTIPLE CHOICE: PAPER 1, PART 1

1 You are going to read an article about the medical condition *synesthesia*. For questions 1–8, choose the answer (A, B, C or D) which you think fits best according to the text.

1 What happens to people with synesthesia?

A They cannot see certain colours.

B They do not see things in the same way as other people.

C They have problems with counting and numbers.

D They are unable to taste and smell most things.

2 What do experts think about synesthesia?

A It is an illness.   C It does not really exist.

B It is imaginary.   D It is possible to prove.

3 How quickly do synesthetes see the triangle in Ramachandran and Hubbard's picture?

A Very quickly.   C The same speed as 'normal' people.

B Very slowly.   D They cannot find the triangle.

4 What colour do synesthetes see the number 4?

A Different synesthetes will see a different colour.

B Most synesthetes think it is orange.

C Most synesthetes think it is green.

D For most synesthetes the colour is constantly changing.

5 What kind of colours do synesthetes see when they look at numbers?

A Vague colours.   C Very precise colours.

B Unpleasant colours.   D Very basic colours.

6 How do many artists feel about their synesthesia?

A They feel depressed.   C It has been a major problem in their life.

B They feel frightened.   D They think it has been beneficial.

7 It is likely that a synesthete knows someone else with the condition because

A a large percentage of people have it.

B people in the same family often have it.

C most people know they have the condition and they tell other people about it.

D it is very common nowadays.

8 How many synesthetes associate the same number with the same colour after a year?

A all of them   C the same number as ordinary people

B about half of them   D the minority of them

Wednesdays are red, but Mondays are green

Look at the numbers at the top of the page. What colours do you see? Probably none as the numbers are all in black and white, but there is a small group of people who would

5 see these numbers in many different colours. These people have the condition *synesthesia*, which means that their five senses react to things in unusual ways. When they hear a sound, they may see a colour. When they

10 touch something, they may smell something too – and smell something that no one else can. These people, *synesthetes*, see, hear, smell and touch things that other people do not. When they see a number, like those at

15 the top of this page, they may see a colour. They may also associate colours with days of the week so that Wednesdays are red and Mondays are green. And this condition is not that rare: experts believe that 1 in 2,000

20 people are synesthetes.

There is an argument that synesthesia is just imagination, that it is not real. But two scientific researchers, Ramachandran and Hubbard have proved that it does exist.

25 They use a picture with five examples of the number 2 mixed up with lots of examples of the number 5, because the two figures look very similar. The examples of number 2 were all placed in the shape of a triangle.

30 When the picture was shown to synesthetes, they instantly saw the triangle made out of the number 2. Most people can only find the triangle by checking every number in the picture.

35 The strange thing is that synesthesia is different for everyone. So one synesthete may say that 4 is blue, and another might say that it is orange. Even more strange is that synesthetes do not just say that the number is red or green: they actually give a detailed 40 description of the colour, such as 'tomato red' or 'lime green'.

So is synesthesia a form of madness? The answer is simple: no. Most synesthetes lead normal lives and often do not know that 45 they see the world differently to other people. Interestingly, many writers, composers and artists have been synesthetes and they credit it with being an inspiration in their work. For many of these people, 50 their artistic life would have been very different if they had not had the condition. Indeed, now that more is known about it, scientists and historians are hypothesising about historical figures who may have been 55 synesthetes.

So finally, how do the experts discover if someone is a synesthete? Firstly, many people with the condition are female, left-handed, and of normal, or higher than 60 normal, intelligence. They possibly have relatives with the condition, as it is genetic. In addition to this, although there are hundreds of different forms of synesthesia, those who associate colours to numbers 65 always associate the same colour with the same number. In tests held in 1993, non-synesthetes did not connect the same colour with a number after one week. Every one of the synesthetes could still identify the same 70 colour with the same number twelve months later.

Grammar

SO, SUCH, TOO AND *ENOUGH*

1 Read the sentences (1–8) below. Match the pictures (a–h) to the sentences.

1 We've got such a lot of things to recycle! ___

2 The bottle bank is so full that I can't put my bottles into it. ___

3 Have we got enough wine for the party? ___

4 The bottle bank is too far for me to carry my bags there! ___

5 I've got too much work to do. ___

6 I haven't got enough work at the moment. ___

7 I'm working on such a complicated project. ___

8 There are so many meetings in my job that I never have time to do any work! ___

2 Complete the sentences with *so*, *such*, *too* or *enough*. Use each word twice.

1 It was _____ a gorgeous house! I wanted to buy it as soon as I saw it.

2 We liked the flat, but it was _____ expensive for us. We couldn't afford it.

3 We couldn't get our chairs into the living room. The door wasn't wide _____.

4 Those are _____ lovely paintings. They look great!

5 I was _____ tired after I'd finished decorating the kitchen.

6 The painting is _____ big to fit in the car.

7 The garden isn't big _____ for a swimming pool.

8 We're _____ happy here that we don't want to move.

CLEFT SENTENCES

3 **Look at the sentences below. Five of them contain a mistake. Find and correct the mistakes.**

1 I thought Denis was the person what sent the email.

2 What had he done was to paint the house green.

3 It's Fiona and Jurgen who is moving house.

4 It wasn't until Walter phoned us that we realised we were late.

5 What I dream of do is sailing around the world.

6 That he did was to ask everyone for money.

7 Doing up the house is how many people spend their weekends.

Pronunciation

SPOTLIGHT ON PRONUNCIATION

Cleft sentences
When using a cleft sentence in speaking, it is usual to separate the subject clause from the rest of the sentence with a short pause before the main verb.

1 🎧 16.1 **Mark the pauses in these sentences using the symbol /, as in the example. Then listen and check your answers.**

1 What I wanted to do/ was knock down a wall between the kitchen and the living room.

2 A quiet house in the country is my lifelong dream.

3 Buying the paint for the whole house is what Pilar was worried about.

4 One person who I really enjoyed meeting was the design expert.

5 It wasn't Tony. It was Ricardo who moved to London.

6 What you will need to do is go on the Internet and find examples of the house design you want.

7 What happened next was very surprising.

8 It wasn't until Andrea looked at her phone that she realised Dino had been trying to call her.

2 **If you are working with a partner, practise saying the sentences in exercise 1.**

Vocabulary

COLOUR AND DECORATION

1 **Complete the words. Write one letter in each space.**

1 The kitchen was painted grey. It was awful: d _ _ _ _ _ –looking.

2 This room is very c _ _ _ _ _ _ _ _ : there are objects and things everywhere!

3 In British cities you see a lot of t _ _ _ _ _ _ _ houses, where all the houses are connected together in a long line.

4 We get the sun all afternoon because the house is south-f _ _ _ _ _ .

5 We've painted the rooms in s _ _ _ _ _ colours like crimson and dark blue.

6 My grandmother lives in a c _ _ _ _ _ _ _ cottage in Cornwall. It's made of yellow bricks and it has roses growing up the walls. It's lovely.

7 We used the wrong colour blue when we painted the bathroom. It was so p _ _ _ that you almost couldn't see it!

8 The walls are very b _ _ _ . Why not put some pictures up?

PHRASAL VERBS

2 <u>Underline</u> **the correct word.**

1 I made that green by mixing *up / through* the blue paint with the yellow, and I really like it.

2 We are *doing / making* up the house because we want to sell it. If you decorate, you can usually get a better price.

3 You're doing a great job working on the garden. Keep it *on / up*!

4 They bought an old windmill and they *turned / brought* it into a home.

5 Jennifer *picked / chose* out the colour for the kitchen. I never know which paints look good.

6 If you have an old house, you have to keep decorating it and repairing things or its condition worsens. You mustn't *let / allow* it go.

7 All the furniture in the room was old and dark, so the red plastic chair really stood *out / off*.

8 We painted the bedroom pink and put up some cheerful new wallpaper to *brighten / lighten* it up a bit.

Listening: self-build

1 🎧16.2 **You will hear an interview with a woman who built her own home, Amanda Boyd. For questions 1–7, choose the best answer (A, B or C).**

1 Where did Amanda get the money to pay for the self-build home?
   A She sold her previous house.
   B She was given it after someone died.
   C She borrowed it from the bank.

2 Why did Amanda choose to self-build?
   A She could not find anywhere that she wanted to buy.
   B She wanted to move to London.
   C She wanted to design her own garden.

3 What was Amanda's biggest problem?
   A getting the money
   B finding somewhere to build
   C designing the house

4 What costs more: self-build or buying a house?
   A Self-build.
   B Buying a house.
   C They cost about the same.

5 Where did Amanda live while her self-build home was being built?
   A with her family
   B on a campsite
   C at her previous home

6 Who gives a house planning permission?
   A national parliament
   B private architects
   C local officials

7 Why do people have problems with planning permission?
   A The buildings look too unusual.
   B The buildings are too large.
   C The buildings are too old-fashioned.

Spelling

SPOTLIGHT ON SPELLING

Verbs ending -en and -n
When a verb is made by adding -en or -n to an adjective, the verb means *to make something become like* the adjective.
Example: white ➡ whiten
   I bought some toothpaste to whiten my teeth.

1 **Replace the adjectives in bold with -en verbs.**

1 You need to **long** the trousers so that they will fit you.

   _____

2 They say that coffee can **high** your awareness, but it just makes me feel bad.

   _____

3 This road is too narrow for modern traffic. The council needs to **wide** it.

   _____

4 We were able to **less** the damage because we prepared carefully for the storm.

   _____

5 They are going to **strong** the walls of the house with steel bars.

   _____

6 The weather might **get worse**. It's very cloudy out there.

   _____

7 In English you can **soft** a request by adding a phrase like 'would you mind'.

   _____

8 We are going to paint the walls white, so that should really **light** the room.

   _____

9 You need to **straight** your tie.

   _____

10 The news of the disaster will **sad** people throughout the land.

   _____

Use of English

1   Read the text below and decide which answer (A, B, C or D) best fits each gap. There is an example at the beginning (0).

When you leave (0) ....*home*...... in the morning, do you turn off every (1) ....? Do you use energy-saving (2) ....? We are all (3) .... about the environment and want to recycle more, but it seems so difficult to lead an environmentally friendly life. Many things that help reduce energy use are expensive. (4) .... panels, for example, are costly because the (5) .... is not yet big enough to make large numbers of these products cheaply.

Some people move to the countryside, but even there it is difficult to live a green life. (6) .... areas tend not to have very good public transport, so you are forced to travel everywhere by car. For people who live in cities or (7) .... areas it is even harder. Although there are more buses and trains, these are often crowded, late or expensive and people end up using their own vehicles to get around. The hectic pace of life means that busy office workers are also dependent on their household (8) .... like dishwashers and microwave ovens.

So what can we do? There are a number of small changes we can make that will have a (9) .... big environmental impact if everyone in society makes them. Recycling household (10) .... , for example, or other small changes such as using the same bag when shopping (11) .... than taking more and more plastic bags. We can also (12) .... environmental charities and try to make a difference by helping them in their campaigns to make our world a better place to live.

0	A house	B building	C bed	D <u>home</u>
1	A switch	B button	C lever	D plug
2	A electricity	B light bulbs	C lampshades	D power
3	A terrified	B occupied	C concerned	D involved
4	A Sun	B Light	C Solar	D Ray
5	A industry	B office	C profession	D activity
6	A Farm	B Urban	C Forest	D Rural
7	A town	B street	C suburban	D centre
8	A appliances	B technology	C machines	D electrics
9	A mostly	B completely	C relatively	D vastly
10	A dirt	B rubbish	C mess	D bins
11	A better	B greater	C rather	D other
12	A indicate	B support	C propose	D obey

2   Read the text below. Use the words given in capitals at the end of some of the lines to form a word that fits in the gap in the same line. There is an example at the beginning (0).

About five years ago my grandparents retired and moved to a (0) ......*cheerful*..... little house quite near Cardiff in Wales. The house is a cottage in a really friendly	**CHEER**
(1) .... It is decorated beautifully: it feels really	**NEIGHBOUR**
(2) .... and I love visiting them.	**HOME**
What is special about the house is that my grandparents have tried to make it as (3) .... friendly as possible. My grandfather has put in solar panels and got a special	**ENVIRONMENT**
(4) .... to provide electricity for the house. He did want the house to	**GENERATE**
be (5) .... by the wind, but it was too difficult to find the equipment. When he realised that there was no real (6) .... of installing wind power, he put in the solar panels. Some people were worried that the solar panels might look strange on the roof, but my grandfather worked	**POWER** **LIKELY**
with a (7) .... to try to make all the technology work with the old building.	**DESIGN**
I was worried at first because it seemed quite an (8) .... project. I thought everything would go wrong and the project would be	**AMBITION**
(9) .... But I was wrong. I think it's because my grandparents	**SUCCESS**
are so (10) .... about it. Of course they were lucky because they had the money to make changes.	**ENTHUSIASM**

Writing: an email to a friend

COMPULSORY TASK: PAPER 2, PART 1

1 In Part 1 of the Writing test, you may be asked to write an email to a friend. Read the exam question below. What information must you include in your reply?

You have received an email from your friend, Katie. Read Katie's email and the notes you have made. Then write an email in 120–150 words using all your notes. You must use grammatically correct sentences with accurate spelling and punctuation in a style appropriate to the situation.

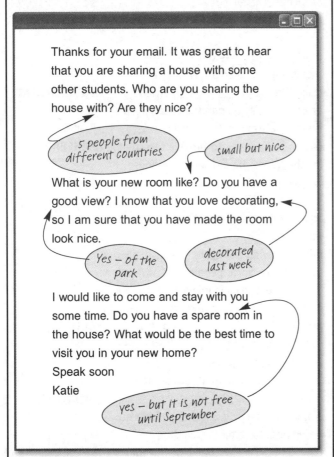

Thanks for your email. It was great to hear that you are sharing a house with some other students. Who are you sharing the house with? Are they nice?

5 people from different countries

small but nice

What is your new room like? Do you have a good view? I know that you love decorating, so I am sure that you have made the room look nice.

Yes – of the park

decorated last week

I would like to come and stay with you some time. Do you have a spare room in the house? What would be the best time to visit you in your new home?
Speak soon
Katie

yes – but it is not free until September

2 Complete the student's answer to the exam question below with a suitable word.

Hi Katie

I've just ¹_____ your email. It's great to ²_____ from you again. My new room is lovely. You ³_____ me in your email who I was living with. ⁴_____ are five other girls in the house from France, Italy, Germany, Sweden and Canada. They're all really nice and I am very happy living here.

⁵_____ for my room, it's small but it's very nice. When I moved in, it ⁶_____ a bit dreary, but last week I painted the walls yellow and I put some posters up too. I've also got some bright artificial flowers ⁷_____ I have put on my bookcase.

You ⁸_____ that you would like to come and visit. We do have a spare room, but someone is staying there until the beginning of September. If you'd like to come after that, you would be very ⁹_____!

Take ¹⁰_____.

Anna

3 Look again at the student's answer in exercise 2. The writer has forgotten to include one piece of information. What did she forget?

4 Now write your own answer to the exam question in exercise 1.

....

....

....

....

....

....

....

....

....

....

....

Speaking

1 **On the CD-ROM included with this workbook there are videos showing two pairs of students in the FCE Speaking test. Watch the first video and complete the interlocutor's questions and statements below.**

1 First of all we'd like to know _____ about you, so erm, where are you from, Waldo?

2 OK, and what do you like about _____ in Colombia?

3 Waldo, do you _____ spending time at home, or do you like to go out?

4 Can you tell me about a day you've enjoyed _____?

5 Who are the most _____ people in your life?

6 So Waldo, it's your turn first. Here are your photographs. They show people _____ in different types of homes.

7 Now here are your two photographs. They show people spending _____ time in the countryside.

8 I'd like you to compare the photographs and say which you think is the best way to enjoy the countryside and _____.

9 Which _____ of activity would you prefer to do, Waldo?

10 First, talk to each other about how _____ these suggestions might be for the events, and then decide which two would _____ to the most people in the town, alright?

11 Bruno, have you ever been to any of these kinds of _____ in your town?

12 Waldo, what is important when _____ where you are going to live?

13 As many people can work from home nowadays with computers, do you think more of us will _____ away from the cities?

14 And do you think that houses will change _____ in the future? What _____ will there be?

2 **Now watch the second video and decide if these sentences are true (T) or false (F).**

1 Adrian and Julian are from the same country. ___

2 Julian is a very sociable person. ___

3 Adrian went to a concert in London. ___

4 Julian only talks about the people in his photographs. ___

5 Adrian prefers the picture showing a winter sport whereas Julian prefers the picture with the fire. ___

6 They do not think the puppet show would appeal to everyone. ___

7 They want to combine the party and the dinner. ___

8 They disagree about the horse rides. ___

9 Adrian does not want to commute a long way. ___

10 Adrian and Julian agree about working from home. ___

3 **If you are working with a partner, look back at the *Spotlight on FCE* Student's Book on pages 162–3 and do the Speaking test tasks together.**

Practice Test

PAPER 1: READING Part 1 (Questions 1–8)

Part 1

You are going to read an extract from an article. For questions **1–8**, choose the answer (**A**, **B**, **C** or **D**) which you think fits best according to the text.

We humans have a high opinion of ourselves – although a visitor from space might wonder why: we spend so much time and energy fighting each other, destroying the environment on which we depend for our survival and behaving like spoilt children. Yet we continue to think of ourselves as the lords of creation.

We think we are superior because we are different from the animals. For a start, we walk upright, have big brains and one of the five digits on each hand is an opposable thumb. As a matter of fact, though, these characteristics are not all unique to our species: several animals can walk upright even if they cannot do it so well; whales, dolphins and the great apes have large brains; and although an opposable thumb is a useful thing to have, it doesn't seem much on which to base a sense of superiority.

Other human abilities and qualities seem more important than physical ones. We believe we are the sharpest knife in the drawer. We look down on the rest of creation because we can use language, make and use tools, and we can grasp abstract concepts and solve problems. The trouble is that the more we learn about other animals, the more we are forced to question how unique our intelligence is.

We now know that the great apes – orang-utans, gorillas and chimpanzees – can also use tools and solve problems. Furthermore, researchers working with gorillas and chimpanzees claim to have taught them to recognise language, respond to it and use it themselves. Scientists argue amongst themselves whether these animals demonstrate 'real' language in the way humans do, but we cannot deny that the great apes are more intelligent than earlier generations believed. Still, these animals resemble us physically. They are one of the family, as it were. Somehow, we don't mind too much if they share our most prized 'human' attribute, intelligence, to some degree.

And of course, dogs are smart. After all, they can be trained to do all sorts of useful things. Yet our egos are
line 39 not threatened by the fact. Perhaps this is because in our relationship with the dog, it is clear who is master (or mistress). And we feel the same about other animals we have domesticated.

Stupid people are often described as bird-brains, but one famous parrot called Alex, whose recent death was widely reported in the press and on television, could count to six, identify colours and had a vocabulary of 150 words. He had the intelligence of a five-year-old and the communication skills of a two-year-old. He could even be naughty in the way a human child is naughty.

Parrots are not the only intelligent birds. Crows in Japan have discovered a new way of obtaining food. They pick up the walnuts lying under trees that grow at the side of roads. Then they take them to crossroads and junctions where they wait until the traffic lights change and it is safe to cross the road. They drop the walnuts on the tarmac and wait for vehicles to drive over them and crack the hard outer shells. When the lights change again, the crows join the pedestrians and pick up the nut.

This is no surprise to people who have contact with parrots and members of the crow family. What is surprising, though, is the discovery that chickens, traditionally regarded as stupid creatures, are a lot cleverer than we suspected. They have a good memory and can recognise other chickens; they use about twenty cries to communicate with each other; they are good at solving problems. If you show a chicken an object and then hide it, it doesn't forget all about the object. The chicken will start to look for it – if it is a desirable object, that is, like a piece of food. In other words, it is capable of understanding that the object has not stopped existing simply because it is out of sight. This ability only develops in human babies between the ages of four and six months.

It is becoming clearer all the time that there is not as much to separate humans from the rest of the animal kingdom as we once thought. Isn't it time we became less arrogant about our supposedly unique abilities and superior intelligence?

1   Humans differ physically from other animals because

  A   few other animals can walk upright.
  B   they have large brains.
  C   other animals do not have five digits.
  D   there is something unique about their hands.

2   The expression 'the sharpest knife in the drawer' implies that humans are

  A   more important than other animals.
  B   more intelligent than other animals.
  C   more dangerous than other animals.
  D   more skilled at using language than other animals.

3   According to the text, some scientists

  A   believe that some apes can use language meaningfully.
  B   think that apes have become more intelligent.
  C   have proved that apes resemble humans.
  D   deny that apes are as intelligent as humans.

4   What does 'the fact' refer to in line 39?

  A   that dogs have replaced people in certain jobs
  B   that dogs can do useful tasks
  C   that dogs are intelligent creatures
  D   that dogs are like other domesticated animals

5   Which statement is true?

  A   Alex was often the subject of television programmes and newspaper articles.
  B   Alex's abilities show that the meaning of 'bird-brain' needs to be revised.
  C   Alex could count up to 150 and identify colours.
  D   Alex's behaviour was unusual for a parrot.

6   Crows in Japan

  A   are more intelligent than crows in other countries.
  B   only cross the street where there are traffic lights.
  C   wait for pedestrians to pick up their walnuts.
  D   have found a way to obtain a certain kind of food.

7   According to the text, chickens

  A   are as intelligent as parrots and crows.
  B   have the ability to hide objects from view.
  C   used to have a good memory.
  D   remember the existence of an object they can no longer see.

8   The writer's purpose is

  A   to demonstrate that humans are not unique.
  B   to prove that animals are as intelligent as humans.
  C   to discuss why certain animals are intelligent.
  D   to explain why human beings are superior.

135

Part 2

You are going to read an article about a television series. Seven sentences have been removed from the article. Choose from the sentences **A–H** the one which fits each gap (**9–15**). There is one extra sentence which you do not need to use.

It was one of the most successful television series for children ever produced. By 1999 it held the record as the longest-running American children's programme. The show? *Sesame Street*. The reasons for its success? They are too numerous to analyse here, but certainly one factor was its ability to appeal not only to pre-school children but to their older brothers and sisters as well.

The series soon became popular beyond the United States. It was watched in 120 countries and there were versions in other languages. **9** [ ] But in spite of this, British children were as delighted as their American counterparts with the show and *Sesame Street* was broadcast from the 1970s right through to the early 2000s.

Sesame Street aims to teach young children letter and word recognition, simple arithmetic and life skills such as road safety and healthy eating. **10** [ ] This area, with its brownstone houses, was inspired by the real-life neighbourhoods of Brooklyn Heights, where some of the show's producers were living at the time.

The puppet characters – known as Muppets – were created by puppeteer Jim Henson. Some Muppets look like people while others resemble animals or monsters. **11** [ ] The idea is that this variety encourages children to be tolerant: we are all different, but no one type of person is better than any other. As Jim Henson commented: 'The only kids who can identify along racial lines with the Muppets have to be either green or orange.'

One of the best-loved 'animal' Muppets in *Sesame Street* is Big Bird, an enormously tall yellow bird who can roller-skate, ice-skate, dance, sing, write poetry and draw. **12** [ ] On one occasion he sang the letters of the alphabet as one long word – and wondered what it could mean.

The 'monster' puppets include Oscar the Grouch, who lives in a garbage can (or rubbish bin, if you are British). His obsession is rubbish (trash or garbage, if you are American). He is a bad-tempered, antisocial creature, but 'the Grouch' does not refer to his personality but his species. And then there is the Cookie Monster. This lovable puppet is covered with blue fur, has huge, globular, protruding eyes. **13** [ ] But he's especially fond of cookies (or biscuits), hence his name.

Other favourites are Bert and Ernie, two of the 'human' Muppets. **14** [ ] One very interesting 'human' Muppet is Count von Count, the vampire. The Count loves to count and will count anything and everything, including the bats that live in his castle. But even though he is a vampire, the Count doesn't suck blood, sleep in a coffin, or change into a bat. This character is especially appreciated by adults, who recognise his resemblance to classic film portrayals of Count Dracula, the most famous vampire of them all. In fact, the Count is an excellent example of why the series appeals to grown-ups, who love its humour.

One imagines it must be hard for the human actors in *Sesame Street*; after all, they have to share the screen with some very telegenic creatures. But they have stood the test of time. They include the Robinsons (an African-American family), the Rodriquez family (a Puerto Rican family), Bob the music teacher and Linda the librarian. In fact, Linda was the first regular deaf character on television. **15** [ ] The fact that these people agreed to appear on *Sesame Street* speaks for the affection which generations of viewers have felt for this remarkable show.

A They vary hugely in shape, size and colour.

B However, when it was first shown in this country, there were some protests, partly because of the show's American flavour.

C They share the basement apartment of 123 Sesame Street and the comic situations they act out are one of the staples of the series.

D It does so through a cast that consists of puppet characters and human actors who live in a fictional part of New York City.

E It is said that several of the characters were based on real-life people in this neighbourhood.

F He can – and does – eat anything and everything.

G Although very talented, he can also sometimes misunderstand things.

H The show has also hosted a galaxy of celebrities as guest stars – sportspeople, entertainers, writers, politicians and even a famous astronaut.

Part 3

You are going to read about four places to stay on holiday. For questions **16–30**, choose from the places (**A–D**).

Which place

has rooms with a sea view?	**16**	
is not visible from the road?	**17**	
is probably not suitable for visitors without a car?	**18**	
is situated in an area where wildlife is protected?	**19**	
is near a beach which can be dangerous at certain times of the year?	**20**	
recommends nearby beaches as being suitable for certain water sports?	**21**	
is situated near a beach where the water is too dangerous to swim in?	**22**	
tempts visitors to buy works of art?	**23**	
caters for disabled people?	**24**	
caters for people who have very young children?	**25**	
is furthest from the coast?	**26**	
has facilities for guests to cook meals out of doors?	**27**	
used to serve another purpose before it became a hotel?	**28**	
attracts animals by providing them with food?	**29**	
grows some of its own food?	**30**	

Winter escapes

If you hate the idea of another miserable winter at home, head south! Here is a sample of the kind of accommodation available to whet your appetite ...

A

The Palm Grove

This small hotel is located on the country's north coast. Unlike more recently-built hotels, the Palm Grove is a low wooden building that combines old-fashioned charm with modern conveniences. It has a fine restaurant and a stunning swimming pool area. Families with babies are welcome and there is twenty-four-hour childcare so parents can relax.

The Palm Grove faces a boulevard fringed with palms. By day the trees provide welcome shade against the tropical sun. The boulevard is all that separates the hotel from the sandy beach, which is visible from all rooms in the hotel. The water is safe for swimmers, but only within the designated area: poisonous jellyfish are a problem in the summer months.

There are numerous boutiques within walking distance as well as several fascinating galleries that exhibit and sell the work of local artists, some of whose works the visitor can see in the lobby of the hotel.

B

Orchid Villas

Situated just two kilometres from the coast, these beautiful villas are surrounded by a thick hedge which screens the complex completely from the main road. There are twelve villas, all of which overlook a lush tropical garden. There is also a swimming pool and fully-equipped barbecue area for those visitors who prefer to dine out of doors. Each villa is independent, with its own garage. There are two-, three- and four-bedroom villas, ideal for families or friends who would like to holiday together.

All areas within the grounds have wheelchair access, and the villas themselves have been carefully designed to be safe for people with reduced mobility and vision.

Orchid Villas are within walking distance of Elias Beach, where swimming is safe within the designated area.

C

Canecutter's Lodge

Canecutter's Lodge is situated twenty kilometres inland and is ideal for visitors in search of peace and quiet. This unusual hotel was once the home of a plantation owner and much of the character of the original building has been preserved. The grounds are surrounded by acres of sugar cane fields, so visitors will not be disturbed by anything other than bird calls. Canecutter's Lodge has a reputation for its excellent cuisine and many of the ingredients are gathered fresh daily from the property itself: guavas, mangoes, granadillas, papayas, bananas and avocadoes.

Visitors who wish to take advantage of what the area has to offer are advised to hire a car. A twenty-minute drive will bring you to several beaches that are excellent for swimming, water-skiing and surfing. A slightly longer journey in the other direction will take you to the tablelands where you can go hot-air ballooning.

D

The Melaleuca

This fantastic hotel is located in the heart of a nature reserve that stretches for kilometres along the coast. The view from the rooms has to be seen to be believed: a tapestry of tropical vegetation including tree ferns, palms and orchids. It is difficult to believe that the beach is a few metres away, hidden from sight beyond the jungle growth. Even the waves can't be heard above the insect and bird calls.

And that, of course, is why visitors come here: to experience the beauty and diversity of plant and animal life in the rainforest. Nature lovers can take advantage of the guided walks organised by the hotel or go off on their own. Alternatively, you can remain in the hotel grounds and watch the creatures that come to feed on the fruit and seeds that the staff put out for them.

For a change of scenery, you can walk along the golden beach, but be warned: saltwater crocodiles are a constant threat in the waters around here and these enormous reptiles have been known to attack and even kill.

PAPER 2: WRITING Part 1

Part 1

You **must** answer this question. Write your answer in **120–150** words in an appropriate style.

1 You have received an email from your college principal asking you to help organise an open day at your college. Read the email and the notes you have made. Then write an email to your principle, using **all** your notes.

From: Marcus Matthews, Principal
Sent: 20th September
Subject: College open day

Each year the college has an open day in October so that members of the public can visit us and see what we do. This year we would like you to help us organise this important event. We are thinking of holding the open day on a Tuesday, but the actual date hasn't been confirmed yet.

Weekend better, say why

As usual there will be exhibitions of work done by students. The art class will exhibit their paintings in the Hall. Can you recommend anywhere for the projects done in science and technology classes?

Yes, give recommendation

Last year the café served food prepared by the cookery class and this was very popular. What other facilities could we provide this year?

Make a suggestion

Finally, we would like this year's open day to be especially enjoyable, so we are looking forward to hearing your ideas!

Regards,

Marcus Matthews

Write your **email.** You must use grammatically correct sentences with accurate spelling and punctuation appropriate for the situation.

Part 2

Write an answer to **one** of the questions **2–5** in this part. Write your answer in **120–180** words in an appropriate style.

2   Your teacher has asked you to write a story for a competition that is being held by a young people's magazine. The story must **begin** with the following words:

> *Chris woke up one morning to find a huge hole where his garden used to be.*

Write your **story**.

3   You recently saw this advertisement on an English-language website.

> ### TRAVEL WRITERS WANTED
>
> We are looking for articles on places of interest. Have you visited anywhere interesting recently, either in your country or abroad? If so, why not write an article about that place and send it to us? Include information on what there is to see and do there, and whether you would recommend the place to other people.
>
> The best articles will be published on our website next month.

Write your **article**.

4   You have had a class discussion on uniforms. Your teacher has asked you to write an essay, giving your opinions on the following statement:

All school and college students should wear a uniform.

Write your **essay**.

Part 1

For questions **1–12**, read the text below and decide which answer (**A, B, C** or **D**) best fits each gap. There is an example at the beginning (**0**).

Mark your answers.

Example:
0 A obsession   **B** interest   **C** enthusiasm   **D** attraction
0 A <u>B</u> C D

Volunteer conservation work

For those of you with an **(0)** ...... in conservation, what could be a better experience than volunteer work in the mountains of South America? At the moment we are running several projects focusing on **(1)** ...... data in the region.

Conservation projects often attract science students; by doing volunteer work, young people can **(2)** ...... valuable experience in the field. But just about anyone can apply to be a volunteer worker as **(3)** ...... skills aren't usually required. However, you need to be fit and **(4)** ...... of doing physical work. You may also have to **(5)** ...... up with the money for your flight to the region, which can be a **(6)** ...... expensive business. Fortunately, many companies and charities will sponsor volunteer workers.

On arrival in an area, you attend a **(7)** ...... of lectures on the local culture of the region. You are also given some basic training that may come in **(8)** ...... in an emergency. **(9)** ...... to say, you will not be given tasks that might expose you to danger. We try to **(10)** ...... the best use of the skills and knowledge each volunteer worker has to offer.

Naturally, it is up to you how much effort you are prepared to **(11)** ...... into a project, but most volunteers come away with experiences that will **(12)** ...... with them for a lifetime.

1	**A** saving	**B** collecting	**C** assembling	**D** bringing
2	**A** achieve	**B** make	**C** earn	**D** gain
3	**A** specific	**B** exact	**C** definite	**D** detailed
4	**A** able	**B** capable	**C** competent	**D** skilled
5	**A** fund	**B** come	**C** pay	**D** afford
6	**A** little	**B** quite	**C** fairly	**D** bit
7	**A** series	**B** sequence	**C** group	**D** chain
8	**A** practical	**B** handy	**C** sensible	**D** necessary
9	**A** Pointless	**B** Unnecessary	**C** Regardless	**D** Needless
10	**A** make	**B** do	**C** give	**D** take
11	**A** insert	**B** put	**C** contribute	**D** go
12	**A** stop	**B** continue	**C** stand	**D** stay

Part 2

For questions **13–24**, read the text below and think of the word which best fits each gap.
Use only **one** word in each gap. There is an example at the beginning (**0**).

Write your answers **IN CAPITAL LETTERS on a separate answer sheet.**

Example: 0 AS

Grow your own

My husband and I have been growing herbs ever since we came here forty years ago.
(0) .... a matter of fact, we cultivate over sixty different kinds. Some are aromatic and a
(13) .... are medicinal, but the majority, like basil and oregano, are for use in cooking. And
of course, we grow others simply **(14)** .... they are so pretty to look at!

I would recommend that anyone **(15)** .... even a small patch of land should grow herbs.
And you don't even need a garden **(16)** .... get started because herbs can also survive in a
plant pot. First of all, **(17)** .... is the pleasure of cultivation: nothing is more satisfying
than watching plants growing. Secondly, **(18)** .... using fresh herbs, you will improve
(19) .... flavour of your cooking. And **(20)** .... , finding out about herbs is fascinating:
the more you learn about these wonderful plants, the **(21)** .... you want to know!

We live in Crete, **(22)** .... the climate is warm and the soil allows us to grow virtually
anything. But if you live in a cooler and wetter climate, you **(23)** .... to take local conditions
into account. Wherever you live, you will find growing **(24)** .... own herbs a worthwhile
experience.

Part 3

For questions **25–34**, read the text below. Use the word given in capitals at the end of some of the lines to form a word that fits in the gap **in the same line**. There is an example at the beginning (**0**).

Write your answers **IN CAPITAL LETTERS on a separate answer sheet**.

Example: 0 IMPORTANT

A great composer

He was undoubtedly one of the most **(0)** .... composers in the history of Western classical music.   **IMPORTANCE**

He was born in Bonn in 1770, the son of a **(25)** .... , but **MUSIC**
moved to Vienna in 1792, where he gained a reputation as a piano
virtuoso. He soon acquired **(26)** .... patrons, and also **WEALTH**
earned money from giving concerts and lessons, and from
sales of his works. He wanted to be financially **(27)** .... **DEPEND**
so he would have the freedom to compose whatever he wanted.

He began to suffer from a **(28)** .... of hearing in his twenties. **LOSE**
By 1814 he was **(29)** .... deaf, but this did not affect **TOTAL**
his **(30)** .... to compose music. **ABLE**

As a result of his **(31)** .... , he began to keep **DEAF**
'conversation books': his friends would 'talk' to him by writing in
these books, and he would reply either in writing or verbally.
Consequently, we have a unique **(32)** .... record of many **HISTORY**
of his conversations. They provide us with **(33)** .... **VALUE**
insights into how he wanted his works to be performed.

He was a difficult man, but he had friends who loved him and were
attracted by his **(34)** .... After a quarrel with one of **PERSON**
his patrons, Prince Lichnowsky, he famously remarked: There are
'and will be a thousand princes; there is only one Beethoven.'

Part 4

For questions **35–42**, complete the second sentence so that it has a similar meaning to the first sentence, using the word given. **Do not change the word given.** You must use between **two** and **five** words, including the word given. Here is an example (**0**).

Example:

0 It might be cold tonight, so you'd better take a coat with you.
CASE
You'd better take a coat with you .... tonight.

The gap can be filled by the words 'in case it is cold', so you write:
Example: 0 IN CASE IT IS COLD

Write **only** the missing words **IN CAPITAL LETTERS on a separate answer sheet.**

35   Despite the traffic, the courier wasn't late delivering the package.

      TIME

      The courier .... despite the traffic.

36   The detective interviewed the suspect this afternoon.

      BY

      The suspect .... the detective this afternoon.

37   'It isn't necessary for you to drive me home,' Francesca told him.

      NEED

      Francesca told him .... to drive her home.

38   There are very few places left on the web design course.

      ANY

      There .... places left on the web design course.

39 It isn't warm enough to take a swim at this time of year.

TOO

The water .... for swimming at this time of year.

40 Students are not allowed to turn on their mobile phones in class.

MUST

All mobile phones .... off before class.

41 If it doesn't rain soon, there will be a water shortage.

UNLESS

There will be a water shortage .... soon.

42 It's time Carlos started that business he's been talking about all year.

SET

Carlos .... that business he's been talking about all year.

Part 1

🎧 PT.1 You will hear people talking in eight different situations. For questions **1–8**, choose the best answer (**A**, **B** or **C**).

1 You hear a young woman talking.
   Why does she want to change her job?

   A She isn't earning enough money.
   B She wants a new challenge.
   C She's been offered a job by a competitor.

2 You hear a woman talking to her friend.
   Where did she get her tree house from?

   A She bought it at the local garden centre.
   B She made it herself.
   C Her neighbours sold it to her.

3 You hear a man complaining to his friend.
   Where has he just been?

   A to the garage
   B to an electrical goods shop
   C to the dentist

4 You hear a woman talking to her friend.
   How does she suggest her friend should travel?

   A by car
   B by plane
   C by boat

5 You hear a man talking to his wife in a shop.
   Which item does the man want to buy?

   A a fridge
   B a washing machine
   C a vacuum cleaner

6 You hear a man talking on the radio about a cinema.
   Why is the cinema going to be pulled down?

   A It is no longer profitable.
   B It doesn't show popular films.
   C It has become dangerous.

7 You hear a teenager who has arrived somewhere for an appointment.
   Why is she late?

   A She left her mobile phone at home.
   B There was a traffic accident.
   C She missed the bus.

8 You hear a woman talking about her skydiving experience.
   How did she feel afterwards?

   A frightened
   B embarrassed
   C thrilled

Part 2

🎧PT.2 You will hear an interview with a man called Bob who runs a sanctuary for horses and donkeys. For questions **9–18**, complete the sentences.

Horse and donkey sanctuary

Some animals in the sanctuary have | 9 |_____| problems.

Approximately | 10 |_____| animals live in the sanctuary.

According to Bob, horses are | 11 |_____| and sociable creatures.

The sanctuary should have more | 12 |_____| to look after the animals.

Penfold sanctuary is looking for | 13 |_____| young volunteers to take part in its summer programme.

Successful applicants would get the chance to learn | 14 |_____|

Transport to the farm will leave from | 15 |_____| each day.

A couple of volunteer helpers will be offered the chance to work | 16 |_____| at the sanctuary after they finish school.

You need to be | 17 |_____| to apply to be a buddy.

Acceptable forms of identity include a passport or | 18 |_____|

PAPER 4: LISTENING Part 3 (Questions 19–23)

Part 3

PT.3 You will hear five different people talking about friends. For questions **19–23**, choose from the list (**A–F**). Use the letters only once. There is one extra letter which you do not need to use.

Which person

A was disappointed by a friend

B felt annoyed with their friend

C let their friend down

D misses a friend

E wants to be like their friend

F doesn't like a friend

Speaker 1	19
Speaker 2	20
Speaker 3	21
Speaker 4	22
Speaker 5	23

Part 4

🎧 PT.4 You will hear an interview with the owner of a gallery. For questions **24–30**, choose the best answer (**A**, **B** or **C**).

24   'Galimoto' is the name of

    A   an African gallery.

    B   a language. | 24 | |

    C   a kind of toy.

25   Tessa was very impressed

    A   by the things children can make out of rubbish.

    B   by the fact that many people in southern Africa are poor. | 25 | |

    C   by the length of time she spent in southern Africa.

26   According to Tessa, the bicycle the child made

    A   had wheels made of sticks.

    B   could be ridden. | 26 | |

    C   was beautifully made.

27   Tessa's gallery exhibits toys from

    A   Africa and South America.

    B   Africa. | 27 | |

    C   South America.

28   In the mornings children will have a chance to

    A   watch how toys are made.

    B   make toys out of wire. | 28 | |

    C   demonstrate their skills to the artists.

29   People who want to see how children in southern Africa make toys will be able to

    A   watch a documentary on DVD.

    B   watch a series on television. | 29 | |

    C   interview children about their skills.

30   Tessa believes that

    A   African children are cleverer than other children.

    B   too many toys are bad for children's creativity. | 30 | |

    C   children in rich countries don't play with toys any more.

PAPER 5: SPEAKING Part 1

Part 1 (3 minutes)

Likes and dislikes
- Do you prefer staying in or going out? Why?
- Do you like music? What sort of music do you listen to?
- Do you prefer listening to music on CDs or your iPod, or going to concerts?
- Tell me about the last concert or show you went to.

Education and work
- Are you studying or working at the moment?
- What are you studying at the moment? Do you like it? Why? / Why not?
- Do you prefer to study at home or in a library?
- Do you work on your own or with other people? Do you like it? Why? / Why not?
- What would your ideal career be? Why?

Free time
- How much free time do you have? Is it enough for you?
- What do you like to do in your free time?
- Do you have any plans for this weekend?
- Do you have a hobby or pastime? How much time do you spend doing this activity?

Holidays and travel
- Where would you like to travel to?
- What kind of holidays do you prefer? Relaxing or exciting? Why?
- What kinds of activities do you like to do on holiday?
- Do you take photos on holiday? Why? / Why not?

PAPER 5: SPEAKING Part 2

Part 2 (4 minutes)

1 Employment

Candidate A
Here are your photographs. They show people working in different environments.
Compare the photographs and say what you think the advantages of working in each environment are.

Candidate B
Say which job you would prefer to have.

2 Excursions

Candidate B
Here are your photographs. They show people on different kinds of excursions.
Compare the photographs, and say what you think the people will enjoy on their visits.

Candidate A
Say which of these excursions you would like to go on.

1 Employment

2 Excursions

Parts 3 and 4 (7 minutes)

Part 3 (3 minutes)

Imagine that someone wants to open a new hotel with hi-tech gadgets. Here are some of the suggestions they are considering.

First, talk to each other about how successful these suggestions might be. Then decide which two would attract most people.

Part 4 (4 minutes)

Would you like to spend time in a hotel like this? Why? / Why not?

Would you like to work in a hotel? Why? / Why not?

What sorts of hotels are most popular with visitors in your country?

What sort of things do people complain about in hotels?

Young people often choose different hotels to older people. Why do you think that is?

Some people say that spending money on an expensive hotel is a waste of money. Do you agree? Why? / Why not?

HI-TECH HOTEL

- 50% off first week's stay

- 40" flat screen TV in every room!

- Free internet access

- Remote controlled lighting

- Jacuzzi in every bathroom

- No room key! Use your fingerprint!

- Pay by credit card only

Listening scripts

Unit 1

🎧 1.1 Listening: friends and family (page 10)

1 *M = Mark, T = Tony*

M Hi, Tony. How are things?

T Hi, Mark. Everything's fine, thanks. I didn't expect to run into you here.

M No, it's not really my sort of thing. But my wife has read the book and she wanted to see it on the big screen.

T Oh, Sandra's here too. Where is she?

M She's just getting some popcorn. I'm starving.

2 I'm babysitting tonight. I quite like it because I'm an only child, so it's good fun to look after Roger and Tom for an evening. The only problem is that the two brothers are always fighting. My aunt said that if I have any problem with them, then I should call her, and she and my uncle will come back home. But they'll be really angry if they have to come home because their children are misbehaving.

3 I've really fallen out with Liam. We used to be great friends, but one day we were on the beach. He was laughing about something and then he stepped on my sunglasses. They just snapped and they were really expensive. He didn't apologise or anything. He just said it was an accident. We had a big argument then and I haven't spoken to him since. He's always calling me on my mobile, but I don't answer the call.

4 Practically everything is finished now. We've made all the arrangements. Unfortunately, we have to get married in winter. My fiancé, Pete, is in the army and we've found out that the only time we can get married is January. That's what life is: if I were marrying an accountant or something, it would be different. The other problem is that my brother can't come because he's working in a hospital in India at the moment.

5 *C = Clara, G = Gary*

C What's wrong, Gary?

G Oh evening, Clara. I'm locked out! I was running around today because I was so busy and I must have dropped my keys somewhere. So, I've fixed all my work problems, and now I have something else to worry about! It could have been worse. I mean luckily it wasn't my wallet or credit cards or anything like that.

C Well, come and wait in my house.

G OK, thanks.

6 This is a picture of my brother. It's so strange that he's a redhead when all of our relatives are quite dark. I remember when we lived in Japan, everyone used to look at him because of it and they thought it was fascinating. He really stuck out. No one was interested in me or my sister, though.

7 Ian and Eric are really alike and people often think they are twins, which isn't true. I look very different to them because they're actually my stepbrothers. Our father was married twice and so Ian and Eric are the children from his first marriage. At the moment they are at university, so I don't see them very much. But if I pass all my school exams, I might go to the same college as Ian next year.

8 I fell in love with her as soon as I met her. It was at my grandfather's house. We were celebrating his retirement with a barbecue and some drinks. There were about a hundred people there. He's a teacher and he invited lots of colleagues from his school, including Rachel. We got talking and later, you know, we started going out. That was how we met.

🎧 1.2 Speaking (page 13)

I = Interlocutor, J = Julieta, P = Philippe

I Good morning.

J Good morning.

P Morning.

I Could I have your mark sheets, please?

J Here you are.

P Yes.

I Thank you. My name is Robert Smith and this is my colleague, Sarah Jones. She's just going to be listening to us. So, what's your name?

J Julieta.

I And?

P My name is Philippe.

I Fine. First of all, I'd like to know something about you. Julieta, where are you from?

J I'm from Zaragoza. In Spain.

I And, do you live alone or do you live with your family?

J I live with my parents. In Zaragoza.

I Do you come from a large family or a small family?

J Er … normal? We are four in my family. I have one older sister, Ana, who has twenty-four years.

I OK. And what about you, Philippe. Where are you from?

P Lille.

I Do you come from a large family or a small family?

P Small. I don't have some brothers and sisters.

I What do your parents do?

P My father is teacher and my mother works as doctor.

I Thank you.

Unit 2

🎧 2.1 Listening: Do you like your job? (page 18)

W = Woman, M = Man

1 I never wanted to work in an office at all. It's all the office politics that I hate. I feel relieved when I get home because I can close the door and forget all the arguments and all the stress. I come here two or three times a day because I need a coffee when I'm at work. I have to have a break from sitting at my desk.

2 When I finally got the letter, I couldn't believe it. The local newspaper had accepted me for their trainee journalist position. I never thought I would get the job. Today was my first day and I was thrilled to be in the office. We print the newspaper on Mondays, and everyone was running around and shouting. I can't wait to see what happens in the rest of the week!

3

W I always wanted to work with the team here in Boston and most of the time it's great. I mean we have the flexitime system and that was Chris's idea. He is a good boss sometimes.

M Yeah, he's always talking to everyone, giving encouragement.

W But there's just one problem. He got the job because he's friends with the company owner, but he doesn't really know anything about the business. He never studied it. He hasn't got a diploma. He doesn't have anything!

M I know. It is a problem.

4 So, Stefan Jung came to the office for an interview yesterday. I wanted you to meet him too. He was excellent and I asked Rachel to send a letter to him offering him the job. I know that I should have asked your opinion too, but if I don't offer him the job now, someone else will. I know we agreed to share all our decisions, but this one time I had to work on my own. We're interviewing again next week. Why don't you do those ones?

5

M I like the company and everything, but I want to do something else for a while.

W Me too. I'm thinking of asking Francis for a sabbatical. I saw a project in Nicaragua where you do voluntary work, protecting the forests and the wildlife.

M That would be great for me too. I studied languages and I'd love to improve my Spanish.

W Would you like me to give you the information? I can send you the weblink if you like.

M Could you? That'd be great.

6 There are over a thousand people working here, so we are a large company. People come from all over the world because these are the headquarters, so it was important to make a space that everyone felt comfortable in. We brought in architects and designers from many different countries, and they all had very interesting ideas. They used a lot of glass, so there's a lot of light. The furniture is very modern and it's a very nice place to work. I think everyone says that they are happy to be in our offices.

7 What a day! This morning a major client asked us to change a delivery at the last minute. It was a delivery of plastic toys and we needed to change the contents of the shipment. There was no one else in the office and it was crucial that we made the change today. Anyway, I managed it. I can laugh about it now, but it was very stressful. I'm sure my boss will be delighted too when he comes back next week.

8 People forget that looking for a job is a full-time job itself. You really have to sell yourself and that's not easy for a lot of people. It takes a lot of time to prepare a CV and to write a letter so it doesn't have any mistakes. It's terrible! One mistake can ruin everything. Personally, I can't wait to start work again and do something useful rather than putting bits of paper in the post and waiting for a reply.

🎧 2.5 **Speaking** (page 21)

I = Interlocutor, E = Eleni, C = Claudio

I Now I'd like you to talk about something together for about three minutes. I'm just going to listen. I'd like you to imagine that you are a student at university and you want to do a part-time job while you are studying. First, talk to each other about the advantages and disadvantages of each job. Then decide which is the best job. You only have about three minutes for this, so once again don't worry if I stop you. Please speak clearly so that we can hear you. All right?

E OK, Claudio. Which picture should we start with?

C The waitress?

E OK. What do you think about it?

C Working as a waiter or waitress is much better than working in an office.

E Do you think so?

C Yes, because you can work at different times. If you work in an office, you work at the same time as classes at university.

E That's true. But the money you get isn't anything like as good as you get in an office.

C Right! OK. So how does the office job compare to the ... uhm the job here? At the swimming pool?

E The life guard?

C Life guard. Uhm ... Is it much different from working in an office, or as a waiter?

E Yes. I think so. I think it's boring if you work as a life guard. You sit down, you watch people. I don't think I like it.

C I see your point. But for me this life guard seems like the best job.

E Why do you think that?

C I like swimming! And life guards ... you don't have to think a lot. You can watch the people swim and think about your university subject. That's very good if you have to study and work at the same time.

E That's a good point.

C Which job would you go for? The life guard too?

E No. I think the tourist information job is the best one.

C It looks fairly similar to working in an office.

E That's right. But if you work in tourist information, you speak to people from many different countries. You can use your languages. And that's good for me because I am a student and I study French and English.

C I see!

I Thank you.

Unit 3

🎧 3.1 **Listening: footvolley** (page 26)

P = Presenter, V = Vera

P Vera, welcome to the show. Today you're going to tell us about the sport of footvolley. What is it exactly?

V That's a good question. Footvolley is a combination of volleyball and football. Usually, it's a game played with four players, two on each side. The game is played just like volleyball except that you're not allowed to touch the ball with your hands. You have to try and kick it back and forwards over the net.

P So, how do you play the game?

V In footvolley you have to kick the ball over the net, but you're only allowed to kick the ball three times before it goes over. You have to be careful too because if you accidentally touch the ball with any part of your body, that counts as a kick.

P And how do you lose points? How do you lose the game?

V If you touch the ball more than three times, you lose the point. Also, no player can touch the ball two consecutive times. You can also lose points if you kick the ball out of the court or if you don't get it over the net.

P It sounds really difficult. Where did a sport like this come from?

V The sport is from my country, Brazil. If you go there, you'll see people playing this on all the beaches. It's very popular. No one is sure exactly which city started footvolley, but it is played all over the country.

P Are there any theories for how it started?

V Yes. Some people think it started as a warm up for a football game – a chance for the players to get ready before the match. Now it's a sport too!

P I must admit that I've never heard of footvolley before. Is it played in other countries too?

V Yes, it's becoming more and more popular. I was recently working in the States, where the sport is becoming very popular. I was training a team over there. There are also footvolley groups starting in many countries including some in Europe. Last month, I was part of a big tournament in Birmingham in the UK. That was very strange for me because they had to have the tournament indoors. There's no beach in Birmingham! I think footvolley will soon be everywhere.

P And you don't just play the sport. You've also produced a series of very beautiful photographs.

V Yes, I had an exhibition in São Paolo last year. That was wonderful for me.

P I think the photographs are excellent. The players look very graceful in your images.

V Thank you.

P And what are your hopes for the future of the sport?

V Personally, I think that one day footvolley will be in the Olympic Games. And why not? It's a wonderful game that you can play on the beach with your friends. It's competitive, but there's always a good atmosphere and that's what a game should be like.

3.4 Speaking (page 29)

1 *I = Interlocutor, J = Julieta*

I In this part of the test I'm going to give each of you two photographs. I'd like you to talk about your photographs on your own for about a minute. OK? Julieta, here are your photographs. They show people competing in activities. I want you to compare the two photographs and say which activity is the most difficult.

J Sì ... I mean yes. In both photographs we can see people competing. In the first photograph they are playing a board game. This is a big room and lots of people are playing the same game. So the first picture is indoors whereas the second picture is outdoors. OK. And they are riding bicycles, in a race. They look very hot and I think you have to practise a long time to do this ... activity. Although I like chess, I prefer the second activity. Because I like to be outdoors and I like cycling very much. Er ... Also, to play chess you must study a lot at home and practise, and it's not very exciting. If you want to go biking, you can go to ... you can go in the countryside and see different places. That is why I prefer the second picture.

2 *I = Interlocutor, P = Philippe*

I In this part of the test I'm going to give each of you two photographs. I'd like you to talk about your photographs on your own for about a minute. OK? Philippe, here are your photographs. They show people competing in activities. I want you to compare the two photographs and say which activity is the most difficult.

P This is very nice. This is a chess competition and lots of people are playing the game. In the second picture we can see a cycle race on the ... road. Both pictures show people in competitions. In each picture there's a different type of competition. In chess you have to use your brain and in cycling fitness is very important. Er ... I think chess is the most difficult activity. Cycling is hard and difficult, but anyone can ride a bike and it's not important to win. In chess you have to think very hard. I think you need a special brain and many people don't understand ... how to play the game. So cycling looks harder, but I think chess is the most difficult activity.

Unit 4

4.1 Listening: special animals (page 35)

1 We used to go there all the time because it didn't cost very much in those days. We used to watch the tigers in their enclosure. They were my favourites. One of my earliest memories is watching them eat an enormous piece of meat that the keepers had thrown into their cage. I remember watching them and imagining what they would do to their prey. Although I think it's cruel to keep animals in captivity like that, I think it does help people understand that animals are important and we need to protect them.

2 We were stupid really. There'd been a film about turtles on TV and I said to my parents that I really wanted one. So my father went to the exotic pet shop and bought a turtle. We were all really excited. Unfortunately, we hadn't done much research on the animals. As it grew up, it became larger and larger. In the end it was so big that we had nowhere to put it. Turtles need a lot of water to live in, you see. So we had to take it to a special sanctuary and they looked after it after that.

3 When we lived in the countryside, there was this really skinny cat that used to come into our garden. He was a stray. He wasn't tame at all. If anyone went near him, he would run away, terrified. But we loved him anyway and we called him Scraggy, which means 'not healthy' or 'messy'. Anyway, my mother was determined to look after him, and although he never trusted us, he did use to eat the food that we left for him. But he'd only eat the food if no one was nearby.

4 The kingfisher is a beautiful bird. It has bright blue feathers and it looks like it should come from Brazil or somewhere in South America. But they live here in Britain. I've only seen one once in my life and it came as a complete surprise. I was eight years old and I was eating breakfast in my kitchen when I saw this bright blue colour outside ... and there it was! A kingfisher. You don't often see a kingfisher in the wild, so it was a special memory for me.

5 Digger was special for me because although I can hear perfectly well, both of my parents are deaf. They were lucky though because there are charities which provide special dogs, hearing dogs, for the deaf. They teach the dogs to listen for particular noises and they can help deaf people in their everyday lives. My parents had Digger, who was one of these dogs, and he was the first pet that we had when I was growing up. I used to take him for long walks before school and after school, and at the weekends. Yeah. I still miss him today, actually.

4.5 Speaking (page 36)

T = Teacher, J = Julieta

T I'd like you to talk about your photographs for about a minute. OK? Julieta, here are your photographs. They show people interacting with animals. I want you to compare the two photographs and say which experience is the most memorable.

J Well, let me see. In the first photo there's a lion and people are on safari. I think they are on holidays. I don't think these people are scientists. There are too many. They are tourists. OK. The second photo shows two girls, riding a white horse. Maybe the young girl is learning to ride a horse. Yes. Both photos show people who interact with animals and I think you remember both ... experiences. But I think the second one is the most memorable because you remember things very strongly when you are very young. I too learned to ride a horse when I was six or seven and I remember it very well. Er ... returning to the first picture, I don't think this is so memorable because people have a lot of holidays nowadays and these experiences are not so important, so special, today.

T Thank you.

Unit 5

5.1 Listening: a ghostwriter (page 42)

I = Interviewer, G = George

I George Moore, thank you for coming in to chat with us today.

G It's my pleasure.

I So we're going to talk about your work as a ghostwriter. First of all, what exactly is a ghostwriter?

G The answer to that question very much depends on who you talk with and what genre the ghostwriter is working in. I can only speak for myself. I write 'autobiographies' for singers, celebrities, and people like that. Basically, the public wants to know about the lives of famous people and the fans want to know what the stars really think. So it's a big publishing industry. The problem is that the stars themselves are often very busy or often are not very experienced writers. So the publisher asks a ghostwriter to help them write the book.

I What do you mean by 'help'?

G It depends on who I'm working with. Actors in the theatre often write very well and they write most of the book themselves. I just correct things or change the order of chapters, that kind of thing. If the person is, for example, a teenage rock star, I would write every word of the book, and the teen star would just read it and make suggestions afterwards.

I How do you write a biography of a teenager?

G Well, a teen rock star has already lived a life that most people can only dream of, and they have had special experiences that they can talk about. Often people like grandparents and parents save news stories from the local newspaper or have videos of early TV appearances and I can use that too to build up the story.

I But it must be really difficult to write the biography of a teenager?

G Not necessarily. I once wrote the history of the music festivals in the 1960s. That was a lot more work because I needed to speak to a huge amount of people and there was a lot to read. That was much harder. I loved the subject though.

I Now, how do ghostwriters get paid?

G Often you get a fee. So the star would get royalties from the book, maybe 10 per cent of every book sold, but the ghostwriter would get a one-off fee. The problem is that people are not buying the book for the ghostwriter's name, so it's difficult to negotiate more money. Sometimes ghostwriters do get royalties. But I never have.

I For many people this would be a dream job. How did you get into ghostwriting?

G When I was a student, I used to write articles for pop music newspapers. After I graduated, I got a job as a reporter on a music magazine – it's not published any more. The editor of the magazine used to write biographies of bands. One year he had too much work on and he had to give up one of his writing projects. He suggested to the publisher that I do the work instead.

I It's not what you know, it's who you know.

G Always.

I One more question. I've looked at your books and you almost never get your name on the cover. Does it hurt you that you don't get recognition for your work?

G Not really because I am very well paid. You have to remember that there are lots of writers out there who write books and don't get their name on the cover: the writers of dictionaries, encyclopedias, etc.

I The world of publishing is quite a confusing world, isn't it?

G It certainly is.

5.5 Speaking (page 45)

E = Eleni, C = Claudio

E So we have to decide on two options to encourage children to read.

C OK. That should be easy to sort out. But there are options which appeal to different people.

E Let's go through the list one by one. OK?

C Yes. Er … comics. In my opinion this is a good idea because young children like comics and picture books.

E But comics are not proper books.

C But it is easy to start reading with comics. You start with comics and then you read other books. No?

E The thing is I think children read comics anyway. So let's move on to the second suggestion and come back to this one.

C Introduce silent reading in school?

E When I was at school, we had an hour of silent reading. Not every day but once a week.

C Yes? I think it's very boring. I can't stand reading in the classroom.

E That's true. I don't think we read a lot. It's not an obvious choice, is it?

C Something that would appeal to me is to invite famous authors to schools.

E Yes! This is exciting! I remember a famous author coming to us in Greece.

C The problem is that maybe it is difficult because writers don't like to visit schools. It can be difficult to find writers.

E Yes, you're right. The national competition is a good idea. A book review is where you read a book and write a description afterwards. It's a good idea because children like competitions and it means that people have to read.

C Maybe. But I think it is good for children who read a lot now. They will like to write a book review. I don't know if children who don't read books start reading for this competition.

E No, I think this is a good idea. I think we should go for it.

C OK, if you think so. But we have two more possibilities. Give every child a free book. Personally, I think this is difficult because it is expensive for the government and you don't know if you give children a book that they want to read that book …

E Maybe it means you give the children a voucher, a piece of paper, that they exchange for a book. Then the children choose.

C Ah! I see. But we don't know. It just says 'give every child a free book.'

E And the book exchange? I think this is a good idea because the children can control it. They decide what to give and take. Children don't have a lot of money and so if they exchange books, then they can read many more books.

C Yes, I quite agree. So to sum up, we have chosen the national competition. Er … and we need to choose one more. I'm weighing up two possibilities: the famous authors and the book exchange.

E Let's try the famous authors. It can be exciting for the children.

C OK. We choose the book review competition and visits by famous authors.

Unit 6

6.1 Listening: travel and visits (page 50)

M = Man, W = Woman

1

M So my plan is that I'll arrive in New York City and then travel by car through Pennsylvania, Maryland, Virginia, right the way down the east coast to Florida. It's a journey that I've always wanted to do.

W That's terrific, Dennis. It sounds really exciting. Can I help you at all?

M Actually, yes. I was wondering if you could put me up for a couple of nights?

W Of course! That's no trouble at all.

2 Well, of course, in the brochure it looked perfect. The hotel was right next to the beach, there was a swimming pool and the rooms looked beautiful. But, when we arrived, things were a little bit different. Don't get me wrong. It was a very high quality hotel and it was nice to be there, but it was nowhere near the beach. Why do they put these things in the brochure if they're not true? It's all quite frustrating.

3 Our Interrail trip around Europe was great fun. The transport ticket was a bit expensive, but that was no problem really. We saw loads of cities and had a great time. There was only one really bad moment. We had to get a train in the morning from Frankfurt to Hamburg and the only train we could get was at 7am. We got there OK, but it was full of commuters and it was packed! We had to stand almost the whole way and it's a long journey. That was the worst thing.

4 That was a marvellous trip to Crete. I knew I had to find something to take back with me. In the end I decided to get a print of one of the pictures at the palace at Knossos. The image is about 3,000 years old. It shows a man leaping over a bull. It's really nice and I've hung it in my living room. Every time I look at it, it reminds me of the fabulous two weeks we spent there.

5

W Come on! You must have the tickets somewhere.

M Er ... yes. They're in my bag. Here.

W Look at the queue for check in! I told you we should have got here earlier.

M It's OK. We're here now.

W How long is it before we take off?

M An hour and a half. Don't worry. Everything is on track.

W I just hope I have time to do some shopping. Oh well.

6

M What about this one? It's a package holiday on a coach that travels through the Alps.

W But look, they take you somewhere every day: castles, museums. I want some time to do other things too. A bit of skiing perhaps. Let's just book our own flights and hotels over the Internet.

M I think the package holiday will be cheaper.

W I'd rather make all the decisions and spend more.

7 The thing that I really wanted to do on the trip was to go diving. The weather had been bad for days and the boats weren't going anywhere. Eventually, though, it cleared up and the sea was calm. I'd already paid up and I was all set to go. Unfortunately, I'd cut my foot a week before and it hadn't healed, so I wasn't able to go on the excursion. It was so frustrating!

8 I don't think it's a job for everyone. I take large groups and show them round the historic centre of the city. I do this about three or four times a day. Some people might think that it's quite boring doing the same thing all the time, but I really enjoy it and you get to meet different people all the time. I also get to use my foreign languages and that's important to me too.

🎧 6.4 **Speaking** (page 53)

I = Interlocutor

I Now I'd like you to talk about something together for about three minutes. I'm just going to listen. I'd like you to imagine that you are in charge of delivering the post to a group of different villages. The pictures show the villages. You have to decide how to deliver

the letters and parcels. First, talk to each other about the advantages and disadvantages of each method of transport. Then decide which is the best way of delivering the post. You only have about three minutes for this, so once again don't worry if I stop you. Please speak clearly so that we can hear you. All right?

🎧 6.5 **Speaking** (page 53)

C = Claudio, E = Eleni

C What do you think, Eleni? How about the small plane?

E No! If we chose the plane, we would have to build a ... somewhere where it could land.

C That would be very expensive. You don't need that for a helicopter. The helicopter can land in a field or somewhere like that.

E But if we delivered the post by plane or helicopter, we would need to have a pilot.

C Is that a problem?

E Well, a pilot is bound to want more money than a postman. They can earn a lot of money. I think the pilot's salary will be expensive.

C If money is a problem, we could always deliver the post by bike. I like the idea because it is good for the environment. There's no pollution.

E That will probably be quite slow. And maybe the villages are a long way away. It will take the postman a long time to get to them.

C Oh no! Every option has problems. We had better make up our minds. What about a speedboat?

E The speedboat? That's very unusual.

C I think it would be very exciting to deliver the post by speedboat. And look! There are rivers between all the villages.

E I think the truck is the best option. That can drive around the villages and deliver the post.

C But look at this village.

E Which one?

C The island. If we used the truck, it wouldn't be able to deliver the post to the island village.

E We could build a bridge.

C I think it is cheaper to buy a speedboat.

E So that's our decision?

C I think so.

E OK, then.

Unit 7

🎧 7.1 **Listening: Domo** (page 58)

P = Presenter, O = Olivia

P Olivia McMath, you're a journalist working in the field of IT and computers, and today you've got something interesting to talk about: Domo. What on earth is that?

O Well, Domo is a robot developed by a team of scientists working at the Massachusetts Institute of Technology (MIT). The team included Aaron Edsinger.

P So what is special about Domo? I mean, there are robots around everywhere these days, aren't there?

O Domo is special because it's different from the sort of robots you see on assembly lines in factories. It doesn't need pre-programmed instructions. The robot can actually interact with the environment around it because it has working eyes and hands, and it's so sensitive that it can pick up an item like a banana.

P But a human being can pick up one of those!

O This may not sound very impressive, but in fact it's something of a breakthrough. Picking things up is very difficult for robots because they don't know when to stop pressing. When robots pick up fragile objects for example, they often smash them into pieces.

P Right. I like Domo's face. Can you tell us something about that?

O It's the face that's Domo's main innovation. Domo's eyes are based on human eyes. For the researchers, this helped them predict where the robot was looking and so how to work with it. Domo can also respond to voice controls and it can 'feel' when someone is touching its body.

P So what's the history of Domo?

O Of course, it didn't come out of nowhere. The robot is the result of three years' work and many sleepless nights on the part of the developers. This is despite the fact that Domo is not the first robot of its type. It was developed based on two previous prototypes known as Cog and Kismet, also developed at MIT.

P But is this just a very expensive toy?

O Far from it. One of the main motivations for the project was the need to develop a robot that could help elderly people. They could continue living an independent life in their own homes with a robot like Domo to help them. Furthermore, the robot has some industrial uses too and its developers are talking about potential use in agriculture, for example. Already the project receives funding from a car manufacturer, so it's clear that there is a commercial usage somewhere.

P Very interesting. Thank you for coming in to talk about it.

7.4 Speaking (page 61)

1 *P = Philippe, J = Julieta*

P I think this would be very useful for people learning English. I like the idea of a list of classic mistakes. For example, I know that I shouldn't say "Last year I studied in England during three weeks", and that it's correct to say "Last year I studied in England for three weeks". Lots of French speakers make the same error.

J I know what you mean, but I don't think you can have a list for every language. So this helps some people but not everyone.

2 *C = Claudio, E = Eleni*

C I don't know about this. I mean, if you use the Internet, it's easy to find an article in English. And if the article is difficult, you can print it and then look up new words in a dictionary.

E Yes, but this does have some questions as well as the text. They can really help you understand a text.

3 *P = Philippe, J = Julieta*

P That's a good idea. I never get the opportunity to see English as it's used in real life. I would really like to watch this, especially if they have the words – what they say – written down on the website too.

J Yes, I think so too. You need to see the words because British people can speak very fast when they speak together.

4 *E = Eleni, C = Claudio*

E For me, this is the best one. When you are preparing for an exam, it's really useful to see what people write. I think it's the hardest part of the language.

C And we could also highlight useful words and phrases that students can learn. Then they can use these in their own writing.

E Good idea. We'll choose this one, shall we?

5 *P = Philippe, J = Julieta*

P I don't think this is a good idea at all.

J Why not?

P This kind of thing never works. Language is just too difficult for a computer program. You can read books which have been changed into English like this and they are ridiculous! Are you happy if we say no and move on to something else on the list?

J Sure. I think it's a bad idea too.

Unit 8

8.1 Listening: victims of crime (page 66)

1 We'd been away on holiday and we'd had a lovely time, so we weren't expecting it at all. But I knew as soon as I came through the front door that something was wrong. The house was very cold and the dining room door was open. We never leave that door open when we're out. Anyway, they'd broken in through the back window. They'd taken everything: the rugs, TV, fridge, everything. It was awful.

2 In the movies it's all very open. Someone comes up to you with a knife and they say they want your bag or your wallet or something like that. In fact what happened to me was that I was walking home one night. It was very late because I'd been to a nightclub with some friends and someone hit me very hard on the back of the head. They knocked me unconscious and I woke up in hospital. I never saw them. But the joke was on the thief. I didn't have any money left. I think they stole about five cents.

3 It happens all the time, doesn't it? I'm a big football fan and I drove down to see an away match. In my car I have a sticker which says 'I support Manchester United', which is my team. Anyway, I think a fan from the other team saw this and while we were at the game, they scratched my car with a key and they broke my wing mirror. Some people say it was my fault, but that's rubbish. It's just football and no one has the right to do something like that to my car.

4 I lost money, but I still think the story is pretty funny. I run a toy store and one day I was counting the money in the till and I noticed something was wrong. I sell these game cards which are very popular with the children and I noticed that an entire shelf was empty. Someone had stolen three boxes of the game cards! I can only imagine it was a child because, to be honest, the cards are almost worthless.

5 You have to be so careful. There I was on holiday and I went to a cocktail bar with my boyfriend. We'd had a lovely day and I was treating him because it was his birthday, so I paid for everything with my credit card. Well, imagine, when I got my bank statement that month, I couldn't believe it. Someone had bought over £1,000 of goods with my card. They'd cloned the card or stolen the number or something, and I'm sure they did it in that cocktail bar. I didn't use my card anywhere else.

8.3 Speaking (page 69)

P = Philippe, C = Claudio, J = Julieta

1

P What do you think about this one, Claudio?

C I don't think it's a good idea. The problem is that you hear these alarms all the time.

J That's right.

C So if you hear one, you don't think 'Oh no, someone's stealing a car'. You think, 'Oh, there's another alarm. How noisy!'

J I'm completely with you on that.

2

J Where are you on this one, Philippe?

P I think this is a very good idea. We have a lot of problems with speeding in my home town. I think that drivers don't care if they drive very fast.

C Exactly.

P You know, the drivers, they don't really care, so you have to do something else. To er ...

J Absolutely. You have to force them to drive with more care.

P Yes. That's it. To force. And for me, this is the most important, because bad driving is very dangerous.

3

J In my country this is very common.

C Is it, Julieta?

J Sure. Every time you buy with your credit card, they ask to see your identity card. It's normal.

P Right.

J This is not a new idea, but I think it's the most effective. If you don't have an identity card, the police don't know who you are, who anyone is.

C I see, but I don't think that they are very useful.

4

P What is this? A western? I have never seen this.

C No, this is important. Sometimes there are dangerous people around and you need to tell everyone. This is a very quick way to tell people 'look out'.

P I see what you mean, but I really don't agree. The photo is terrible. This could be anybody.

C That's true, but it is important to say to people, 'Be careful'.

J OK, so do we think this is effective or not?

5

C We haven't talked about this picture yet, have we?

P No, we haven't. Julieta?

J These are CCTV cameras, aren't they? I don't know if these really work. The problem is that they are everywhere, so people don't think 'Oh no, there's a camera'. Look at the picture. The boy is doing graffiti and the camera stops nothing.

C I see what you mean.

J And also you can cover your face so nobody sees you.

P Good point. Anyway, the pictures you get from these cameras are often not very clear.

C Maybe. But sometimes they are useful after a crime. The police have caught lots of criminals by using these cameras.

J True.

Unit 9

🎧 **9.2 Listening: favourite dish** (page 75)

1 I've been living in London for a long time now, but I still love going home to Napoli, to Naples, to see my family. It's very special, of course. And because my parents run a pizzeria, I grew up in the kitchen, and I love going back and making a real Margarita pizza in the restaurant. We always eat together too after we've made the pizzas. In some countries people don't eat lunch on Sundays together any more because the traditional family is breaking up, but my family always eat together.

2 Normally, if I have visitors round, I just look in the fridge to see what I can rustle up. But sometimes I do something special. One thing that I always enjoy preparing is trout with boiled potatoes and some fennel. You just slice the fennel and put it in the trout. Then you heat up the oven, and bake it for ten minutes or so, something like that. I suppose what's special for me is not the cooking, but the fact that I often go and catch the trout myself in the river near my house.

3 I'm a vegan, so I don't eat meat, cheese, eggs or anything. I've become a pretty good vegan chef. My favourite is a recipe that a friend of mine gave me for a casserole with tomatoes and three kinds of beans. You need to chop all the vegetables up and put them in a saucepan. I always add extra chilli to spice it up and it's delicious. Even my friends who eat meat think it tastes great.

4 I love to prepare ... in my language, it's *tête de veau*. I suppose you say 'cow's head' in English. Perfectly good food, but nowadays butchers don't often sell it. This stuff goes straight in the bin. But people have been eating this for hundreds of years and I think it's important to keep the old traditions up. So, if I have friends round, I sometimes cook this. Admittedly, I do check with everyone beforehand, just to check that they will eat it. Most people say yes.

5 Now that I'm studying in Europe, I can go to Chinese restaurants here. But I have to say that the Chinese food in this country is not the same as the food we eat in my country, especially where I come from, north of Beijing. So I often invite friends to my house to cook real Chinese food for them. Although the food tastes different, they always eat everything up. What I love to prepare most of all is very simple: fried rice. It's easy, it's delicious, and if you use the right rice, it always reminds me of home.

🎧 **9.3 Speaking** (page 77)

I = Interlocutor, P = Philippe, J = Julieta

I Imagine that you are looking after a group of children aged five to seven for the day and you have to prepare lunch for them. Decide together which things in the picture you would prepare and tell each other why. Spend about two or three minutes doing this.

P OK Julieta, where shall we start?

J How about with the salad? I think this is a good option because is very healthy with lots of vegetables, tomatoes, lettuce.

P Hmm ... In my opinion this is very healthy, but sometimes children don't like to eat salad. If they don't like it, they won't eat it. And then you could have lots of hungry children. That would be terrible!

J Well, what would you suggest?

P How about the hamburgers and chips? Kids love eating that!

J Philippe, do you really think that's a good idea? Burgers and chips have lots of fatty ... no, lots of fat.

P But it's only for one day, it's not a big problem.

J I don't know. I don't agree.

P Er ... OK.

J Let's turn to the next picture. I think this is OK, some ice cream. I mean ... if the children eat the salad first, then it's OK to have the ice cream.

P So are you suggesting that we choose this one? I think chocolate ice cream is like burgers. They are no good to eat.

J It's OK. I like ice cream. Now, what about to drink?

P I think we should give the fizzy drinks. Children love them. It'll be like a party. This is a good idea.

J I hear what you're saying, but I think this one might cause some problems.

P Oh, why?

J The children are very young. I have a little cousin and when he drinks sodas, he gets very excited ...

P Hyperactive.

J He runs around everywhere. This could be a problem if we give them fizzy drinks.

P I see. Are there any pictures that we haven't talked about yet?

J Yes. This one. The sandwiches.

P Maybe we should give them sandwiches and orange juice.

J I think maybe you're right. With the ice cream too.

P No ice cream.

Unit 10

🎧 **10.1 Listening: a ghost hunter** (page 83)

D = David

D I was very much an amateur ghost hunter. I never did it professionally or anything like that. What happened was that I was a student of Computer Science at university in Scotland. One day, when I was on vacation, my neighbour told me about a strange experience that she'd had. Apparently, she'd been staying in a bed and breakfast in the Scottish Highlands. One night when she was getting ready for bed, suddenly the room felt very cold, and all of a sudden the curtains just opened. Then they closed. But there was no one else there. Well four friends and I decided to investigate this. We stayed at the same place in the same room, and we stayed up all night. Of course, we saw nothing at all. Nevertheless, I was interested in the story, so I set up a website called *Your Weird Events*. The idea was that people could log on to the site and leave their own ghost stories there. If there were any interesting stories, we would go and investigate them. Unfortunately, we only got messages from foreign countries. And you know, we were students and we couldn't afford to go to any of them. So it all came to nothing really. And to be honest, nowadays, I don't really believe in ghosts anyway.

10.2 Speaking (page 85)

I = Interlocutor, C = Claudio

I In this part of the test I'm going to give each of you two photographs. I'd like you to talk about your photographs for about a minute. OK? Claudio, here are your photographs. They show people performing magic tricks. I want you to compare the two photographs and say which trick is the most entertaining.

C Er ... I'm sorry. Could you repeat the question please?

I Of course. Here are your photographs. They show people performing magic tricks. I want you to compare the two photographs and say which trick is the most entertaining.

10.3 Speaking (page 85)

C = Claudio

C OK. Both photos show magic tricks. In the first one we have a magician and a girl, and she is above the floor. This is called levitation, isn't it? It looks like he is on the stage in a theatre or somewhere like that. Now, in the second picture we have another magician and he's doing a card trick, and everybody looks amazed. The question is which trick is the most entertaining. Well, the first picture certainly looks entertaining, but the thing is that the magician is on stage and the audience just sits and watches. For me it's really boring. I much prefer the second picture. This is a lot more entertaining because the magician is very near and you can see what he is doing. You can try to see the 'trick'. I think that's definitely the better of the two.

Unit 11

11.1 Listening: spending money (page 90)

1 At the moment we're saving up to go on holiday. This year we really want to go to Australia and it's difficult taking the kids, because you have to buy five tickets for the flight. That's really expensive. We are staying with my husband's brother, so the accommodation is sorted. The thing is that there are so many other things I want to buy, but I can't because of this.

2 On Saturdays I work at the local pet shop. They don't pay me very much, but I do get a 20 per cent discount on everything in the shop. But I think it would be better if I didn't get the discount because I buy so many things in the shop for my dog and my cat. Some weeks I spend more there than I earn.

3 I don't normally splash out like that. But we'd all finished our exams and we wanted to celebrate in style, so we all went to this really posh restaurant in the centre of town. The food was delicious and it was great fun, but I got through my month's allowance in one night. It was the same for us all. I wish I hadn't done that.

4 We had just moved into a new house, our first home, and so we were having a housewarming party. My wife and I went to the supermarket and we put all this expensive food in the trolley: lobster, champagne, everything. Well, when we got to the check-out, it came to something like £300. So we actually went back around the shop putting things back on the shelves!

5 I saw this beautiful top in a department store and it was perfect for me, so I had to have it. It cost me a lot of money, but for media professionals there's tremendous pressure on women to look good. I don't buy expensive clothes on a whim or because I'm vain or anything. Expensive clothes are an essential purchase.

6 My husband is driving me mad. He'll go to the shops to buy bread and come back with a new set of golf clubs. He's constantly doing things like that and it's impossible! I mean, take the golf clubs: he already had a set in the garage! And another thing, he never discusses anything with me. I am very careful and I always pay off my credit card at the end of the month. I think very hard before I buy something expensive, but nothing seems to stop him.

7 My parents give me quite a lot of pocket money. In fact if I ask my dad for some money for a comic or something, he usually gives it to me. But actually I don't really buy anything except crisps and sweets. We don't get them at home and I love them, so that's where all my money goes. I'm lucky because I've got loads of uncles and aunts, and they're always buying me toys and games. So I don't have to buy those either.

8 There are so many options and I haven't made my mind up. In my last job everyone paid into a really good pension scheme, but now I have to arrange one for myself and I don't really know what to do. Some people have told me not to pay into a pension scheme and to put my money in the stock market instead, but I don't think that's very sensible.

11.4 Speaking (page 93)

C = Claudio, E = Eleni, P = Philippe, J = Julieta

C What the pictures have in common is that they show customers talking to salesmen. Some people are in the department store and the woman is in a market or a shop. Er ... Both the salesmen seem to be very friendly. In the second picture the girl is asking to try some of the spices.

E These pictures show very similar situations. One thing that is the same in the pictures is that the customers are really going to buy something. I think that in the first picture that they are going to buy a TV. Maybe they are asking about a special deal. They might want to know if the DVD player is included in the price or if the TV has a guarantee ... or something.

P We can see the same thing happening: the customers are asking questions. The girl is asking if she can taste some of the food in the sacks. In the other picture they are asking the salesman some question about the special features of the TV. In each picture the salesman looks very friendly and that's very good.

J There isn't a big difference here: we can see people thinking about buying something. They are talking to the shop assistant in one picture and a merchant in another one. The pictures show the same sort of thing. The people are trying to get a good price, I think. With the merchant sometimes you can haggle to get a good price, but sometimes you can get a special deal in department stores too. They look different, but they are very similar really.

Unit 12

12.1 **Listening: San Francisco earthquake** (page 98)

P = Presenter, D = Denise

P On April 18 1906 San Francisco was devastated by an earthquake that destroyed almost 30,000 buildings and left 3,000 people dead. Denise Wei is here today to talk about the legacy of that event. Denise, what happened after the earthquake hit?

D The problem was that before this earthquake, people didn't know anything about the San Andreas Fault: that's the line along California where earthquakes can take place. It was this earthquake that revealed that the Fault existed and so when the earthquake struck, the city of San Francisco wasn't very prepared at all.

P Was the centenary of the event marked in any way? What did people do to remember what happened?

D Lots of things. Firstly, they built a memorial to the earthquake victims and there was an exhibition of what happened. There were some other more unusual events too.

P Such as?

D The artist Liz Hickok made a model of the city out of jello. She lit the sculpture from underneath and even made videos of parts of the city shaking to represent what might happen in an earthquake.

P And can we still see this sculpture?

D Unfortunately, you can't see it any more. They disposed of it after it started to go mouldy. You couldn't even eat it.

P Extraordinary. Now, returning to more serious matters. San Francisco was hit by another earthquake a few years ago, wasn't it?

D That's right. On 17 October 1986 an earthquake measuring 6.9 on the Richter scale hit San Francisco. That's a very large quake and in the end some 63 people lost their lives.

P But 3,000 people died in 1906. Why were the casualties so few in 1986?

D Because people knew the city was in danger from earthquakes, buildings and roads were built to survive an incident like this. Having said that, people were still surprised by how much damage there was. Many roads and bridges collapsed, and they were built to survive. But the main reason why there were so few casualties was the San Francisco Giants baseball team were playing a big match in the baseball World Series and lots of people had left work early to watch the game.

P Thank goodness for that. So two earthquakes have hit San Francisco. Are people worried about the future?

D In a word, yes. People in California talk about the Big One, a huge earthquake that might hit in the future with enormous damage.

P How probable is that?

D Seismologists estimate that in the next 25 years there is a 60 per cent chance of San Francisco being hit by an earthquake greater than 6.7 on the Richter Scale.

P That is terrifying!

12.4 **Speaking** (page 101)

1 *C = Claudio, E = Eleni*

C I don't think this is a good idea at all.

E Why not?

C If people want to give money for charity, then they can just give you the money. I don't see why you should run a marathon in …

E He's in fancy dress, isn't he?

C That's right, in fancy dress. This doesn't work for me.

2 *P = Philippe, J = Julieta*

P What about this picture, Julieta? We do this a lot in my country.

J Really? I don't see the point of doing this. The thing is, OK, lots of people will sign up and they say they agree with you. But governments get this kind of thing all the time and when it arrives, they just file it somewhere or they throw it away. This is not an effective solution to the problem.

3 *C = Claudio, E = Eleni*

C How about the market stall?

E In this case I don't think this is the best option.

C Why not?

E Well, to have something to sell, you need to make something to sell. That takes a lot of time and also you don't know if people will buy your products. I don't think it's a bad idea, but I think some of the other ones are better.

4 *J = Julieta, P = Philippe*

J Does this really work? I'm not sure.

P What's the problem?

J If you do a show like this, you have to hope that people will come. What if nobody comes to the event? That would be a disaster.

P OK, I see your point.

Unit 13

13.1 **Listening: a journalist** (page 106)

P = Presenter, L = Linda

P Linda, did you always want to be a journalist?

L No! When I was little, I wanted to be Britain's first female prime minister. But Margaret Thatcher beat me to that. I don't think I would have been a very good leader anyway. But I was always interested in politics and news. And I think when I was fifteen, I decided I would be a journalist.

P How did you get your big break?

L At university I was the editor of the college newspaper and I wrote some of the stories too. At the end of my degree, I wrote to my local newspaper and asked them for some work experience. They took me on for six months.

P Did you get paid for that?

L I got paid nothing. I did it to learn about the job and it was hard work. It was very different after being the boss on the student paper to being the office junior.

P Did you enjoy it?

L I didn't enjoy my first week at all. My first job was typing editorials: my boss dictated them to me and I remember I spelt the town name Sherborne incorrectly. My boss really shouted at me for that mistake, and I wasn't being paid anything!

P How do you spell Sherborne?

L S-H-E-R-B-O-R-N-E. I remember now!

P Did you report on any stories during the work experience?

L Yes! The first story I wrote was a showbiz one. There was a famous singer living locally and I went with another reporter to interview her. He asked the questions and I just took notes. But the next day the other reporter didn't come into work because he had to go to hospital to have an emergency operation. So I wrote the story from my notes. I used that story to apply for jobs later on and that was how I got my first paid job on a music magazine.

13.3 **Speaking** (page 109)

1 *I = Interlocutor, J = Julieta*

I What do you think is the best way of getting news?

J Hmm … That's an interesting question. I have to say the radio. On TV they don't really have enough time to discuss all the complicated issues. On the radio they have a lot of time to talk and you can hear experts speak.

2 *I = Interlocutor, P = Philippe*

I Do you often read newspapers or watch the news on TV?

P I have to think about this one. I read a free newspaper if there's one in the station. And I sometimes watch the news when I'm cooking because we have a TV in the kitchen. But I don't think I'm very interested in the news.

3 *I = Interlocutor, C = Claudio*

I Is it important for people to watch the news?

C It really depends. I think if there is a big story, then it's important that the public know what's going on: if there is a weather problem or something like that. But often there isn't really any big news, so it's not necessary to find out what's going on all the time.

4 *I = Interlocutor, P = Philippe*

I What are the advantages and disadvantages of getting news over the Internet?

P I've not really thought about this before. Er ... it's a very quick way of getting information, of course, and you can get a lot of different opinions too. I think it's good as long as you use the sites from serious newspapers or news services. Otherwise you don't know who wrote the news that you're reading.

5 *I = Interlocutor, J = Julieta*

I Do you like reading about celebrities in newspapers and magazines?

J I absolutely love it. I can't get enough gossip to be honest. I think everyone really likes to read about that sort of thing. I buy two or three gossip magazines each week. I think I'm a bit addicted!

6 *I = Interlocutor, C = Claudio*

I What part of the newspaper is most interesting to you?

C Personally it's the crossword. I love doing it in my coffee break when I'm at work. Sometimes I work on it all day and I always have to buy the next day's newspaper to see what answers I didn't get.

Unit 14

🎧 14.1 **Listening: clothes and fashion** (page 113)

1 We were going on holiday to the Maldives and I bought my husband some shorts. They were dark blue, his favourite colour, and they fitted him perfectly. They weren't too trendy or anything like that, so that was OK too. The thing was there was a big flower on the back of the shorts and he wouldn't wear them because of that! Ridiculous!

2 *S = Son, F = Father*

S Where's my coat? It's raining.

F Hang on – you can't go looking like that!

S Why, what's wrong? This is my best shirt.

F But you can't wear jeans to a wedding. It looks too scruffy.

S I'm sixteen, not sixty! I can wear what I like.

F Go and change.

3 *D = Daughter, M = Mother*

D I love that dress! Can I have it?

M Oh, but it's so old-fashioned, darling. I bought it thirty years ago. The only place you can wear this is in the theatre.

D No, no it's really retro! That's cool now.

M But you've got a wardrobe full of clothes! Why would you want this?

D You can't get a tie-dye dress like that any more. Please?

M Well, OK. Here you are.

4 I'm so frustrated. I bought this shirt and it doesn't fit. I wanted to try it on, but it was in a market and there wasn't a fitting room. It

was a great price and the label said it was my size, so I bought it anyway. And now I find it's far too big for me. Next time I'm going to order online. There's a site which has some really great clothes.

5 *W = Woman*

W1 What about this necklace?

W2 Oh yes! It suits you perfectly. I'd get that if I were you.

W1 I don't know. Maybe it's a bit too trendy for me.

W2 I think it's good to have some trendy jewellery. You've got quite a lot of classical rings and bracelets already.

W1 But my new earrings?

W2 I know, but you can wear it with some other earrings. Trust me, the necklace is you. It really complements the colour of your eyes.

6 *M = Mother, S = Son*

M Stop! Don't throw that shirt away!

S But there's a hole in it, and I've had it over a year.

M It's only a small one. I can sew it up and no one will notice.

S That's a lot of trouble and it didn't really cost very much anyway.

M But I like it and stripes look good on you. Come on. Give it to me.

S Oh, all right then.

7 I used to go shopping there a lot, but I don't any more. The funny thing is that when I bought clothes there it was very pricey, but now things cost the same as anywhere else on the high street. The thing is, yes the clothes look very stylish, but they don't last. Look at this shirt. When I bought it, it had a design of a football tournament. I've washed it three times and now the design is really faint. You can't see it. I don't think that's good enough.

8 *W = Woman, M = Man*

W I shouldn't have worn these high heels – they are killing me!

M Next time choose a more comfortable costume, like me.

W I don't think I would look good dressed as a tiger. I feel much better as Marilyn, but the shoes are so uncomfortable. Oh, look at Martin!

M Ooh, that shirt really clashes with those trousers!

W To be fair, the invitation did tell us to dress adventurously!

🎧 14.2 **Speaking** (page 114)

I = Interlocutor, E = Eleni, C = Claudio

I Do you think young people spend too much money on clothes and fashion?

E I think so, yes. Some of my friends always want to go to the most expensive shops and they spend a lot of money on clothes, but there are cheaper shops. I think it's a bit ridiculous.

C But don't you think that sometimes you have to go to the expensive shops? I think that brand names are very important and clothes with brand names are only sold in department stores and expensive shops.

E But do you really need the brand name? After all, if clothes look good, the name is not important.

C What I mean is that if you want to look good, you need to buy quality clothes, designer clothes, big brands. You have to pay a lot of money for that.

E Yes, but we're speaking about young people. They don't need to spend a lot of money on designer clothes.

C I suppose not. But if your friends have the best clothes, you want them too.

E So their parents have to spend money on these clothes.

C Not necessarily. Many of my friends have jobs, and they study and work. So they can buy their own clothes.

E All the same, I think there are better things to spend your money on when you're young.

C Such as?

E Er ... DVDs, music, going out.

C This is the same as buying clothes. When you are young, you spend money on enjoying yourself! Buying clothes is fun.

E I suppose so. But I still think they spend too much money on clothes.

I Thank you.

Unit 15

🎧 15.1 **Listening: works of art** (page 122)

1 When I was living in Cairo, I used to see the statue of the pharaoh Ramses II all the time. It's a wonderful statue and very impressive, and it was one of my favourite things in the city. It shows the pharaoh standing with a large beard and it's made from grey stone. Unfortunately, it's not there any more. The problem was that it was being damaged by pollution and so about twelve months ago, it was taken to Giza, which is one of Egypt's major archaeological sites. Basically, the experts think that it will be easier to preserve there.

2 Surprisingly, most of the tourists who come to London don't know it's there. It's ridiculous really because there are very few sculptures by Michelangelo. Actually, there is only one Michelangelo sculpture in the UK and that is a round sculpture of the Madonna and Child which is in a gallery, the Royal Academy, in London. It's not easy to find even when you're in the museum, however. So you might need to ask someone where it is. I think that it's a wonderful work of art. I often go and look at it when I'm in town.

3 In our local museum at Delphi we have a famous statue of a charioteer, which we call *Iníochos* in Greek. It's about 2,500 years old, made of bronze and it's a wonderfully lifelike portrait. Amazingly, it still has the original glass eyes that bronze statues used to have and it seems to be looking into the distance. Its left arm is broken, which is a pity. Nevertheless, it's a miracle that the sculpture survives at all. Some archaeologists found it buried in Delphi about 100 years ago and it's thought that it's by the great sculptor Pythagoras of Rego.

4 If you go to the north of England, just outside of the city of Gateshead, you can see The Angel of the North. This is a giant statue of a man, as tall as four buses. The man's arms are actually wings, and they are huge: as long as a Boeing 767. I love it and I often drive over there to look at it. Anyway, it's by Antony Gormley, who is one of Britain's most important living artists, and he modelled it on himself – except for the wings of course.

5 It's a lovely picture that my niece did of a landscape, showing some black and white cows in a green field. The sky is very blue and the whole picture is lovely to look at. She's only eight, but I think that this is great. You know, interestingly, Picasso liked children's art. He said, 'At twelve years old I could draw like Raphael, but I needed a whole lifetime to learn to paint like a child.' When I look at this picture, I know exactly what he means.

🎧 15.3 **Speaking** (page 125)

1 *J = Julieta*

J Well, let me see. Here we can see some people in an art gallery. In the foreground a girl is looking at some abstract art, I think it is, and er ... in the background a man is looking at some very small pictures. I can't see what they are ... photos perhaps? The other picture shows a street festival of some kind. It looks like a procession and the person is dressed in fancy dress. Well, I think intellectual people like art galleries and it is a good place to go if you are a quiet person and you like to think a lot. Regarding the second picture, I think perhaps this is more for party people, people who like to have a good time. But everyone likes going to an art gallery sometimes and I think most people enjoy parties too.

2 *P = Philippe*

P OK. The second photo shows some people in a procession. They are waving signs and maybe there is dancing and noise. They are celebrating something, while in the other photo the people are looking at ... art. They are in a gallery or a museum. I don't think these two people know each other, actually. So both photos show people doing something in their free time. I think being in a place like this, a gallery, is quite boring. I wouldn't enjoy it. But going back to the other picture, I think this looks like a lot of fun. There is a large crowd in the background and people are having a good time, so I think it would be good for me too. I like to go out and do things.

Unit 16

🎧 16.2 **Listening: self-build** (page 130)

I = Interviewer, A = Amanda

I Today we're going to talk to a woman who built her own home: Amanda Boyd.

A Good morning.

I First question. What exactly is self-build?

A Instead of buying an existing house, you start from scratch and build your own home. This doesn't mean that you actually put all the bricks and mortar together yourself. You can employ builders and architects to construct the house.

I So why did you decide to do it?

A Two reasons. Firstly, I inherited a lot of money from my aunt, so there was no need for a mortgage. Secondly, I was living in a terraced house in London, which was nice, but I wanted to live somewhere else in the country with a lawn and a drive and all those other things. There didn't seem to be anywhere like that on the market, so I decided to build my own.

I What was the most difficult thing?

A As I say, I had the finance. Designing the house and building it was easy because a company did all of that for me. The main thing was finding the land. Lots of people are self-building and a lot of the best land has already been bought. There was nowhere to put my house! It took a long time to find a place.

I Was it very expensive?

A Actually, it doesn't cost as much as buying a house because when you self-build, you just pay for the land, the materials and the work.

I I see. Where did you live while your house was being built?

A I stayed in my old place because I didn't need to sell it. Other people who self-build stay with relatives. One couple lived for six months in a caravan on a campsite!

I Amazing. Now, do you have any other hints for people out there?

A Yes. In the UK we have planning permission. This means that before you build something, you need to get approval of your architect's plans from the council, the local government. Many people when they start a self-build want to build a very exotic or modern house: lots of glass, something like that. But the local government often refuse plans like that because the house will stand out too much from the others in the local area. You have to be sensible.

I Amanda, thank you for talking to us.

A My pleasure.

Practice Test

PT.1 **Part 1** (page 148)

1 Well, it isn't like I don't earn enough – I get by. And I have to say the salary is quite competitive. But that's not always enough, is it? The job just isn't exciting any more! I went to an agency who found me another job which sounded really good: the money is even better and the position is the same as the one I have now. But then I thought, what if I take that job and I feel the same again six months down the line? So I said to myself, it's time to find something completely different.

2 We've had our tree house for years now. The kids have never grown out of it even if they've grown too big for it! Of course, I wasn't keen at all at first. The kids asked for one every time they saw them at the local garden centre, but it just seemed a bit dangerous to me. However, the neighbours were moving abroad and they couldn't take theirs with them. They offered it to us and I thought, well, why not? It was certainly cheaper than buying one from a shop!

3 Honestly, that's the last time I go there. It's like pulling teeth getting those people to do their job properly! First, they made me wait for three hours and then they charged me forty pounds to change one wire. Can you believe that? It's not a classic car, it's only an old runabout!

4 Yes, you're right. It's by far the best way because you can take as much stuff as you can fit in, and you can leave and arrive when you like. Flying would definitely be quicker and cheaper if you were going on your own. But as there are two of you, it would work out pretty expensive. There's the ferry, of course. That takes six hours, so you might make it in time – but it would be touch and go. I'd be a bit worried about being at the wheel for so many hours, but I suppose you can take it in turns.

5 M = Man, W = Woman

M We don't need to buy everything this minute. For a start, the carpets aren't being delivered for another month, so we won't need a vacuum cleaner for a while.

W Yes, I know, but we could get the washing machine and the fridge. Oh, look! What about this one?

M That's far too big! There's just the two of us and we don't buy a lot of food. I think we should go for the smaller model.

W OK, and I suppose we can continue using the washing machine at the launderette until we can afford to buy a really good one.

6 Local residents will be sad to hear that the Royal Cinema, which hasn't operated for years, will be pulled down next month. Of course, the cinema hadn't been making money, and young people, especially, preferred the popular new cinema complexes with their wide screens, Dolby Sound, and what have you. But it was hoped that the building could be converted into an arts centre. Unfortunately, there are problems with the building's structure and experts say that it has become a threat to safety.

7 Hi! I'm really sorry. I hope I didn't keep you waiting long. I forgot to take my phone with me and so I couldn't call you to let you know. The bus was a little late and then there was a huge car crash right in front of us – the bus just missed it by centimetres. So then the bus driver had to get out and give a statement to the police when they turned up and we were all …

8 Well, I was petrified from start to finish! I'd agreed to jump out of a plane for charity. I thought that once I was up there, I would be fine. But when they opened the plane door, I froze – the thought of having to jump out was too much. Once everyone had taken the plunge, the plane landed … with me still in it. Back on the ground,

everyone was thrilled. But I just felt humiliated. I paid the money to the charity, of course, but never again!

PT.2 **Part 2** (page 149)

I = Interviewer, B = Bob

I Now, if you're fed up with city life and want to get back to nature, we might have just the thing for you. This morning we join Bob Sanders from the Penfold Horse and Pony Sanctuary. Bob, welcome.

B Thank you. Nice to be here!

I So Bob, first of all, why don't you tell us exactly what it is that you do at the sanctuary?

B Well, Penfold Sanctuary looks after unfortunate horses, ponies and donkeys. They come to us for different reasons – some have been treated badly, some are too old to work and have been discarded by their owners. We even have a couple with emotional problems! At any given time, we have around fifty animals staying with us on our farm.

I That's fantastic! Now, you have some news to share with our listeners.

B That's right. Well, as you can imagine, looking after so many animals takes a lot of time and a lot of money. Horses are very friendly, sociable animals and it's a pity we don't have more full-time employees. Then we could give them the attention they really need. But we think that members of the public could help. This summer we want to give young city dwellers the chance to come and get to know our friends on the farm and lend a hand.

I That sounds like a fun opportunity. How does that work?

B We have a number of horses and ponies that are in need of a bit of care and company, and we want to choose twenty teenage volunteer 'buddies' to pair up with each of the animals and spend some time with us during the summer holidays.

I And what kind of things will the buddies get to do?

B Anything that takes their fancy really. All the horses need care, and so their buddies would undertake to feed and exercise them, as well as clean out the stables. They would also have the opportunity to learn how to ride if they don't already know how. This would also enable them to exercise the horses and ponies in the best possible way, of course.

I That's great! But the sanctuary is quite a trek from the city centre. How will the buddies 'get to work', so to speak?

B We have a large minibus, which will pick them up outside the Town Hall every day at 8am.

I Wow! It's tough getting up that early, especially during the summer break!

B Yes, we realise that, but there's a good reason for it. You see, we're hoping that one or two of the buddies might be interested in joining us as full-time animal carers when they've finished school. It's important that buddies have the dedication to get up early every morning and be there to catch that bus!

I Well, listeners, anyone out there who's interested in animal care as a career should really go for this. It's a wonderful opportunity. Bob, how can someone who is interested in this project apply to be a 'buddy'?

B Well, we're guessing that this might be quite a popular thing and as we only have a few places, we'd like applicants to send us a short composition saying why they'd like to work at the farm with us this summer. Five hundred words should do it.

I Is there anything else?

B Yes, all applicants should be fourteen to sixteen years old, so along with your composition, you'll need to send proof of your age. This can be in the form of a photocopy of your passport or birth certificate. You should also send us a consent letter from your parent or guardian stating that he or she agrees to your work experience at Penfold Farm.

I That's great, Bob. Thank you very much. I hope you'll come back in September and let us know how it all went.

B I most certainly will. And thank you very much for allowing me to come on the show today.

I Now, listeners, grab a pen and paper, because coming right up is the address …

🎧 PT.3 **Part 3** (page 150)

1 Gerry's always been a really good friend – he's always been there for me, which makes the whole thing worse, really. He was quite upset when I told him I wasn't coming on the trip. We'd been planning it for months and we even paid a deposit for the accommodation, but what was I supposed to do? I can't get time off work, so it isn't my fault! I did try to explain.

2 I've never really been very trendy. At school I would always copy the other kids, not because I wanted to fit in so much but because I really didn't have a style of my own. Nothing's changed much there! Now Hannah on the other hand, she's a different story. She always looks so great – I don't know how she does it. I don't think I've ever seen her wearing something that looked wrong or didn't suit her. If I had her fashion sense, I'd be thrilled!

3 We've hung around as a group since were small kids. It's always been the six of us. Of course, other friends have come and gone, but us lot have always stuck together. I don't know why it's like that, it just is. Actually, come to think of it, it seems a bit daft because we've all grown up now – and grown apart in so many ways. In fact, there's one person in the group that I'm not even that keen on any more. But I guess it's hard to break years of habit.

4 I hadn't seen Jessica for years, not since school. We'd promised to keep in touch when we went to college, but then I moved away and we just drifted apart. When I heard there was going to be a school reunion, I couldn't wait! I was so excited at the thought of seeing her again! We chatted about the reunion by email and arranged to meet beforehand for a coffee, so when she didn't turn up, I was devastated. I just don't understand why she didn't turn up.

5 Pete moved to Australia, now let's see … it must be five years ago now. Wow! Doesn't time fly! We were best buddies and I guess we still are in a way. I'd love to go and visit him, but it's Australia – it's just so far away and so expensive. Then there's work: it's so hard to take off enough time for a long trip like that. Sure, we keep in touch. Things are much easier nowadays with instant messaging and webcams, but it's not the same as seeing each other face to face, is it?

🎧 PT.4 **Part 4** (page 151)

I = Interviewer, T = Tessa

I November is an exciting month for art lovers, with plenty to see, especially in the city's smaller galleries. Today on *Culture Corner*, I'm pleased to welcome gallery owner: Tessa Hartley. Tessa, first of all, your gallery has an interesting name: Galimoto. For the benefit of our listeners, that's spelt G–A–L–I–M–O–T–O. Does the name mean anything?

T Yes, it does. It means 'car' in Chichewa – that's a language spoken in south central Africa. But it also refers to a type of toy.

I How come you named your art gallery after a toy?

T Well, some years ago, my husband went to southern Africa on business, and I was lucky enough to be able to go with him. It was my first time in Africa, and we were there for several months. I loved it there! The way people face life is fantastic. In spite of being poor, they are so kind and cheerful, and I couldn't believe how inventive the children are! You see, most people are too poor to buy toys, so kids make their own out of the things others throw away: wire, tin cans, bits of rubber, things like that. But you mustn't imagine these toys are simple. They're lovely – made with such care and love for detail. I once watched a child making a bicycle using wire. The bicycle had a rider, also of wire. The child attached a long stick to the toy, and when he pushed the bicycle with the stick, the wheels actually turned. Even more amazing, the pedals went up and down. And I thought: these aren't just toys, they're works of art! That's when I got the idea of opening a gallery devoted to children's toys.

I I must say, Tessa, it sounds great! Where do the toys in your gallery come from? Africa?

T There are toys from Malawi, Zimbabwe and South Africa, but other African countries are represented too. And next year we have plans to travel to South America; we hope we'll discover some wonderful young artists there as well. Because, I must stress this, I firmly believe that these toys are works of art. That's why they are exhibited with the artist's photo, name, age and a note of where they're from. We think it's very important for people to know who made each object.

I I see that a number of events will be held at the gallery this month. Can you tell us a little about them?

T Well, three young artists whose work is on sale will be demonstrating their skills at the gallery every weekend from 2pm to 4pm, so children will have the chance to see how these toys are made. There will also be daily morning workshops where children can make toys themselves out of wire. We're sure these events will be very popular, and many schools have expressed an interest, so we advise people to book in advance.

I I'm sure many adults would like to take part as well!

T Yes, we think so too, and at the moment we're also involved in making a one-hour documentary showing how children in southern Africa make toys. It includes interviews with these children: we learn about their daily lives, how they learnt their skills, and what they'd like to do when they grow up. The documentary will be broadcast on television later this year. If you miss it, you can order the DVD from our gallery's website.

I Tessa, time for one more question. What makes these African kids so creative?

T Well, that's a difficult question. Actually, I believe kids everywhere are creative, but in richer countries they don't know the joy that comes from making things themselves. I mean, why make a toy when your bedroom is already full of toys from a shop?

I Well, Tessa, thank you for being with us today. And now listeners, if you would like more details …

Answer key

Unit 1

Reading

1 1 C 2 B 3 A 4 C 5 D 6 B
   7 C 8 A 9 D 10 B
2 1 expecting 4 thrilled 7 Practically
   2 dilemma 5 overseas 8 grow up
   3 heritage 6 bullying

Vocabulary

1

	¹f	i	a	n	²c	e		
					o			
³r		⁴s	p	o	u	s	⁵e	
e		i			s		x	
l		b			i		t	
a		l			n		e	
⁶t	w	i	n	s		⁷i	n	l a w
i		n				n		
v		g				e		
e		s				d		
s								

2 1 d 2 c 3 b 4 a
3 1 b 2 f 3 e 4 a 5 d 6 c

Grammar

1 1 are growing up 5 Do you usually send
   2 eats 6 she is playing
   3 is changing 7 are getting
   4 speaks
2 1 owns (*state verb*)
   2 are thinking (*active verb*)
   3 doesn't believe (*state verb*)
   4 is having (*active verb*)
   5 like (*state verb*)
   6 tastes (*state verb*)
3 1 She has written five letters.
   2 She has been jogging.
   3 She has been cleaning the house.
   4 She has broken a plate.
   5 She has made a cake.
   6 She has been working on the computer.

Spelling

1 1 periodically 3 logically 5 genetically
   2 Tragically 4 Economically 6 sympathetically

Listening

1 1 C 2 B 3 B 4 A 5 C
   6 B 7 A 8 C

Use of English

1 1 fitness 5 membership 9 length
   2 cultural 6 eventually 10 strength
   3 professional 7 restlessness
   4 sponsorship 8 personal
2 1 which *or* that 6 of 11 so
   2 have 7 is 12 a
   3 Her 8 their 13 When
   4 at 9 for 14 in
   5 because 10 well 15 with

Writing

1 1, 3, 4, 6, 8
2 (Possible answers)
   Paragraph 1 Your general impressions of the trip.
   Paragraph 2 A description of interesting locations that you went to. A description of your trip to the capital city.
   Paragraph 3 What your accommodation was like. A description of some food.
3 1 g 2 e 3 a 4 c 5 b 6 f
   7 d   f is a compliment

Speaking

1 1 Julieta says that she lives with her parents.
   2 Julieta says she comes from a normal family: four people (Julieta, her parents and her sister). Philippe says he comes from a small family. He doesn't have any brothers and sisters.
   3 Philippe's father is a teacher and his mother is a doctor.
2 1 There are four of us in my family.
   2 I have one older sister, Ana, who is twenty-four.
   3 I don't have any brothers and sisters.
   4 My father is a teacher and my mother works as a doctor.

Pronunciation

2 Question 3 has a different pronunciation. The intonation falls at the end of the question because this is a question made without a question word. Questions made with a question word (*who, which, why, when*, etc.) have a rising intonation.
3 1 rises 4 falls 7 falls
   2 falls 5 rises
   3 rises 6 rises

Unit 2

Reading

1 1 C 2 D 3 A 4 B 5 A 6 B
   7 D 8 C 9 A 10 D 11 B 12 C
   13 A 14 D 15 C
2 1 e 2 d 3 b 4 g 5 c 6 h
   7 a 8 f

Vocabulary

1

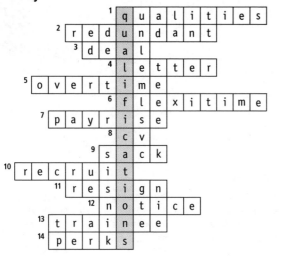

```
                    1 q u a l i t i e s
              2 r e d u n d a n t
                 3 d e a l
                        4 l e t t e r
        5 o v e r t i m e
                        6 f l e x i t i m e
            7 p a y r i s e
                        8 c v
                 9 s a c k
    10 r e c r u i t
              11 r e s i g n
                    12 n o t i c e
              13 t r a i n e e
              14 p e r k s
```

2 1 e   2 a   3 c   4 f   5 d   6 b
3 a 1, 6   b 2   c 4, 5   d 3

Spelling

1 1 illustrator   4 translator   7 ski instructor
    2 sailor   5 decorator   8 doctor
    3 director   6 editor

Grammar

1 1 The harder you work, the **quicker** you get promotion.
    2 I don't think my new job is as interesting **as** my old one.
    3 *correct*
    4 We're **busier** this year than last year.
    5 London is the **most** expensive city in Europe.
    6 *correct*
    7 Working as a manager is **more difficult** than working as a secretary.

2 1 You need to go on a training course to learn how to use the new program. It's a **bit** more complicated than the software we were using before.
    2 The new office is as good **as** the old one.
    3 I have to do **a** lot more overtime in my new job than in my old one.
    4 My job is **far** too easy. I want a job with more responsibility.
    5 The job in Berlin pays €30,000 and the one in Madrid pays €29,000. So the money is **almost** the same.
    6 My new project is easy. It isn't anything **like** the project that I've just finished. That one was a nightmare!
    7 I don't think working as a journalist is **any** more difficult than working as an editor.

Listening

1 1 A   2 B   3 A   4 C
    5 A   6 C   7 B   8 A

Pronunciation

2 underline = stress, *italics* = schwa
    org*ani*s*a*tion
    *po*ss*e*ssions
    inter*na*tional
    in*for*mation

qualifi*ca*tion
*po*werful
*cer*ti*fi*cate
com*pu*ter

3 The word in *italics* is pronounced with the schwa in the b sentences.

4 1 the first example of *to*
    2 have
    3 the second example of *you*
    4 a

Use of English

1 1 a assessment
        b improvement
    2 a application
        b communication
    3 a successful
        b doubtful
    4 a reference
        b existence
    5 a ability
        b similarity

2 1 A   2 D   3 D   4 A   5 A   6 C
    7 C   8 D   9 A   10 D   11 B   12 D

Writing

1 1 B   2 A   3 B   4 C   5 A   6 C
2 a 2   b 5   c 1   d 3   e 4   f 6

Speaking

2 They forget to talk about the job delivering pizzas.
3 1 start   3 so   5 think
    2 it   4 compare 6 for

Unit 3

Reading

1 1 H   2 B   3 E   4 A
    5 G   6 C   7 F
2 1 demanding   5 bulk up   9 sacred
    2 talisman   6 stew   10 trace back
    3 bout   7 soles
    4 one-sided   8 grip

Vocabulary

1 1 golf   3 darts   5 chess
    2 sailing   4 wrestling 6 croquet
2 1 archery   6 tennis
    2 volleyball   7 badminton
    3 synchronised swimming   8 tenpin bowling
    4 table tennis   9 snowboarding
    5 American football   10 karate (*also* judo)
3 1 I like **board** games like chess and backgammon.
    2 *correct*
    3 We played tennis on a grass **court.** It was really different to playing on clay.
    4 We played golf yesterday and Sarah **beat** me!
    5 Zinedine Zidane used to play **for** Juventus and Real Madrid.
    6 *correct*
    7 We played a game of football at our local stadium, but the **pitch** was terrible.
    8 I think darts is my favourite **game.**

Grammar

1 1 c   2 f   3 b   4 e   5 a   6 d

2
1. Laura **could** ride a bike when she was five: she learned really quickly.
2. When we got to the slopes, we discovered that we needn't **have** brought our skis.
3. You **don't** need to buy bowling shoes. You can rent them at the bowling alley.
4. You **are** supposed to wear special shoes when you play golf.
5. I wasn't able **to** beat Suzanne at tennis.
6. You had **better** start training if you want to run the marathon in July.
7. Andy **wasn't** able to save the goal.

Spelling

1

a	d	e	l	i	g	h	t	f	u	l	l	c
g	k	r	o	d	k	t	l	h	p	w	f	o
o	e	t	e	u	p	m	v	o	a	g	o	l
l	x	w	a	a	w	a	e	p	f	y	r	o
b	w	c	m	o	d	i	w	e	i	j	g	u
e	g	o	n	h	z	f	b	f	b	b	e	r
a	r	e	n	c	t	u	u	u	u	e	t	f
u	a	i	f	d	v	b	n	l	h	l	f	u
t	t	y	a	o	e	v	e	n	t	f	u	l
i	e	w	s	s	r	r	p	a	n	r	l	x
f	f	p	o	w	e	r	f	u	l	l	l	a
u	u	o	z	r	e	u	j	u	b	y	d	n
l	l	g	r	a	c	e	f	u	l	l	m	r

Listening

1 a 1, 2   b 3, 4, 6, 7   c 10   d 5, 8, 9

2
1. two
2. three
3. court
4. Brazil
5. warm up
6. the States / USA
7. beach
8. photographs
9. the Olympic Games
10. competitive

Pronunciation

1 a 5   b 3   c 6   d 2   e 4   f 1

4 bending, best, van, bars, vote, buyer, very

Use of English

1
1. mustn't go / must not go
2. is good at
3. weren't able to / were not able to
4. from time to time
5. had better tell
6. aren't supposed to / are not supposed to *or* 're not supposed to
7. don't have to / do not have to
8. keeps beating

2
1. contestants
2. inhabitants
3. intelligence
4. correspondence
5. entrants *or* entries
6. patience
7. difficulty
8. expensive
9. impressive
10. competitive

Writing

1
1. excited
2. exciting
3. amazing
4. amazed
5. boring
6. bored
7. disappointing
8. disappointed

Speaking

1 Julieta (candidate 1)

2
1. whereas
2. Although
3. show
4. type
5. looks

Pronunciation

1 /ɑːʒ/: camouflage, collage, espionage, garage (*US English*), massage
/eɪdʒ/: cage, enrage, stage
/ɪdʒ/: cottage, courage, damage, encourage, garage (*UK English*), heritage, image, manage, message, village

Unit 4

Reading

1
1 D   2 B   3 C   4 A   5 D   6 B
7 C   8 B   9 A   10 D   11 A   12 D
13 A   14 B   15 C

2
1 e   2 g   3 a   4 c   5 f   6 j
7 h   8 b   9 d   10 i

Vocabulary

1
1. wild
2. tame
3. breed
4. instinct
5. endangered
6. pet
7. prey
8. train
9. habitat
10. extinction

2
1 of   2 to   3 on   4 with
5 in   6 for   7 of

Spelling

1
1 a   2 c   3 b   4 a   5 b   6 c
7 a   8 b   9 a   10 c   11 b   12 c

Grammar

1
1. Mark and Steve **get on well** together. They are great friends.
2. I was so poor that I **lived off rice**. It was all I ate.
3. Some journalists have revealed that big business is destroying wild animal habitats in Africa. I wonder how they **found it out.**
4. *correct*
5. I have some complicated instructions that I want you to **carry out.**
6. You shouldn't **look down on** environmental activists. They are trying to help all of us.
7. *correct*
8. One of the most exciting things about Indonesia is that explorers are **coming across new species** all the time.

2
1 a   2 much *or* any   3 any   4 Few   5 Hardly   6 number   7 little   8 Each *or* Every

Use of English

1
1 C   2 C   3 A   4 D   5 A   6 C
7 B   8 D   9 A   10 C   11 B   12 D

Writing

1 You must say whether you enjoyed your trip to the rescue centre. You need to say whether the trip is suitable for young children (there is a play park, but seeing the injured birds might upset children). You need to suggest somewhere to stay (a local bed and breakfast).

2
1 d   2 b   3 g   4 c
5 a   6 h   7 e   8 f

Listening

1 1 B   2 D   3 A   4 F   5 C

Pronunciation

1 1 grew up is linked with /w/ and larger and larger is linked with /r/
   2 see a is linked with /j/

2 1 /r/   3 /w/   5 /j/
   2 /w/   4 /j/   6 /r/

3 Sentences 1, 3, and 5 make the linking sound from a letter which is already in one of the words. Sentences 2, 4, and 6 add a linking sound.

4 1 too old /w/, for a /r/, two-hour /w/
   2 there another /r/, way of /j/
   3 tea and /j/, Tina and /r/

Use of English

1 1 terrifying   5 successful   9 nervous
   2 breathe   6 mysterious   10 attacker
   3 imagination   7 majority
   4 harmless   8 extremely

Speaking

1 a, b, c, d, f, i

Pronunciation

1 1 white   3 rail   5 ring
   2 right *or* write   4 wail *or* whale   6 wing

2 1 a   2 a   3 b   4 b

Unit 5

Reading

1 1 B   2 D   3 D   4 A   5 B   6 C
   7 B   8 D

Vocabulary

1

1 c l a s s i c
2 c h a p t e r
3 v i l l a i n
4 h e r o i n e
5 n a r r a t o r
6 f i c t i o n
7 p l o t
8 s e r i e s
9 s c e n e r y

2 1 mortified   4 furious   7 delighted
   2 ridiculous   5 devastated
   3 terrified   6 exhausted

3 1 slurp   3 glared   5 gasping   7 strolled
   2 limping   4 giggling   6 sipped   8 sighs

Grammar

1 1 f   2 a   3 e   4 c   5 b   6 d

2 1 it had disappeared
   2 the audience were clapping for ten minutes
   3 had been writing all night
   4 I was working in the garden
   5 I was reading a novel
   6 it had been stolen

Spelling

1 1 furious   5 vicious   9 unconscious
   2 gorgeous   6 nervous   10 religious
   3 *correct*   7 *correct*   11 *correct*
   4 curious   8 victorious   12 delicious

Listening

1 1 C   2 A   3 A   4 C
   5 B   6 A   7 B

Pronunciation

2 Words with stress on the second syllable from the end: appearances, appropriate, embarrassment, enthusiasm, experienced, mysterious, necessarily, personality, professional, retirement
Exceptions: centimetre, characteristic, disappearance, disappointment, realistic, sympathetic

3 The stress in the adjectives that end -ic is on the penultimate syllable (one from the end).

4 When a word ends in -ion, the stress is on the penultimate syllable (one from the end).

Use of English

1 1 in   5 the   9 not *or* never
   2 by   6 who   10 whose
   3 fact   7 had   11 more
   4 it   8 down *or* along   12 as

2 1 C   2 D   3 C   4 B   5 A   6 A
   7 D   8 C   9 B   10 B   11 D   12 A

Writing

1 1 Yes.
   2 No.
   3 No. The story does not include the sentence 'I suddenly realised that I was lost.'
   4 Yes.
   5 Yes.

2 (Possible answer)
The text below shows a possible answer using the past continuous and past perfect. The correct punctuation has been used for thinking and direct speech. The eight misspelt words have been corrected and appear in bold. The text now also includes the sentence 'I suddenly realised that I was lost'.

Bus 149
Five years ago I was studying in Finland. One night I went out with some friends and I went to get the last bus home to the **village** where I lived, Kivenlahti. My friends all lived in Helsinki so I was alone, waiting for bus 149.
   Strangely, there were two buses that night with the number 149. My usual bus was 149X but lots of people had **already** got on that one. The other bus was empty so I thought "It'll be much more **comfortable** on a bus with nobody on it" and I got on the 149Y.
   I was tired and **fell** asleep. Eventually I felt a hand on my shoulder. The bus driver was waking me up. He said something **which** I didn't understand. I could only say "149 Kivenlahti?" But the driver said "No, 149X is Kivenlahti." I looked around in **panic**. I had got on the wrong bus and we were in a dark forest covered in snow. I suddenly realised that I was lost.
   The driver told me not to worry and then, in the **middle** of the night, he drove me home!

Speaking

1 They choose to invite famous authors to speak to schools and to have a national competition with prizes for the best book review.

2
1 But there are options which appeal **to** different people.
2 I **can't** stand reading in the classroom.
3 It's not **an** obvious choice, is it?
4 **Something** that would appeal to me is to invite famous authors to schools.
5 **Personally**, I think this is difficult because it is expensive for the government
6 Yes, **I quite** agree.

3 1 d 2 f 3 b 4 a 5 c 6 e

Unit 6

Reading

1
1 B 2 C 3 D 4 A 5 D 6 C
7 B 8 A 9 C 10 D 11 A 12 D
13 B 14 C 15 B

2
1 a number of
2 all to yourself
3 The highlight
4 a treat
5 Eventually
6 even so
7 like something out of
8 nothing short of
9 nowhere more so
10 even by its standards

Vocabulary

1
1 *correct*
2 What time are you **checking in to** your hotel?
3 We can **show you around** the city and the old town this afternoon.
4 When we get to Vilnius, we're **meeting up with** some friends.
5 *correct*
6 We're **setting off** at 5pm. That's when we're leaving.
7 We were waiting for Rachel and Robert all afternoon, but they never **turned up**.
8 The match is **kicking off** in five minutes!

2 1 off 2 up 3 off 4 back 5 up 6 back

Grammar

1 1 d 2 c 3 f 4 a 5 b 6 e

2
1 due
2 to receive
3 I'll just answer
4 Shall
5 will have gone
6 is driving
7 be flying ... be going

Spelling

1

British English	American English
-our, e.g. *rumour*	-or, e.g. *rumor*
-ise, e.g. *realise*	-ize, e.g. *realize*
-re, e.g. *centre*	-er, e.g. *center*
-ogue, e.g. *catalogue*	-og, e.g. *catalog*

Note that -ize is becoming increasingly common in British English.

2 British

3
2 American English
3 British English
4 American English
5 American English
6 British English
7 British English
8 American English
9 American English
10 British English
11 American English
12 British English
13 British English
14 British English
15 American English

Listening

1
1 B 2 A 3 C 4 B
5 B 6 C 7 A 8 C

Pronunciation

1
1 /dʒ/ 3 /j/ 5 /tʃ/
2 /tʃ/ 4 /dʒ/ 6 /j/

3 church, you'll, gin, yet, general, use, chair, jaw

Use of English

1
1 what 5 be 9 of
2 is 6 during 10 If
3 from 7 addition 11 Take
4 by 8 have 12 could *or* can

2
1 would rather go
2 time we bought *or* time to buy
3 had better book
4 could always go
5 the first time (that)
6 does it take *or* will it take
7 as soon as I get
8 if we didn't eat / if we did not eat

Writing

1
1 You are writing a report on the transport system of your home town.
2 To discuss how to get to your home town from the nearest airport and how to travel around.
3 A language school / Other foreign students.

2
The following report outlines
It aims to
One suggestion when travelling by metro is to write down
Alternatively
Another possibility is
On the one hand
on the other
To sum up

Speaking

2
1 together 4 decide 7 worry
2 listen 5 each 8 hear
3 imagine 6 way

3 They choose the speedboat.

4
1 If we chose the plane, we **would** have to build a ... somewhere where it could land.
2 But if we **delivered** the post by plane or helicopter, we would need to have a pilot.
3 Well, a pilot is bound **to want** more money than a postman.
4 If money is a problem, we could **always** deliver the post by bike.
5 We **had better** make up our minds.
6 I think it **would** be very exciting to deliver the post by speedboat
7 If we used the truck, it wouldn't **be able to** deliver the post to the island village.

Unit 7

Reading

1
1 F 2 G 3 A 4 H
5 E 6 B 7 D

2
1 barely
2 warriors
3 paced
4 to hold their own
5 signed
6 narrowly
7 void
8 narrowing

Vocabulary

1

			1	o	b	s	e	s	s	i	o	n	
		2	s	c	r	e	e	n					
			3	s	e	t	b	a	c	k	s		
	4	h	o	m	e	p	a	g	e				
			5	l	i	n	k	s					
6	i	n	n	o	v	a	t	i	o	n			
7	b	r	a	i	n	c	h	i	l	d			
8	p	i	o	n	e	e	r						
			9	p	r	o	t	o	t	y	p	e	
			10	m	o	u	s	e					
		11	i	m	a	g	i	n	a	t	i	o	n
12	a	t	t	a	c	h	m	e	n	t			

2   1 into   2 on   3 up   4 into   5 in   6 up

3   1 with   3 of   5 up   7 from
       2 out   4 to   6 forward

4   a look up to   d keep out of   g run out of
       b look forward to   e get away from
       c stand up to   f come up with

Grammar

1
1. Oh no! I've forgotten **to tell** Mika about the party!
2. I would like **to see** what the world is like in a hundred years' time.
3. *correct*
4. Do you remember **visiting** the Kremlin when we were in Russia?
5. *correct*
6. Sorry, I didn't mean **to stop** you while you were working.
7. This equipment is out of date. It needs **replacing**.
8. I told them to do some work, but they went on **reading** the newspaper.

2   1 in developing   3 to see   5 to think
       2 to look after   4 having   6 telling

Spelling

1

e	s	p	j	u	d	g	e	m	e	n	t	a
n	a	a	f	g	o	l	z	o	i	b	v	i
c	c	r	y	e	b	q	a	v	u	k	u	z
o	h	j	r	v	n	t	y	e	e	l	l	y
u	i	e	f	a	r	g	u	m	e	n	t	a
r	e	s	u	l	n	k	q	e	t	o	d	d
a	v	q	p	e	e	g	u	n	c	n	f	v
g	e	r	o	n	p	k	e	t	s	s	e	e
e	m	g	o	v	e	r	n	m	e	n	t	r
m	e	b	d	i	b	v	v	o	e	k	e	t
e	n	a	e	r	c	o	d	g	x	n	v	i
n	t	x	d	o	e	n	t	f	p	g	t	s
t	a	w	z	n	p	w	j	w	i	y	o	e
y	f	l	k	m	b	l	e	j	b	e	i	m
p	l	a	c	e	m	e	n	t	s	n	k	e
i	v	o	d	n	y	a	n	g	y	t	c	n
g	l	i	x	t	z	d	w	t	e	x	s	t

Note that *judgement* can also be spelt as *judgment*.

---

2   1 environment   2 argument

Listening

2   IT, scientists, assembly line, pre-programmed, breakthrough, innovation, developers, prototype, potential

3
1. assembly lines *or* an assembly line
2. a banana
3. fragile objects
4. human eyes
5. voice
6. three years
7. prototype
8. elderly people
9. agriculture
10. a car manufacturer

Pronunciation

1   a 3   b 1   c 2   d 5   e 6   f 4

Use of English

1

1	connection	5	shopping	9	consultant
2	technological	6	criticism	10	natural
3	argument	7	wider		
4	security	8	drawing		

Writing

1   1 d   2 h   3 b   4 f   5 a   6 g
       7 c   8 e

2   1 cutting edge   3 lifelike   5 downside
       2 scene   4 villain   6 All in all

Use of English

1
1. didn't remember to buy / did not remember to buy
2. went on playing
3. looking forward (to going) to
4. regret deleting
5. tried to fix
6. needs to be checked *or* needs checking
7. stopped using
8. succeeded in solving

Speaking

1   Pair 1 e   Pair 2 g   Pair 3   a
       Pair 4 d   Pair 5 c

2

1	very useful	5	so too	9	of thing
2	you mean	6	this is the best	10	a bad idea
3	know about	7	could also		
4	That's a	8	at all		

Unit 8

Reading

1   1 B   2 A   3 D   4 B   5 C   6 A
       7 D   8 B   9 A   10 D   11 C   12 A
       13 C   14 D   15 B

2

1	numerous	5	colossal
2	an institution	6	within
3	forced to	7	run-down
4	the state	8	bail

Vocabulary

1

Crossword answers:
- 1 (across) speeding
- 2 (down) deter
- 3 (down) theft
- 4 (across) forgery
- 5 (down) jury
- 6 (across) prosecution
- 7 (down) service
- 8 (across) fine
- 9 (across) vandal
- 10 (down) larsonist
- 11 (across) probation
- (down) shoplifter

Grammar

1
2 This is the hotel where the murderer was caught.
3 The police want to speak to the man whose car was parked outside the bank during the robbery.
4 Three people were working in the jewellery store on Wednesday when several watches and pairs of sunglasses were stolen.
5 The police interviewed five people who had reported the vandalism in the railway station.
6 No one knew the reason why the crime had taken place.
7 These are the keys which/that were stolen last night at 11pm.

2
1 *No commas needed.*
2 The police released the man, who then sold his story to the newspapers.
3 My father, who you met last year, is now writing a detective novel.
4 Our head office, which is being decorated at the moment, is on the top floor of this building.
5 *No commas needed.*
6 Matt Damon starred in *The Bourne Ultimatum*, which was directed by Paul Greengrass.

3
1 This is the building which was built by Sir Norman Foster. *or* This is the building that was built by Sir Norman Foster.
2 That is the man whose dog is outside.
3 *correct*
4 *correct*
5 Denise is the woman who comes from France. *or* Denise is the woman that comes from France.
6 Do you know the name of the man who is working here tomorrow? *or* Do you know the name of the man that is working here tomorrow?
7 *correct*
8 I think November 19th is the day when we are having the party. *or* I think November 19th is the day on which we are having the party.

4
1 to   2 on   3 in   4 for

Spelling

1
1	irresponsible	6	immoral	11	imprecise
2	immature	7	irregular	12	immortal
3	inaccurate	8	improbable	13	irresistible
4	illogical	9	inappropriate	14	incapable
5	irrelevant	10	illiterate	15	impolite

Listening

1
1 the fire brigade, matches
2 a shelf, a store, a till
3 to break, to scratch
4 a bag, to hit, a knife, a wallet
5 a bank statement, to clone, a credit card, the number
6 to break in, the front door, holiday, a window

2 1 F   2 D   3 C   4 B   5 E

Pronunciation

1
	a		b	
1	a	noun	b	verb
2	a	noun	b	verb
3	a	verb	b	noun
4	a	noun	b	verb
5	a	noun	b	verb
6	a	verb	b	noun

2
	a		b	
2	a	re<u>jects</u>	b	<u>re</u>jects
3	a	con<u>duct</u>	b	<u>con</u>duct
4	a	<u>record</u>	b	re<u>cord</u>
5	a	<u>produce</u>	b	pro<u>duce</u>
6	a	pro<u>ject</u>	b	<u>pro</u>ject

Use of English

1
1	to	5	a	9	in
2	to	6	the	10	of
3	when	7	will	11	is
4	them	8	who *or* that	12	and *or* while

2
1	C	2	B	3	A	4	B	5	C	6	C
7	B	8	D	9	A	10	C	11	D	12	B

Writing: an article

1
1	g	2	e	3	d	4	f	5	i	6	a
7	b	8	h	9	c						

Speaking

1
Extract 1 d   Extract 2 a
Extract 3 b   Extract 4 e
Extract 5 c

2
1 That's right.
2 completely with you
3 Exactly ... Absolutely ... That's it
4 Is it ... Sure ... Right
5 I see
6 I see what ... That's true ... OK
7 Good point ... Maybe ... True

Unit 9

Reading

1
1	D	2	B	3	E	4	A
5	H	6	C	7	F		

2
1	buzzwords	4	Originally
2	originate from	5	dominates
3	a wide range of	6	to domesticate

Vocabulary

1
1	boil	4	grill	7	stir
2	sprinkle	5	chop	8	roast
3	slice	6	fry		

2
1	spicy	4	dry	7	sour
2	salty	5	sparkling	8	bland
3	well-done	6	raw		

Pronunciation

1

answer	island	sandwich
calm	knight	sword
castle	knitting	vegetable
chocolate	palm	Wednesday
cupboard	pneumonia	whole
guardian	psychiatrist	yacht
guess	salmon	

Grammar

1
1	used to love	4	are used to
2	can't get used to	5	have got used to
3	used to	6	aren't used to eating

2
1 My father worked for the post office for five years.
2 *correct*
3 I studied at Bristol University from 1993 to 1996.
4 *correct*
5 Bill Clinton was president of the USA for eight years.
6 We travelled across Asia from January to June 2003.

3
1 *Not possible to change.*
2 My family would always eat lunch together on a Sunday.
3 We would always go on holiday to the same seaside village.
4 *Not possible to change.*
5 *Not possible to change.*

Spelling

1

p	m	y	n	o	i	s	y	i	c
g	s	t	o	n	y	u	y	t	o
k	g	a	r	l	i	c	k	y	l
w	a	s	h	a	b	c	b	d	k
e	p	t	p	a	s	m	o	k	y
j	i	y	g	i	f	q	n	p	o
z	u	g	h	x	c	k	y	i	r
a	t	i	u	r	r	y	a	i	p
g	t	i	c	y	b	o	j	o	q
o	v	m	s	y	d	n	o	s	y

2 Garlicky. A *k* is added to the word *garlic* before the *-y* ending.

Writing

1
Fast food restaurants are good for society: 1, 4
Fast food restaurants are bad for society: 2, 3, 5

2
1 That must be
2 It is clear that
3 This results in
4 It is said
5 this is the case
6 It is important therefore that people
7 On balance it seems
8 The main problem is that
9 There is some truth in the statement
10 It depends on what is meant by

Listening

1
1	F	2	B	3	A	4	D	5	C

Vocabulary

1
1	e	2	a	3	c	4	b	5	d

2
1	Keep, up	3	breaking up	5	ate, up
2	spice, up	4	chop, up		

Use of English

1
1 take care of
2 got used to driving
3 take his inexperience into account *or* take into account his inexperience
4 put off
5 take her for granted
6 used to spend
7 is Martina getting on
8 we ate

2
1	a	5	on	9	that *or* the
2	without	6	the	10	in
3	at *or* in	7	which *or* that	11	for
4	have	8	much	12	so

Speaking

1
1	d	2	a	3	b
4	e	5	f	6	c

2
1	P	2	J	3	J
4	P	5	J	6	P

Unit 10

Reading

1
1	C	2	C	3	A	4	D
5	C	6	B	7	A	8	C

Vocabulary

1
1	round *or* circular	3	square
2	triangular	4	rectangular

2
1 The police have received reports of **spherical** objects in the sky.
2 What is the **width** of the football pitch?
3 We'd like to know your **height** and weight.
4 *correct*
5 I was surprised by the **softness** of the material. It felt lovely and smooth.
6 I saw this **colourful** summer dress and I really wanted to buy it. It was all the colours of the rainbow.
7 Do you know the **length** of the garden?
8 *correct*

3
1	d	2	f	3	e
4	a	5	b	6	c

4
1	off	4	off	7	down
2	down	5	off	8	off
3	down	6	down		

Grammar

1
1 You should read his email right away! It **could** be important – we don't know.
2 He **must** have been in a hurry because he ran out of the room.
3 I know she spoke French but she might **not** be from France because we also have students here from Quebec.
4 It may not **have** been the postman. We get a lot of people here delivering junk mail.

5 You **can't** have seen Diana at the station: she's in Lithuania at the moment!

6 He says he's a detective so he must **be** from the police.

2
1	must have been	6	must have found
2	can't have been	7	must have run
3	might have made	8	can't have done
4	might have sent	9	must have been
5	must have happened		

Note that you can use *couldn't have* instead of *can't have* in sentences 2 and 8.

Writing

1 You must include 2, 4, 6, 7, 8.

2
1	f	2	e	3	a	4	b
5	c	6	g	7	h	8	d

3 The writer forgot to say how to get the tickets.

Spelling

1
1	friend	4	review	7	chief
2	experience	5	perceive	8	inconceivable
3	receipt	6	deceive		

2
1	neither	5	foreign	9	species
2	ancient	6	proficient	10	height
3	efficient	7	weird	11	science
4	neighbour	8	protein		

Listening

1
1 amateur
2 Computer Science
3 neighbour
4 bed and breakfast
5 curtains
6 four friends / some friends
7 nothing (at all)
8 Your Weird Events
9 (their own) ghost stories
10 foreign countries

Use of English

1
1 doesn't seem that / does not seem that
2 seems that *or* seems like *or* seems as though
3 might have forgotten
4 is rare to see
5 give a reason for
6 have no idea
7 apart from
8 no point (in) telling

2
1	C	2	B	3	A	4	A	5	C	6	B
7	B	8	D	9	B	10	A	11	D	12	D

Speaking

1 Could you repeat the question please?

2
1	first one	7	the thing is
2	called	8	really
3	like	9	much
4	like that	10	lot more
5	The question	11	the two
6	certainly		

3 certainly, really, much, a lot more, definitely

Pronunciation

2
1	a Q	b C		4	a C	b Q
2	a Q	b C		5	a Q	b C
3	a C	b Q		6	a C	b Q

Unit 11

Reading

1
1	B	2	C	3	D	4	A	5	D	6	C
7	B	8	D	9	A	10	B	11	C	12	C
13	A	14	D	15	B						

2 Sabine: on the spot
Dirk: instantly
Amandine: right then and there
Walter: just like that

2
1	c	2	f	3	a	4	b	5	d	6	e

Vocabulary

1

```
1 d i s c o u n t
2   b u d g e t
3 b r a n d s
4   o u t
5   o f f e r
6 w h i m
7   d e a l
8 b a r g a i n
```

2
1	off	3	by	5	to
2	around	4	up	6	aside

Grammar

1
1 I wish I **had studied** harder when I was at university.
2 If I **had** a million euros, I would buy a yacht and sail around the Mediterranean.
3 If it **rains** tomorrow, you'll need to take an umbrella.
4 *correct*
5 If my boss **hadn't left**, I would still be working for the company.
6 *correct*
7 If you **worked** in the shop, you would be able to buy watches, rings and jewellery at half price.

2
1 If the shop still has those nice earrings, I **will** buy them.
2 I would get the DVDs online if I **were** you. They're cheaper.
3 If I **had** known that you can only cook this dessert in a microwave, I wouldn't have bought it.
4 Customers can return products to the store **provided** that they are not damaged in any way.
5 I'll go to the shop as **long** as you do the washing up.
6 **Should** I see Eric, I'll ask him to call you.
7 Don't buy anything **unless** you really want to.

3
1	a	2	b	3	a	4	a	5	b	6	a

Spelling

1
1	h	2	k	3	e	4	m	5	c	6	i
7	b	8	g	9	f	10	d	11	l	12	a
13	j										

Listening

1
1	B	2	B	3	A	4	C
5	A	6	A	7	C	8	A

Pronunciation

1
1	e	2	c	3	g	4	f
5	b	6	a	7	d		

2 *The stress could be placed in six different places.*
WE don't want to watch the concert tomorrow.
We DON'T want to watch the concert tomorrow.
We don't WANT to watch the concert tomorrow.
We don't want to WATCH the concert tomorrow.
We don't want to watch the CONCERT tomorrow.
We don't want to watch the concert TOMORROW.

Use of English

1
1 wish I had helped
2 did the bank lend you
3 you mind if I tell
4 wish I hadn't told / wish I had not told
5 would go *or* could go
6 comes to
7 unless you phone
8 if I were you

5
1 A	2 D	3 B	4 C	5 A	6 B
7 D	8 D	9 B	10 C	11 A	12 C

Writing

1
1 f   2 b   3 d   4 g   5 a   6 e
7 c

Speaking

1 Picture 1: department store, a special deal, included in the price, a guarantee, special features, shop assistant
Picture 2: to try, spices, to taste, sacks, merchant, to haggle

2
1 What the pictures have **in common** is that they show customers talking to salesmen.
2 Both the **salesmen** seem to be very friendly.
3 These pictures show very **similar** situations.
4 One thing **that** is the same in the pictures is that the customers are really going to buy something.
5 We can see the same thing **happening**: the customers are asking questions.
6 In **each** picture the salesman looks very friendly.
7 There isn't a big **difference** here: we can see people thinking about buying something.
8 The pictures show **the** same sort of thing.

Unit 12

Reading

1
1 C   2 D   3 F   4 A   5 H   6 G
7 E

2
1 d   2 f   3 g   4 a   5 c   6 h
7 b   8 e

Vocabulary

1
2 drought   6 volcanic eruption
3 earthquake   7 famine
4 flood   8 tidal wave
5 tornado

2

3
1 died		4 was killed		7 was lost
2 raised		5 devestated		8 disappeared
3 rose		6 was destroyed		

Grammar

1
1 knowing   3 even   5 Although
2 Despite   4 fact   6 Nevertheless

2
1 a   4 Ø   7 Ø
2 The   5 the   8 the
3 a   6 the

Spelling

1
-*os*: radios, videos, studios
-*oes*: potatoes, tomatoes, heroes
-*os*/-*oes*: mangos/mangoes, dominos/dominoes, volcanos/volcanoes

Listening

1
1 B   2 A   3 B   4 C
5 C   6 A   7 B

Pronunciation

1
1 the answer /ði:/, the question /ðə/
2 the end /ði:/, the book /ðə/
3 the orange /ði:/, the banana /ðə/

2
1 /ði:/   3 /ðə/   5 /ði:/
2 /ðə/   4 /ðə/   6 /ðə/

Use of English

1
1 a business   b blindness
2 a catastrophic   b energetic
3 a drinkable   b believable
4 a recovery   b bravery
5 a survivors   b demonstrator

2
1 C	2 D	3 A	4 A	5 D	6 A
7 B	8 C	9 D	10 B	11 D	12 D

Writing

1
1 this problem   6 their
2 these places   7 even though
3 this   8 Instead
4 They   9 this
5 In this case   10 it

2 (correct spellings given)
paragraph 2: information, batteries, special
paragraph 3: elderly, heavy
paragraph 4: Finally, available, separated

Speaking

1   a 3   b 2   c 5   d 1   e 4
2   Pair 1 1   Pair 2 3
Pair 3 5   Pair 4 2
3   1 I don't think this is a good idea **at** all.
2 This doesn't work **for** me.
3 I don't see the point **of doing** this.
4 This is not **an** effective solution to the problem.
5 In this **case** I don't think this is the best option.
6 I don't think it's a bad idea, but I think some of the other **ones** are better.
7 Does this really work? I'**m not** sure.
8 **What** if nobody comes to the event?

Unit 13

Reading

1   1 C   2 A   3 B   4 C   5 A   6 D
7 A   8 C

Vocabulary

1

	h	e	a	l	t	h		w	e	e	k	l	y
	o								d				
	r				p				i		p		
	o	b	i	t	u	a	r	y			o		
	s				p				t		l		
	c				a				o		i		
	o		j	o	u	r	n	a	l	i	s	t	
	p				a				a		t		
	e		w		z				l		i		
			e		z						c		
	h	e	a	d	l	i	n	e			s		
			t										
		s	h	o	w	b	i	z					
			e										
c	o	r	r	e	s	p	o	n	d	e	n	t	

2   1 going   4 ahead   7 up
2 broke   5 up   8 leak
3 out   6 out

Grammar

1   2 Rich said that he hadn't seen Tina.
3 Maria asked if I was going to buy a newspaper. *or* Maria asked if we were going to buy a newspaper.
4 The schoolteacher said that it would be a nice day tomorrow.
5 The policeman said that no one could go in the building.
6 Katy asked if Simon had heard the news.
7 Joe said that they had been asking him questions.
2   1 When we left, our parents warned **us** not to speak to people who seem too friendly.
2 Gemma advised me **to** compare prices on the Internet.
3 His sister reminded **him** to post the letter.
4 He didn't apologize **for** arriving late.
5 When the teacher spoke to Jim and me, he suggested **we** do an exam preparation course.
6 They criticized the people **who** didn't do the work.
7 I recommended **he** ask for some help from our teacher.

Spelling

1   1 1 a   2 a   3 b   4 b   5 b   6 a
7 a   8 b   9 a   10 a
2   *-able*: advisable, believable, notable
-eable: changeable, knowledgeable, manageable

Listening

1   1 prime minister   6 editorials
2 politics and news   7 the town name
3 college newspaper   8 a (famous) singer
4 nothing   9 hospital
5 office junior   10 a music magazine

Pronunciation

1   1 b   2 b   3 b   4 a   5 b   6 a
7 b   8 a   9 b   10 a   11 b   12 a

Use of English

1   1 by   5 able   9 of
2 a   6 own   10 to
3 for   7 it   11 who
4 as   8 much   12 which
2   1 B   2 A   3 C   4 C   5 A   6 A
7 D   8 C   9 C   10 A   11 D   12 A

Writing

1   1 d   2 f   3 a   4 b   5 e   6 c
2   1 I saw Mike. He was running to the station.
2 There is a Canadian student in the class who speaks English and French.
3 The person that they are looking for isn't here.
4 I worked in Switzerland for six months.
5 "Can anyone see my pen?" he asked.
6 It cost me €1,999.99!
3   1 I think that's Gary's **wife's** car.
2 Eight **students'** answers were right.
3 Tina's **brothers** go to the same school as me.
4 *correct*
5 I couldn't find **Charles'** phone anywhere.
6 We were surprised by **people's** response to the questionnaire.
7 *correct*
8 **Everybody's** answer is wrong.

4

Hi Anders

I'm really pleased that you're coming to London to study English. I think that you will have a great time when you are over here.

In your last email, you asked me to help you find some accommodation. The good news is that you will be able to stay in James' room while you are here, because he is going to Madrid to learn Spanish over the summer. The bad news is that you will have to leave the room in September when he comes back, but it will be easy to find somewhere else then.

You also asked me how to get to the house from Heathrow Airport. The best way is to get a Travelcard, which you can buy at the station. It costs £6.70. I was planning to meet you at the airport, but unfortunately, on that day my university puts up a notice with all the students' exam results and I need to go and see it. Anyway, I'm really looking forward to seeing you in a fortnight! Speak soon,

Tony

Speaking: topic discussion

1 1 f   2 b   3 a   4 e   5 d   6 c

3 a It really depends.

b I have to think about this one.

c Personally

d I absolutely love it.

e I've not really thought about this before.

f That's an interesting question.

Unit 14

Reading

1 1 B   2 C   3 A   4 D
   5 C   6 C   7 A   8 A

Vocabulary

1

		¹f	a	d	e			
		²c	r	a	z	e		
		³c	o	o	l			
	⁴t	r	e	n	d	y		
	⁵f	a	d	s				
	⁶c	l	a	s	h			
⁷r	e	t	r	o				
⁸f	l	a	i	r				
		⁹s	t	y	l	i	s	h

2 1 hang   3 try   5 take   7 dress
   2 turn   4 do   6 let   8 take

Grammar

1 1 The city **was destroyed** by a volcanic eruption.

2 I couldn't believe that he was being **questioned** by the police.

3 *correct*

4 Many synthetic fibres, like nylon and polyester, are **used** in clothes manufacture.

5 *The Name of the Rose* was written **by** Umberto Eco.

6 The window had been opened **with** a screwdriver.

7 The washing machine **has ruined** my new shirt!

2 1 had their heads shaved

2 had her windows cleaned

3 has her shopping delivered

4 are having the walls painted *or* are going to have the walls painted

5 had it repaired

6 is having his eyes tested

Listening

1 1 C   2 C   3 B   4 A
   5 C   6 A   7 B   8 A

Spelling

1 1 flower   4 site   7 heels
   2 jeans   5 complements
   3 dye   6 hole

2 1 sight   4 whole   7 die
   2 flour   5 compliments
   3 genes   6 heals

Speaking

1 They disagree because Claudio thinks it is not a problem to spend too much money on clothes because you need to buy brand names to get good quality. Eleni thinks that there are better things to spend money on when you are young.

2 1 don't you think   5 suppose not

2 After all   6 the same

3 I mean is   7 suppose

4 but we're

3 b

Use of English

1 1 made him wear

2 let me leave

3 allow us to wear

4 need to be watered *or* need watering

5 has to be given *or* must be given

6 am having mine repaired *or* am having my car repaired

7 has his house cleaned

8 were being designed by

2 1 a hunger   b anger

2 a fashionable   b miserable

3 a trendy   b handy

4 a width   b depth

5 a exploitation   b imagination

Writing

1 The first student is writing about a village. The second student is writing about a town.

2 a I spend a lot of time walking down the country lanes.

b One problem is that it's quite noisy especially in the morning as you can hear all the commuters driving to work.

c The house is a really traditional little place close to the sea

d There are large numbers of red-brick houses all around

e There is a little shop nearby which is covered in ivy,

f a view of the river.

3 2 wrinkles   4 freckles   6 dyed
   3 skinny   5 messy

Pronunciation

1 1 c   2 b   3 b   4 a   5 c

Unit 15

Reading

1 D	2 A	3 H	4 C
5 F	6 B	7 G	

1 g	2 d	3 a	4 f
5 b	6 h	7 e	8 c

Vocabulary

1

¹c	e	r	e	²m	o	n	y		
u				e					
s				m					
t		³p	o	r	t	r	a	i	t
t	⁴f		r						⁵m
m	e		i			⁶s			u
	s		a			t			s
	t	⁷l	a	n	d	⁸s	c	a	p	e
	i					i			u
	v					t			m
	a					u			
⁹g	a	l	l	e	r	i	e	s	

2

1 out		4 up		7 through	
2 off		5 out		8 off	
3 after		6 out		9 in	

Grammar

1
1. No sooner **had** he given her the answer than she started to laugh.
2. Not **only** did he break the window, but he also lost the house keys!
3. **Hardly** had they sent the email than they realised they had made a terrible mistake.
4. No **longer** does the government ask people to apply for this form by going to their offices.
5. No sooner had he left the room **than** the whole class started arguing.
6. **Not** only had he not done his homework, but he also hadn't brought any of his books to school.
7. Not only did they cancel the flight, but they **also** refused to pay us our money back!

2
1. Hardly had David started shouting than **Maria walked** out of the room.
2. *correct*
3. No sooner **had the police arrived** than he admitted he was responsible for the fraud.
4. *correct*
5. Not only **did she break** the vase, but she also broke the mirror.
6. *correct*
7. Hardly **had I arrived** at work than the telephone started ringing.
8. *correct*

Spelling

1

	a		b	
1	a dairy		b diary
2	a lose		b loose
3	a trial		b Trail
4	a exiting		b exciting
5	a desert		b dessert
6	a choose		b chose
7	a assurance		b insurance
8	a quite		b quiet

Listening

1 1 C 2 F 3 A 4 E 5 B

Pronunciation

1

1 Unfortunately		6 Amazingly
2 Basically		7 Nevertheless
3 Surprisingly		8 Anyway
4 Actually		9 interestingly
5 however		

2 They pause after the sentence adverb in sentences 1, 2, 3, 4, 6, 7 and 8. They pause before the sentence adverb in sentence 5. They pause both before and after the sentence adverb in sentence 9.

3
2. He didn't tell anyone the bad news, | surprisingly.
3. They did not ask the cost of the painting, | however, | because they weren't interested in buying it.
4. This is a very dangerous expedition. Nevertheless, | I want to be involved in it.
5. Basically, | they weren't really interested in art.
6. Actually, | I have a degree in History of Art.

Use of English

1
1. don't mind if / do not mind if
2. make up your mind / make your mind up
3. you mind working
4. sooner had I told
5. only did he
6. took me in
7. going through
8. take part in

2

1 relationship		5 unlikely		9 historical
2 remarkable		6 recently		10 explanation
3 infamous		7 impressive		
4 discovery		8 building		

Writing

1

1 b	2 e	3 c	4 g
5 a	6 d	7 f	

2
1. We all put on fancy **dress**: I was dressed as a pirate.
2. **It** was crowded everywhere: it was difficult to move.
3. The best part of carnival is when a huge **procession** walks though the main street of the city.
4. Several people have been invited **to** our party tomorrow.
5. It's **a tradition** in carnival that women can cut off men's ties. *or* It's **traditional** in carnival that women can cut off men's ties.
6. The whole city **goes** crazy during Carnival.

Speaking

1 Student 1 c   Student 2 a

2

1 let		4 while
2 foreground, background		5 both
3 Regarding		6 going

Unit 16

Reading

1
1 B	2 D	3 A	4 A
5 C	6 D	7 B	8 A

Grammar

1
1 f	2 h	3 c	4 a
5 e	6 g	7 b	8 d

2
1 such	4 such	7 enough
2 too	5 so	8 so
3 enough	6 too	

3
1 I thought Denis was the person **that** sent the email.
2 What **he had done** was to paint the house green.
3 It's Fiona and Jurgen who **are** moving house.
4 *correct*
5 What I dream of **doing** is sailing around the world.
6 **What** he did was to ask everyone for money.
7 *correct*

Pronunciation

1
2 A quiet house in the country | is my lifelong dream.
3 Buying the paint for the whole house | is what Pilar was worried about.
4 One person who I really enjoyed meeting | was the design expert.
5 It wasn't Tony. It was Ricardo | who moved to London.
6 What you will need to do | is go on the Internet and find examples of the house design you want.
7 What happened next | was very surprising.
8 It wasn't until Andrea looked at her phone | that she realised Dino had been trying to call her.

Vocabulary

1
1 dreary	4 facing	7 pale
2 cluttered	5 strong	8 bare
3 terraced	6 cheerful	

2
1 up	4 turned	7 out
2 doing	5 picked	8 brighten
3 up	6 let	

Listening

1
1 B	2 A	3 B	4 B
5 C	6 C	7 A	

Spelling

1
1 lengthen	5 strengthen	9 straighten
2 heighten	6 worsen	10 sadden
3 widen	7 soften	
4 lessen	8 lighten	

Use of English

1
1 A	2 B	3 C	4 C	5 A	6 D
7 C	8 A	9 C	10 B	11 C	12 B

2
1 neighbourhood	6 likelihood
2 homely	7 designer
3 environmentally	8 ambitious
4 generator	9 unsuccessful
5 powered	10 enthusiastic

Writing

1 You must explain that you are sharing a house with people from five different countries and to describe them. You must describe your room: it's small but nice. You need to describe your view, which is of the park. You need to explain that you decorated the room last week. You need to explain that Katie can visit you but not until September when the room is free.

2 (Possible answers)
1 received *or* got *or* read
2 hear
3 asked
4 There
5 As
6 was *or* seemed *or* felt *or* looked
7 which *or* that
8 mentioned *or* said
9 welcome
10 care

3 She forgot to mention the view of the park.

Speaking

1
1 something	8 why
2 living	9 type
3 prefer	10 successful, appeal
4 recently	11 events
5 important	12 choosing
6 living	13 move
7 free	14 much, differences

2
1 F	2 T	3 F	4 F	5 T	6 T
7 T	8 F	9 T	10 F		

Practice Test

PAPER 1: READING

Part 1

1 D [these characteristics are not all unique to our species: ... and although an opposable thumb is a useful thing to have, it doesn't seem much on which to base a sense of superiority.]

2 B [We believe we are the sharpest knife in the drawer. ... The trouble is that the more we learn about other animals, the more we are forced to question how unique our intelligence is.]

3 A [Scientists argue amongst themselves whether these animals demonstrate 'real' language in the way humans do.]

4 C [And of course, dogs are smart. After all, they can be trained to do all manner of useful things. Yet our egos are not threatened by the fact.]

5 B [Stupid people are often described as bird-brains, but ... Alex ... could count to six, identify colours and had a vocabulary of 150 words. He had the intelligence of a five-year-old and the communication skills of a two-year-old.]

6 D [they take them to crossroads and junctions where they wait until the traffic lights change and it is safe to cross the road. They drop the walnuts on the tarmac and wait for vehicles to drive over them and crack the hard outer shells. When the lights change again, the crows join the pedestrians and pick up the nut.]

7 D [If you show a chicken an object and then hide it, it doesn't forget all about the object. ... it is capable of understanding that the object has not stopped existing simply because it is out of sight.]

8 A

Part 2

9 B	10 D	11 A	12 G
13 F	14 C	15 H	

Part 3

16 A [The boulevard is all that separates the hotel from the sandy beach, which is visible from all rooms in the hotel.]

17 B [these beautiful villas are surrounded by a thick hedge which screens the complex completely from the main road.]

18 C [Visitors who wish to take advantage of what the area has to offer are advised to hire a car.]

19 D [This fantastic hotel is located in the heart of a nature reserve that stretches for kilometres along the coast.]

20 A [The water is safe for swimmers, but only within the designated area: poisonous jellyfish are a problem in the summer months.]

21 C [A twenty-minute drive will bring you to several beaches that are excellent for swimming, water-skiing and surfing.]

22 D [saltwater crocodiles are a constant threat in the waters around here and these enormous reptiles have been known to attack and even kill.]

23 A [fascinating galleries that exhibit and sell the work of local artists, some of whose works the visitor can see in the lobby of the hotel.]

24 B [All areas within the grounds have wheelchair access, and the villas themselves have been carefully designed to be safe for people with reduced mobility and vision.]

25 A [Families with babies are welcome and there is twenty-four-hour childcare so parents can relax.]

26 C [Canecutter's Lodge is situated twenty kilometres inland.]

27 B [There is also a swimming pool and fully-equipped barbecue area for those visitors who prefer to dine out of doors.]

28 C [This unusual hotel was once the home of a plantation owner and much of the character of the original building has been preserved.]

29 D [Alternatively, you can remain in the hotel grounds and watch the creatures that come to feed on the fruit and seeds that the staff put out for them.]

30 C [Canecutter's Lodge has a reputation for its excellent cuisine and many of the ingredients are gathered fresh daily from the property itself: guavas, mangoes, granadillas, papayas, bananas and avocadoes.]

PAPER 3: USE OF ENGLISH

Part 1

1 B	2 D	3 A	4 B	5 B	6 C
7 A	8 B	9 D	10 A	11 B	12 D

Part 2

13 few	17 there	21 more
14 because	18 by	22 where
15 with	19 the	23 have
16 to	20 finally or lastly	24 your

Part 3

25 musician	29 totally	33 valuable
26 wealthy	30 ability	or invaluable
27 independent	31 deafness	34 personality
28 loss	32 historical	

Part 4

(|| shows where the answer is split into two parts for marking purposes)

35 delivered the package || on/in **time**

36 was interviewed || **by**

37 (that) he || didn't **need**

38 are || hardly **any**

39 is || **too** cold

40 **must** be || turned/switched

41 **unless** it rains

42 should/ought to || **set** up

PAPER 4: LISTENING

Part 1

1 B	2 C	3 A	4 A
5 A	6 C	7 B	8 B

Part 2

9 emotional	14 how to ride
10 fifty/50	15 the Town Hall
11 friendly	16 full-time
12 (full-time) employees	17 14 to 16
13 twenty/20	18 birth certificate

Part 3

19 C	20 E	21 F	22 A	23 D

Part 4

24 C [It means 'car' in Chichewa – that's a language spoken in south central Africa. But it also refers to a type of toy.]

25 A [kids make their own out of the things others throw away: wire, tin cans, bits of rubber, things like that]

26 C [They're lovely – made with such care and love for detail. I once watched a child making a bicycle using wire. ... And I thought: these aren't just toys, they're works of art!]

27 B [There are toys from Malawi, Zimbabwe and South Africa, but other African countries are represented too.]

28 B [There will also be daily morning workshops where children can make toys themselves out of wire.]

29 A [The documentary will be broadcast on television later this year. If you miss it, you can order the DVD from our gallery's web site.]

30 B [Actually, I believe kids everywhere are creative, but in richer countries, they don't know the joy that comes from making things themselves. I mean, why make a toy when your bedroom is already full of toys from a shop? I think toys are like chocolate: a little is delicious, but too much makes you sick.]

Credits

Photo credits